SUN & MOON SIGNS

Sun & Moon Signs

An Astrological Guide to Love, Career, & Destiny

Marisa St. Clair

GRAMERCY BOOKS
NEW YORK

This 2007 edition is published by Gramercy Books, an imprint of Random House Value Publishing, a division of Random House, Inc., New York, by arrangement with Amber Books.

Gramercy is a registered trademark and the colophon is a trademark of Random House, Inc.

Random House
New York • Toronto • London • Sydney • Auckland
www.valuebooks.com

Printed and bound in Dubai

A catalog record for this title is available from the Library of Congress.

ISBN: 978-0-517-23058-9

10 9 8 7 6 5 4 3 2 1

CONTENTS

INTRODUCTION

*E*very man, woman and child is born with a distinct and different destiny. There are no exceptions. Everyone, no matter how humble, has cosmic significance and a part to play in the life of the universe. This is innate and inescapable, and goes beyond the tiny boundaries of nation, creed and colour.

As we live out our lives on planet Earth, we are, however unknowingly, acting in a greater drama and reacting to impulses that come from distant astronomical bodies, stars and planets millions of light years away. Sceptics pour scorn on the idea that far-distant Saturn, for example, can have any effect on our lives, as the ancient art and science of astrology teaches. But the fact is that we are sparks of energy inhabiting bodies made of the same stuff as the stars, responding like tiny radios to the distant messages they send to Earth.

Each infant carries within it a double blueprint for life: its genetic programming and the pattern of character that comes from the astrological 'clock' that was set in motion at the moment of birth. No one knows the full extent of genetic influence, although it seems to be astonishingly far-reaching, but the power of the horoscope has been well known to the wisest men and women for many, many centuries.

Our Sun and Moon Signs provide essential inside information about our destinies. They reveal the secrets of who we really are, and why we are here, laying out before us our potential, the sort of joys and achievements our character-istics may bring about, and warn us of problems to be overcome through the triumph of free will.

Read *Sun and Moon Signs* with an open mind and discover who you really are.

Marisa St Clair
LONDON 1999

Finding Your Sun Sign

Aries	21 March – 20 April
Taurus	21 April – 21 May
Gemini	22 May – 21 June
Cancer	22 June – 22 July
Leo	23 July – 23 August
Virgo	24 August – 22 September
Libra	23 September – 23 October
Scorpio	24 October – 22 November
Sagittarius	23 November – 21 December
Capricorn	22 December – 20 January
Aquarius	21 January – 18 February
Pisces	19 February – 20 March

THE ELEMENTS

Up to the beginning of the Age of Enlightenment – the modern scientific era – in the 18th century, it was commonly believed that everything, including human beings, was made up of the four elements: Earth, Air, Fire and Water. These were thought of as the building blocks of life, and each astrological sign had a predominance of one or another. Each created its common characteristics, although too much of any of the elements can produce an unbalanced personality.

EARTH SIGNS

Those signs ruled by Earth are Taurus, Virgo and Capricorn. Each manifests the element in different ways. However, in all cases, Earth makes those born under these signs tend to be more practical, sensible and stable than most. They are better 'grounded' or, to put it in another way, they keep their feet on the ground. Whereas others may rush off on madcap schemes or sit around and day-dream, those born under Earth Signs roll up their sleeves and quietly get on with the job. For example, Arians may be the great explorers and adventurers of the zodiac, but it is Taureans who follow behind, set up camp for them and arrange for provisions to be sent ahead up river. Taureans are 'the salt of the earth', the plodders who may strike the more dynamic and extrovert signs of the zodiac as being uninspired, but who are invaluable and upright members of society.

Virgoans, always organized, tidy and efficient, are the analysts and notekeepers who keep track of records, accounts and archives so that society knows its history. They are the ones who ensure that the great exploits of the Arian adventurers are known to posterity. Capricornians always have an eye to the future, planning ahead for a rainy day from their lofty mountain peaks, like the Goat that symbolizes their sign. And if they are occasionally dour and pessimistic – thanks to the influence of their ruling planet Saturn, who nevertheless encourages them to be disciplined and careful – then they succeed all the more in keeping the wilder excesses of the Fire and Air Signs under control.

WATER SIGNS

The Water Signs are Cancer, Scorpio and Pisces. They are emotional, intuitive and often psychic, strongly in touch with the hidden, mysterious side of life and with the ebb and flow of unseen energies. Like the ocean tides, they have surges of inspiration and bursts of euphoria, or they can be plunged into gloom and introspection. Cancerians are emotionally tied to their homes and families; like their sign, the Crab, they jealously guard their own particular little rock pool, hiding their softest feelings under a hard shell.

Scorpians are the occultists and profound thinkers of the zodiac, very sexy and magnetic, but sometimes too intense. They are the still waters that run deep – very, very deep.

Pisceans' emotions can lie undisturbed for long periods, then suddenly rise to the surface. They can be fast and elusive – slippery customers sometimes – and change direction for no apparent reason, often against their own best interests. But, like the other two Water signs, they operate almost entirely through their feelings, which can be very positive when set against the dour practicality of a Capricornian or the most reliable investment banker of a Taurean. They give depth to the adventures of the Arian and the madcap schemes of the Geminian, and reveal some of the mysteries of the Universe, which is never a bad thing.

AIR SIGNS

The Air Signs are Gemini, Libra and Aquarius. These inspirational, communicative signs of the zodiac can talk alot of 'hot air', and their ability to cause a 'wind of change' to run through society is a mixed blessing.

This tendency is viewed with horror by the Earth signs, to whom all chance is fraught with danger. Often the Air Signs are blown this way and that by sudden enthusiasms and conflicting, contradictory opinions, but they can throw new light on apparently intractable problems. It is their influence that helps sweep away outmoded ways of doing things, bringing in all manner of brave new worlds. Geminians talk and act fast, and live life at a furious pace, often doing several things at once – one of which is forever talking on the telephone. Librans are more cool and collected, the arbiters and diplomats of the zodiac, but they can be great ditherers, prone to sudden reversals of opinion.

Aquarians, the idealists and New Agers of the zodiac, can move swiftly if their crusading zeal is fully engaged, and their motivation is razor-sharp. If they feel something is best for mankind, they will go for it, dropping everything else, including all thoughts of personal comfort or gain. However, they can also be irritatingly nebulous and 'airy-fairy', often lost in their dreams of creating a brave new world while failing to make their mark on this one.

FIRE SIGNS

The Fire Signs are Aries, Leo and Sagittarius. Consumed with passion – which all too often, however, takes the form of self-love and burning ambition – these are the natural stars of the zodiac. They are fired up with motivation, and sparks really fly when they get going. It is difficult to keep a Fire Sign doing things at a measured pace (steady old Taureans can sometimes do it, though) because their enthusiasms soon spread like wildfire, catching the imaginations of more and more people. Fire Signs are the leaders – especially Leo, King of the Jungle, the most regal and imperious of all the signs of the zodiac.

They do, nevertheless, have great warmth and charisma, and light the way for others to follow. Arians can burn with a cold flame or with the raging fires of revolution. Either way, their passion is based on a childlike – even childish – desire to get their own way, without any thought for the future or the feelings of others. But they are willing to go where others fear to tread, and without them human progress would always be a great deal slower and more difficult.

Sagittarians are the great enthusiasts of the zodiac, sparky and constantly generating yet more energy. Like the centaur-archer and the horse-man of their sign, Sagittarians can rush into things, galloping at the gate that is never going to open magically at the last minute, or shooting very wide of the mark. But they will pick themselves up and start again, uncomplainingly, forever encouraging more timid souls, while keeping their own eyes on new horizons.

BALANCE

B alance is essential where the elements are concerned. Each of them may provide us with what is necessary for life – drinking water, food, air to breathe and warmth – but once out of control, they are highly dangerous. When the Earth is unbalanced, earthquakes rip cities apart almost without warning, killing thousands and making millions homeless in just a few terrifying seconds. Landslides and avalanches also come out of nowhere, to flatten human settlements like matchwood. Presently, we are suffering from our failure to understand that the Earth needs respect. By tearing down the rainforests, we have created almost unimaginable problems through the accumulation of greenhouse gases. At the same time destruction of natural habitats is threatening the world's wildlife at a horrifying pace.

Fire is both Man's best friend and most terrifying enemy. Without campfires, early groups of humans would never have survived, but once out of control, fire destroys everything in its path and is no respecter of people. Bushfires regularly create rings of terror around some of the world's most prestigious residential areas – Malibu Beach and the South of France, for example – sometimes taking the lives of rich and poor alike. Fear of fire is ingrained in us. The police advise people who are being attacked to shout 'Fire' in order to get help because, sadly, few would come running at a call of 'Rape!'.

Air is essential for life, allowing us to breathe and draw the sun's rays into our bodies. Fresh air is balm to the soul, too, and can do wonders for the burnt-out townie or someone recuperating from illness. Windmills are also gaining in popularity as an alternative form of energy because they are clean, renewable and safe. Too much air, on the other hand, can be terrifyingly violent – taking the form of hurricanes and tornadoes, smashing up all before them. In 1987, even temperate Britain suffered one of the most violent storms of its history – though it was, incorrectly, called a hurricane – in which over 40 people died and countless others were injured, made homeless or in some way traumatized. Those who live in the United States' 'hurricane zone' or 'tornado alley' know how helpless even the most sophisticated and advanced of us can be against the full force of Nature.

Water, too, is life. We can do without food, if we have to, for weeks, but without water we will die a horrible death in days. We drink it – in increasing quantities as bottled mineral water – bathe in it, swim in it and sail on it. We dive under it, too, although only one per cent of all the oceans of the Earth has been explored, and even then not exhaustively. But most of all, we are water: over 70 per cent of our bodies is water, which is why we constantly need to top it up. Even mild dehydration can lead to a host of unsuspected problems, such as headaches and lack of concentration. But if water rages out of control, we are swept away into oblivion, a threat that is increasingly likely as the oceans and seas rise due to global warming. Already we are seeing a marked increase in floods and tidal waves. At least once before in Mankind's history large areas of the inhabited Earth were destroyed by a great flood, an event recorded in the myths of cultures all around the world. Noah, who built the Ark to escape the flood, is the best-known protagonist in such stories. In addition, the lost continents of Atlantis and Mu were believed to have come to an abrupt end in some kind of massive flood, perhaps caused by a massive volcanic eruption.

When two elements – Fire and Earth – come together in the form of volcanic eruptions, major cataclysms result. In turn, the other two elements are affected. Volcanic ash pollutes the air for months, even years, causing meteorological disturbances, while molten lava gushing into water results in plumes of hissing steam and undrinkable, unnavigable water.

It is no wonder that the ancients tried to placate the gods of the elements with sacrifices. In Hawaii, some locals still worship the goddess Pele, who lives in volcanoes, in order to avert her wrath.

We may go about our daily lives without much thought for the symbolism of the four elements, but the unconscious mind deals in such imagery, and dreams often speak to us, symbolically, of our relationship with Earth, Air, Fire and Water.

DREAMS

In dreams, Earth tends to symbolize the need to keep our feet on the ground, tackle practical matters and get in touch with our true natures.

Flying and soaring dreams represent the element of Air, as do those involving storms and wind. Flying is often a very positive image and can relate to being an ambitious and successful 'high flyer', or, at least, the desire to be one.

Flying dreams can also refer to deep, often hidden, desires to explore the Higher Mind, to get to know the mysteries of spirituality and the esoteric. Storms and wind symbolize a fear of uncontrolled passion or emotional upheaval, or of being swept away by some over-whelming force.

Fire in dreams also refers to passion, although it may be of an intense and short-lived nature. It can be initiatory, a 'baptism of fire' that relates to a difficult rite of passage that you are, or will be, facing in order to be cleansed in preparation for greater things. Fire also symbolizes the quick wits and sharp intellect of clever, bright people.

Water almost always signifies emotion or the secrets of the unconscious mind. Deep water is the depth of feeling or the place where your true self may be found, deep down. Raging water, as in tidal waves, means great passion or emotional upheaval, which can sweep you away. Rain can mean tears.

MAGIC

In magic and all kinds of esoteric lore, the elements are important, each being ruled by an archangel (see The Angelic Hierarchy on page 22). Each is also assigned to a point of the compass. The ruler of Fire is Michael, assigned to the South; Raphael rules Air and the East; Gabriel rules Water and the West; and Uriel rules the Earth and exercises dominion over the North.

In that most modern of 'magical' systems, the Sino–Japanese art of *feng shui*, which, although ancient in the Orient, is new to the West, the elements must be balanced within each building to maximize harmony and luck. A simple way of doing this is to light candles (being very careful never to leave them unattended) to symbolize the element of fire. Use scented joss sticks and/or door chimes for Air. A discreet scattering of salt around the corners of the rooms symbolizes the Earth and is believed to keep evil influences away. Indoor fountains, fish tanks or even a few puffs of water from a plant sprayer will bring the element of Water into balance.

Colours of the Zodiac

Traditionally, each sign of the zodiac has its own colour, which is believed to be 'lucky'
or magically empowered for those born under that particular sign. In general, the
colours are associated with the ruling planets and are symbolic of their attributes. Many
people find that they feel most comfortable when wearing their sign's colours, and often
choose them without knowing the astrological background.

Aries

Ruling planet: Mars.

Colour: Shades of red, usually the most vivid. Red is the colour of energy, revolution, aggression, war and raw sexuality. Wearing red gives energy and promotes a sense of optimism and motivation, although some may find it too abrasive and combative.

Taurus

Ruling planet: Venus.

Colour: Green – shades of the verdant earth and the spirit of nature. Green is calming and meditative, and can be used to help balance the energies of mind, body and spirit. Too much green, however, can cause lethargy. It was once associated with witchcraft (because it symbolizes the cult of fertility and nature). Consequently, some older people dislike it.

Gemini

Ruling planet: Mercury.

Colour: Yellow or gold. This is the colour of speedy communication and of healing. It is energetic without being confrontational (like red) and is also the colour of optimism and of 'sunny' temperaments. Too much yellow, however, can discourage realistic long-term planning.

Cancer

Ruling planet: the Moon.

Colours: Pale blue and silver. These aid the flow of intuition and constructive and revelatory dreaming, and put Cancerians in touch with their secret, psychic selves. However, these colours can lead to unrestrained and inappropriate daydreaming. Cancerians must remember that the chores have to be done sometime!

Leo

Ruling planet: The Sun.
Colours: Gold, yellowy-orange and sometimes red. These are the colours of ambition and extroverts, of bold Leos who seek the limelight. More timid people can benefit from wearing them, but naturally strong personalities may need to tone them down.

Virgo

Ruling planet: Mercury.
Colour: Rich brown and russet reds. These colours anchor the individual to the Earth, balancing the Mercurian potential for 'flightiness'. Many people find brown depressing, however, so it should be used in light touches and with some care.

Libra

Ruling planet: Venus.
Colours: Royal blue and rose-pink, the colours of love, care and emotional stability. Pink, in particular, encourages affection and romanticism, although it can wear off pretty quickly!

Scorpio

Ruling planet: Pluto.
Colours: Black and red. Dramatic, uncompromising and sexy, these are 'dangerous' colours, especially when used together. They are the colours of mistresses rather than of wives. Wear them only if you mean it.

Sagittarius

Ruling planet: Jupiter.

Colours: Dark blue and purple. Expansive, luxury-loving and gregarious Jupiter also has a regal streak – hence the royal colour purple. Although it is a difficult colour to wear, it can, nevertheless, bestow dignity.

Capricorn

Ruling planet: Saturn.

Colours: Dark brown, black and grey. Introspective and wintry, those born under the sign of the Goat need to escape from, rather than use, their sign's traditional colours or at least cheer themselves up with brighter, more positive and outgoing colours such as pink, yellow or red.

Aquarius

Ruling planet: Uranus.

This is unique in the zodiac for traditionally having all the colours of the rainbow – sometimes all at the same time.

Pisces

Ruling planet: Neptune.

Colours: Sea green and mauve. Evocative of the ocean, seaweed and myths about mermaids, these greens encourage the ebb and flow of emotion, but should be worn sparingly. Pisceans need to get their feet on the ground occasionally.

THE ANGELIC HIERARCHY

According to ancient tradition, each planet is governed by one of the great archangels, who are also rulers of certain aspects of human life. The following pages list the planets and signs they rule, their areas of influence and their special day of the week.

The Archangel Michael

Michael

Archangel of the Sun. Governs Leo. Rules human destiny, ambition, monetary gain, careers and motivation.
Day: Sunday.

Raphael

Archangel of Mercury. Governs Gemini and Virgo. Rules writing and all forms of communication and learning as well as healing.
Day: Wednesday.

Anael

Archangel of Venus. Governs Taurus and Libra. Rules matters of the heart, romance, art and music.
Day: Friday.

Gabriel

Archangel of the Moon. Governs Cancer. Rules femininity,
intuition and all matters psychic.
Day: Monday.

Samuel

Archangel of Mars. Governs Aries.
Rules assertiveness, bestows courage
and protects against danger from violence or fire.
Day: Tuesday.

Sachiel

Archangel of Jupiter. Governs Sagittarius.
Rules financial gain, windfalls and material luck.
Day: Thursday.

The Archangel Raphael

The Archangel Gabriel

Cassiel

Archangel of Saturn. Governs Capricorn. Rules property,
land and legacies, and also matters concerning the elderly,
the Eastern belief of ultimate justice through rebirth, karma,
and the fate of humanity.
Day: Saturday.

Uriel

Archangel of Uranus. Governs Aquarius.
Rules magic, astrology, mysticism and sudden change.
Day: Uriel is not associated with any particular day.

Azrael

Archangel of Pluto. Governs Scorpio.
Rules death and rebirth, the mysteries of the afterlife and karma,
and buried treasure.
Day: Azrael is not associated with any particular day.

THE GREAT YEARS

The Great Mother

Most people are aware that we are about to enter the Age of Aquarius, but what of the preceeding ages? What influence has each Age – or Great Year – had on the development of the human race? Each Great Year is approximately 2500 years long – the length of time it takes for the Sun to travel backwards through each sign of the zodiac. The influence of any Great Year can be felt up to 500 years beforehand and as many after, so it is an oversimplification to state, categorically, that the Age of Aquarius will begin in the year 2000. Its influence has been very strong for some time. Traditionally, each Great Year may also be influenced by its polar sign, that is, its opposite sign in the 'wheel' of the zodiac. The dates used in the following pages are approximate. (The more modern term BCE, meaning Before the Christian Era, is used instead of BC, Before Christ, and CE, the Christian Era, is used instead of AD, Anno Domini, the Year of Our Lord.)

THE AGE OF LEO

10000-8000 BCE

This is as far back in time as our knowledge of human civilization goes. Although Man existed for thousands of years before this time, it was only around the 11th century BCE that people left permanent examples of their art and craft behind them for posterity. The beautiful and marvellously lifelike cave paintings found at Lascaux in the south of France and at Altamira in Spain reveal the high standards of primitive art and demonstrate the creative fire of Leo.

This was a highly significant time for the Earth: the last great Ice Age was ending, the survivors emerging into a warmer, more welcoming world. Perhaps, for this reason, in many areas the Sun became the focus of worship that often involved blood sacrifice. As far as we can ascertain, for the people of the Age of Leo, the daily rising of the Sun was a miracle that must be sustained by supplication and appeasement. The memory of the Ice Age must have created great global anxiety about the death of the Sun.

By modern standards, of course, life was extremely hard and precarious. The earliest humans led a nomadic life, hunting animals, gathering food and, later, living in caves. However, with the emergence of farming and civilization around

6000–4000BCE, dwellers in cities were no longer universally concerned with finding food. This meant that some were free to explore more spiritual and philosophical pursuits – a reflection of the polar sign of Aquarius.

Recently, some writers have suggested that the Age of Leo began at a specific dateline, and that the Great Sphinx at Giza in Egypt, generally accepted as being built around 2250BCE, was much older, being originally the likeness of a giant lion, positioned to face the rising of the sun at the beginning of this Great Year. This is a very romantic notion, but unfortunately the facts do not support it: it is impossible to state with any accuracy when the Age of Leo began.

THE AGE OF CANCER

8000-6000 BCE

With the proliferation of settlements, the importance of the family and the home became paramount, and, as becomes the sign of Cancer, the role of women became more defined. No longer were they as likely to have to help fend off marauding wild animals or join the men in hunting for food to scrape together an existence. The milder climate encouraged the

development of basic agricultural skills, the hunter-gatherers became farmers and fishermen, and their womenfolk perfected the domestic arts and concentrated on motherhood.

It was a time of great fertility, as reflected in the widespread worship of the Great Mother and the religious observance of the seasons of the year and phases of the Moon (Cancer is ruled by the Moon – see The Ruling Planets). Many figurines

depicting the Great Mother have been found dating from this time. They show her as great-breasted and full-bellied, the epitome of beauty in a time when fecundity was all, and well-padded females were more likely than their skinny sisters to last through the winter.

Many modern anthropologists believe that people in those days were totally ignorant of the basic facts of conception and probably believed that women were the sole progenitors of their offspring. This bestowed an air of great magic and mystery on women, hence the intense fervour of early goddess worship.

There was also widespread veneration of the Moon at this time, partly because of its very Cancerian link with the cult of women.

The polar influence of earthy, Saturnine Capricorn introduced elements of caution and constraint to the early settlements. Life, always precarious, was usually short, the average lifetime was only about thirty years.

THE AGE OF GEMINI

6000-4000 BCE

By now mankind had recovered from the trauma of the Ice Age and was beginning to develop intellectually, as becomes the Age of Gemini. Ruled by Mercury (see The Ruling Planets), Gemini is the sign of communication and self-expression, of quick-wittedness and movement. Consequently, this was the era when the first known alphabets were formed and the art of writing was standardized within several civilizations, including those of Egypt and China. Some people believe, as befits a time of movement, that this was when the wheel was invented, enabling people to expand their horizons, both literally and figuratively.

Due to the polar influence of Sagittarius, it may also have been the time when early, horse-like animals were first tamed and put to work. Because Man was now relatively mobile, human nature, unfortunately, demanded that he become covetous and quarrelsome. Consequently, this Age saw the beginnings of larger-scale territorial battles. Bows and arrows were probably invented at this time, again thanks to the polar influence of Sagittarius.

Gemini's ruling planet Mercury governs all matters connected with commerce, and it was during the Age of Gemini that trading began in earnest between far-flung settlements. Thanks also to the adventurous Sagittarian influence, these trade routes may have encompassed vast tracts of land and even the oceans. This was a time of enormous expansion and discovery.

THE AGE OF TAURUS

4000-2000 BCE

This is the age of the greatest builders of history, when astonishing temples and pyramids were constructed on both sides of the Atlantic: in Egypt, Crete and Sumer to the East; and in Central and South America to the West. The precision and solid, Taurean beauty of these giant buildings remains unparalleled to this day, and the mystery of their true purpose is still baffling. However, what is certain is that they were built to last, a typical Taurean trait.

This was also the time of the great bull cults of the Minoans on the island of Crete and in Babylon and Egypt. Murals in the very ancient ruined city of Knossos in Crete depict lithe female acrobats entertaining the court by leaping over the heads of bulls. In Egypt at this time, the bull was venerated as the physical embodiment of the Father god, Ptah, and of Osiris, the dying-and-rising consort and half-brother of the mother goddess Isis. Bull bones were discovered in the pyramid at Dashur. It is thought that a bull was sacrificed as a gift to Osiris, then buried in state to represent him. He was then believed to rise again three days later, as Osiris did in legend.

Bulls were venerated throughout this period as embodiments of strength, virility and stamina,

and although they were eaten and used as beasts of burden, they were also honoured as noble beasts.

The polar influence of Scorpio, the sign of occult secrets, death and rebirth, was particularly strong at this time in Egypt, where the priests intoned instructions over the embalmed bodies of the newly dead on how to navigate the perils of the afterlife. It is often said that the ancient Egyptians were obsessed with death, but the truth is that they constantly celebrated life – in parties, festivals and through drug-taking. They saw death as a natural rite of passage to a new spiritual life for which Mankind ought to be prepared.

Ruins of the ancient city of Knossos in Crete

THE AGE OF ARIES

2000 BCE–0 CE

The Age of Aries was the age of conquest, of pushing back the boundaries and striking out for new land and new adventures. Arian physicality was embodied in the Greek cult of the male body, while the emphasis on beauty and strength is clearly to be seen in the sculpture of the time.

The most striking example of Arian energy and ambition was surely that of Alexander the Great, the Macedonian king and military leader who conquered most of the then known world by the time he was in his early thirties. Then, reputedly, he wept because there was nothing left for him to conquer. Single-handedly he changed the world, leaving behind an ineradicable legacy. He chased the hated Persians from Egypt and, after his premature death in 323BCE, left the land of the Nile to his general, Ptolemy, who founded a Macedonian dynasty of pharaohs. So began the Greek occupation of that mysterious land, which only ended with the suicide of Queen Cleopatra in 30 BCE.

Later, the Age of Aries saw the irresistible rise of the Roman Empire, which was characterized on the one hand by the establishment of many of the precepts of western civilization and, on the other, by relentless brutality.

The polar influence of Libra was exemplified by the development of the democratic ideal in Greece, and the rise of formalized justice in both Greece and Rome.

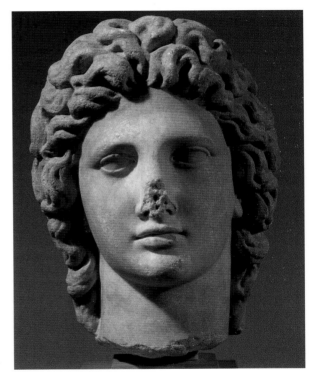

Alexander the Great, conqueror of the world who, reputedly, wept because he had nothing left to conquer

THE AGE OF PISCES

1-2000 CE

Synchronized, perhaps coincidentally, with the birth of Jesus and the rise of Christianity a century or so later, came the Age of Pisces. The early Christians used the secret symbol of the fish to signify Jesus's name.

The beginning of the Age of Pisces also coincided with the rise in popularity of the cult of Isis throughout the Roman Empire. Her temples have been discovered as far north as Paris. She was known as 'stella maris', Star of the Sea, and was the patron of sailors and navigators. For nearly four centuries her cult, in one form or

another, was a serious rival to Christianity.

The Piscean qualities of compassion and forgiveness were characteristic of both of these religions.

Pisces can be evasive and, at worst, deceitful, and the last 2000 years have witnessed an astonishing series of half-truths or downright lies: from the continued insistence that the Earth was flat, even though the principle that it was round had already been expounded, to the machinations of the early Church, which was determined to twist the original Gnostic teachings and customs into something more misogynistic, callous and mundane. With the danger of a spread of scientific and other knowledge, which had long been the preserve of the Church, came the pressure to cover up and conspire in order to control the masses.

The polar influence of Virgo can be seen in the worship of the first, or Virgin, aspect of Isis and similar goddesses such as Diana and, later, the Virgin Mary. The extension of the cult of virginity can be seen in the insistence on priestly celibacy and the demonization of pleasure.

The Virgin Mary with the infant Jesus, whose symbol was the fish

THE AGE OF AQUARIUS

2000-4000 CE

The New Age begins with a celebration of the Age of Pisces and, hopefully, a serious and honest appraisal of its successes and failures. Then, it is time to move on – and there is no better influence under which to do so than Aquarius.

The last hundred or so years have seen an extraordinary upsurge of Aquarian idealism and the burning desire to change things for the better. This process accelerated rapidly as the 21st century loomed ever closer. In the West, at least, women finally won the vote; medical and social breakthroughs meant that many hitherto fatal illnesses could now be eliminated and most pain is easily treatable. Thanks to better housing, diet and education the average life expectancy is still shooting upwards. Women need no longer be crushed by endless childbearing, thanks to reliable contraception. The breakdown of old class barriers means greater equality in education and career opportunity. Rape and child abuse are now treated as serious crimes. And powerful organizations such as the United Nations attempt, though not always successfully, to keep the world safe. But, perhaps, the character of the Age of Aquarius has been most strikingly exemplified by the pushing back of the frontiers of space exploration and beaming back to Earth images from the surface of Mars – including the much-discussed 'face' seen above.

However, no one doubts that all these and many other examples of recent progress can be matched by countless instances of terrible injustice and the phenomena of social breakdown. It may be thought that the Aquarian revolution could not come at a better time ,but, since the influence of each Great Year is felt many years before it technically comes into effect, there must be a suspicion that many of these modern ills have happened because of the Age of Aquarius.

It is also worth considering what form the polar influence of Leo will bring to our brave new world. Will it mark an era of new paternalism, perhaps even benign dictatorship? Powerful forces are at work, politically and astrologically, which are already making themselves felt in the societies of the West. Increasingly, democratic governments are demonstrating, time and time again, that they do not hesitate to use the iron hand in the velvet glove. So far, they have acted only against criminals or those who threaten human rights in many parts of the world. This is an interesting development, for it exemplifies a mix of Aquarian freedom and the demonstrations of strength for which Leo is famous. But will it stop there? How far will Aquarian idealism and Leonine power take us?

This is not an easy balance to maintain, and the road ahead into the heart of the new Great Year may well be rocky. In this more than in most things, it is surely true that only time will tell.

THE GENDERS

Traditionally, the twelve signs of the zodiac are divided into masculine and feminine,
although of cvourse both men and women are born into each.
The characteristics were assigned to the genders aeons ago, well before Women's
Liberation or Political Correctness, and may now seem old-fashioned to many.
However, the signs do seem to be grouped according
to the appropriate gender.

THE MASCULINE SIGNS

The Masculine signs are Aries, Gemini, Leo, Libra, Sagittarius and Aquarius. Masculine traits do tend to be accentuated in the Fire signs, which are Aries, Leo and Sagittarius.

Masculine signs are dominant and assertive, often to the point of being pugnacious, and extroverted. They are natural leaders and rulers, showing fiery initiative and are fiercely protective of others in their care. They are pioneers and visionaries, conquerors of new lands and the first

to achieve great things. They tend to tackle things themselves and can be impatient with others who are less assertive.

Negatively, Masculine signs can be egotistical, arrogant and cruel, and dismissive of the needs and feelings of others. They can be trouble-makers and rebels – violent, belligerent and inclined to subversion.

THE FEMININE SIGNS

The Feminine signs are Taurus, Cancer, Virgo, Scorpio, Capricorn and Pisces. Feminine traits tend to be accentuated in the Water signs Cancer and Pisces.

These signs present gentler, more passive qualities. They are the carers and the nurturers,

inclined to take a back seat and worry over the well-being of others. They are artistic and in tune with their intuition, and may be psychic. Self-evidently, these are the motherly, sisterly, signs,

with all the attendant positive and negative characteristics. They tend to be the power behind the throne, rather than movers and shakers, although many are great achievers, especially in the modern, more egalitarian world, where their qualities are encouraged.

Negatively, the Feminine signs can be fussy, possessive, mean-minded, vindictive, cringing, clinging and over-emotional.

Aquarius, the sign of the coming Age, is endowed with both Masculine and Feminine traits, although it is traditionally categorized as Masculine.

The Ruling Planets

Until the 18th century, astrologers knew only the planets of our solar system that could be seen with the naked eye: Mercury, Venus, Mars, Jupiter and Saturn. (For the purposes of astrology, the Sun and the Moon are also counted as planets even though the Sun is a star and the Moon is the satellite of Earth.) Uranus was discovered in 1781, Neptune in 1846 and Pluto was first seen in 1930. Many astrologers believe that the existence of other heavenly bodies – such as the rumoured Vulcan, which hypothetically exists within the orbit of Mercury – is about to be confirmed. Astrologers will then have to agree which signs these 'new' planets will rule, and what human characteristics their discovery will accentuate.

THE SUN

The Sun, around which nine planets and their satellites revolve, is the life-giver of our solar system. Without it, everything would die. It is about 93 million miles (150 million kilometres) from Earth and is so large that approximately 110 Earths could be fitted inside it.

Many ancient civilizations worshipped the Sun, seeing in its brightness the potential perfection of Man. Zeus, Helios, Mithras, Ra, Atum and Aten were just some of the many Sun gods who were venerated millennia ago. Lucifer, now seen as synonymous with Satan in the West, was originally a beneficent Sun-god. His name simply means 'light-bringer', or illuminator of the spirit. The goddess Diana was known as 'Diana Lucifera', and Mary Magdalene was also called 'Mary Lucifera' by the early Gnostic Church, in honour of their power to illuminate the souls of men. It seems that Luciferans were not the evil Satanists of popular imagination, but were in reality adherents of a Gnostic belief system that celebrated personal knowledge of, and enlighten-ment by, the light of God. Gold and kingship are associated with the Sun, the ruler of Leo and archetypical sign of royalty, nobility and worldly achievement.

A scarab, a symbol of solar power

Its fire inspires loyalty, *joie de vivre* and ambition. However, Sun-subjects can be ruthless, patronizing and overbearing, and their fire can die very quickly, leaving them lazy and downcast.

The day that was originally sacred to the Sun was, of course, Sunday.

Lucifer the light-bringer

37

THE MOON

The Moon orbits the Sun together with the Earth, and meanwhile also circles the Earth approximately once every 27.5 days. The Sun's illumination gives the illusion that the Moon grows and diminishes in size or waxes and wanes, producing the three major phases of New Moon, Full Moon and Dark of the Moon. When the orbiting Moon completely masks the Sun, it creates the spectacular phenomenon of a solar eclipse. This is now thought to have limited astrological significance, although once, like the Moon itself, it was believed to have a major effect on human life.

However, the Moon does have a major role to play in the drama of life on Earth. It causes tides to ebb and flow, and induces certain types of behaviour in animals. The hatching of baby turtles, for example, takes place under a Full Moon. Many animals become restless and aggressive at this time. Research strongly suggests that human beings are similarly affected. Indeed, the term 'lunatic' comes from the Latin luna, meaning Moon. Many people believe that sleeping in the light of the Full Moon helps women regulate their menstrual cycle. Some research indicates that the Moon also affects plant life, both on land and in the depths of the oceans.

In mythology, the Moon is traditionally associated with women, whereas the Sun is honoured as a very male god. The Moon is the Queen of Heaven, a title also given to the Egyptian goddess Isis and, later, to the Virgin Mary. The Moon is associated with magic, spell-casting and seduction, which is why the other great lunar goddesses Circe and Hecate are considered to be enchantresses. So strong was the distrust of the latter's power by the early Church that she became associated with Hell.

However, the ancient Egyptians also had a Moon deity, the goddess Tsukiyomi. The Moon was the first heavenly body to be reached by manned spacecraft. In 1969 Neil Armstrong became the first man to step on the surface of the Moon, famously declaring it to be 'One small step for Man ... a giant leap for Mankind'. As he planted the Stars and Stripes in the lunar dust, the Moon belongs, technically, to the United States.

Cancerians are ruled by the Moon, which is believed to make them emotional, caring and nurturing, although they can become easily distressed and possessive. The Moon is traditionally associated with silver.

The sacred day of the Moon is Monday.

VENUS

Our nearest neighbour in the solar system, Venus, is 160 million miles (260 million kilometres) from Earth, and is usually visible at night. It takes 225 days to orbit the Sun.

Venus has always been associated with beauty, harmony and love. The name comes from the Roman goddess of love, who also governed cosmetics, clothes and all finery and luxury. The negative side of Venus is expressed in venereal diseases, which were once

Hathor, Egyptian goddess of love and beauty

thought to be caused by an excess of Venusian influence.

The Greek name for Venus was Aphrodite, while the Egyptians worshipped several love-and-beauty goddesses – Isis, Hathor and the cat-headed goddess, Bast. In Christian iconography the nearest saint to Venus – although of course the Church has never celebrated female sexuality – is Mary Magdalene. In Scandinavia, the goddess of love was Freya, who gave her name to Friday.

Venus rules both Taurus and Libra, endowing them both with an appreciation of beautiful things and a lusty love of good sex. Both, in their own way, seek harmony – Taureans, with their need for stability, hate anything that rocks the boat, while Librans' distaste for confontation underscores all their relationships.

The sacred day of Venus is Friday.

The cat-headed Egyptian goddess Bast

MERCURY

This tiny planet, the nearest to the Sun, is just 3000 miles (4880 kilometres) across, with a year of 88 days – the second-fastest-moving heavenly body after the Moon.

Mercury was the name of the Roman messenger god, ruler of communication, whose great energy always kept him on the move. To help him travel fast he had little wings on his ankles and helmet. In Greek mythology he was Hermes, who gave his name to the legendary body of learning known as the Hermetica, which inspired thousands of great names over the centuries, from Leonardo da Vinci to Sir Isaac Newton. Although many scholars once believed that Hermeticism originated with the Greeks, there is increasing evidence that they had merely adapted much older Egyptian wisdom.

The Egyptian version of Mercury was Thoth, god of wisdom, healing and time. Known as 'Thrice-great Thoth', he was worshipped in the form of an ibis-headed man. His secrets were jealously guarded in temples specially dedicated to him in ancient Heliopolis, and passed on only to initiates who had proved worthy of them.

In Scandinavia, the messenger god Loki was also a trickster. So was the Native American Heyeohkah, the mocking version of the creator god, who, nevertheless, showed kindness and compassion to Mankind. All the mercurial gods share the same dual nature. They are both trickster and friend of the human race.

Mercury gave his name to quicksilver, the beautiful and unusual liquid metal, which – being a cumulative poison – is also deadly. It was of enduring fascination to generations of alchemists who sought for centuries to turn base metal into gold.

Gemini and Virgo are both ruled by Mercury. Typical Geminians are truly mercurial – quick-witted, fast talkers, energetic and volatile. However, there can also be an element of the trickster in them.

Virgoans are great communicators but at a slower pace than Gemini. They think before they speak and can be immensely entertaining, with a highly developed – often self-deprecating – sense of humour.

The 20th century, with its unprecedented advances in communication – from the transmission of the first radio signals to the Internet – has been an archetypally Mercurial epoch.

The sacred day of Mercury is Wednesday.

Left: *The Roman god Mercury*
Right: *The Egyptian god of war, Seth*

MARS

Mars is the fourth planet beyond the Sun. Due to its extremely elliptical orbit, Mars can pass as close to the Sun as 129 million miles (208 million kilometres), and takes 687 days to circle it.

Mars was the Roman god of war, from whom we derive our word 'martial', although the preferred cult among soldiers of the Roman Empire was that of the Persian sun-god, Mithras.

The nearest equivalent to Mars in Greek mythology was Ares, who featured in many epic poems. He was seen as the destroyer, which perhaps explains his lack of cult worship. Possibly, like the Egyptian Seth, he was seen as a god too dangerous to invoke. In India, the destroyer was female – the many-armed goddess Kali, who tore men apart in her bloodlust.

The Egyptians had no god of war as such, but worshipped Horus, the hawk-headed son of Osiris and Isis, who represented courage and valour, Sekhmet, the ferocious lioness-headed goddess of revenge and mighty Seth, god of destruction and the implacable enemy of Osiris and Horus.

Known as the 'red planet' because of the colour of its dusty, eroded, lava-strewn surface, Mars recently became the subject of much excited controversy when pictures taken of its surface in the 1970s were re-examined and it was noticed that they seemed to reveal the existence of artificial structures in the Cydonia region. There appeared to be vast, five-sided pyramids, a gigantic 'amphitheatre' – and, most dramatic and exciting of all – a 'face' (See Aquarius, The Great Year). Usually described as leonine, this massive 'structure' looked out into space – as if intended as some kind of a message for us. However, pictures sent back to NASA by the Mars Global Surveyor in the late 1990s revealed that the 'face' was no more than a trick of the light – or was it? Amid claims of conspiracy and cover-up, Mars continues to guard its secrets jealously.

Arians are ruled by war-like Mars, as are highly Scorpians (although the latter are now also ruled by Pluto).

Mars gives Aries its fiery zeal, courage that often amounts to foolhardiness and its explosive temper. It bestows on Scorpio its red-blooded sense of drama and angry passion.

Tuesday is sacred to Mars.

Mars, Roman god of triumph in war

JUPITER

A far-distant 484 million miles (778 million kilometres) from the Sun, the planet Jupiter measures a massive 90,000 million miles (145,000 kilometres) across. It is the largest heavenly body in our solar system, although much of its mass is composed of hydrogen and helium. It has 16 moons, two of which, Ganymede and Callisto, were discovered by the Italian astronomer Galileo Galilei in 1610. Jupiter naturally emits radio waves, which have confused and temporarily excited beyond compare amateur astronomers who frequently think they have finally made contact with extra-terrestrial beings! Jupiter was the Graeco-Roman god of plenty, also known as Jove or, in ancient Greece, Zeus. He was the protecting father-god of the city of Rome. The Egyptians had no god of plenty, but sometimes the

Earth god, Geb, and Ptah, the father god, were worshipped for their benef-icence. In many cultures it was the fertile Earth Mother who bestowed all material blessings on her children, so the seasons of the year became associated with her waxing and waning fecundity.

Traditionally deemed a 'lucky' planet by astrologers, Jupiter is the ruler of Sagittarius, and is associated with joy, plenty, philosophy and all manner of academic study. Happy-go-lucky and naturally disposed to be optimistic, Sagittarians do seem to embody the air of cheerful expectancy conjured up by the image of Jupiter. They accept that anything can happen but have little fear for the future, feeling instinctively that fate will take care of them, and it usually does. Sagittarians are often happiest with their head buried in a book.

Jupiter's sacred day is Thursday.

Zeus, the Greek father god

The winter Solstice, time of the festival of Saturnalia

SATURN

At 74,600 miles (120,000 kilometres) in diameter, Saturn is the second-largest planet in our solar system. It is 887 million miles (1427 million kilometres) away from the Sun, which it takes 29 years to orbit. The largest of its 12 moons is Titan. Saturn is surrounded by many hundreds of rings, which are composed of chunks of rock and ice.

The god Saturn originally governed the agricultural arts and skills, but later he gave his name to one of Rome's favourite festivals – Saturnalia, in which the dark of winter was enlivened with music, dancing, feasting and more than a little lechery. This usually took place at the winter solstice of 20–21 December, although when the Christians took over and sanitized the feast day of Saturnalia, it was moved to 25 December to encompass other pagan festivals, including the celebration of the birth of gods such as Dionysus.

Because Saturn was once thought to lie at the remote edge of the solar system, it has come to represent coldness, distance and limitation. Many of the old astrologers were repelled and frightened by Saturn, a view reflected in the adjective 'saturnine' – meaning gloomy, taciturn and somewhat sinister. However, we now know that Saturn does not mark the edge of the planetary system, and astrologers no longer consider it to be totally negative in its influence on Mankind.

Saturn rules Capricorn (and, more controversially, Aquarius), bestowing the mixed blessing of great karmic lessons on those born under the sign of the Goat. It can bring restrictions in its wake, and can make its subjects inclined to be narrow in outlook. However, it is also the bringer of tenacity and the wisdom that comes from learning the hard way.

The day sacred to Saturn is, of course, Saturday.

The Roman festival of Saturnalia

THE
MODERN
PLANETS

URANUS

Four times the size of Earth, Uranus was discovered in 1781 by William Herschel. It is nearly 1785 million miles (2875 million kilometres) from the Sun, which it orbits every 84 years. Uranus is surrounded by many rings and has four moons.

In Greek mythology, Uranus was the son of the Great Mother, from whose incestuous mating were born all the creatures of the Earth. He was caught by Saturn, who came at the head of an army, and vengefully castrated. From his severed testicles grew the goddess of love, Aphrodite.

Uranus is associated with abrupt upheaval, like the Tower struck by lightning in the Tarot pack. His rulership of sudden and ruthless change highlights the impermanence of life and the way in which all of Man's greatest achievements and

Aphrodite, who grew from the severed testicles of Uranus

material wealth can be swept away in an instant. This is fate at work at its most dramatic.

Astrologically, Uranus governs Aquarius, bestowing the ability to be forward-looking, original and idealistic. The negative aspects of Uranus as a ruling planet are its tendency to make Aquarians too eager to sweep away the old, to be shocking and to seek 'kicks' in unusual and even dangerous ways.

This planet is now increasingly seen as the 'cult' ruler of futuristic fantasy such as science fiction and of space exploration.

Uranus has no sacred day.

NEPTUNE

The strange, eccentric path of Uranus suggested to 19th-century astronomers that it was affected by the proximity of an unknown planet – which they finally discovered in 1846. This was Neptune, which is approximately 28,000 million miles (45,000 million kilometres) away from the Sun, which it takes 165 years to orbit. Neptune has two moons.

Neptune was the Roman version of the Greek god of the sea, Poseidon. He was often depicted as a bearded man rising from the depths clutching a trident, the symbol of his power. Interestingly enough, he was ruler of the ocean in relatively male-dominated societies, but in Egypt – which was comparatively egalitarian – it was a goddess, Isis, who governed the sea. She herself was often pictured sailing across heaven in her sacred barque, and was known as 'Star of the Sea', a title later given to the Virgin Mary.

Poseidon was said to be the name of the city or main island of Atlantis, the legendary continent that many believe sank beneath the Atlantic Ocean in around 10,000 BCE. A highly advanced civilization, for which many technological wonders have been claimed, it was destroyed by a volcanic eruption – some say as divine retribution for the wickedness of its inhabitants. The survivors then went their separate ways, bestowing their great knowledge upon the peoples with whom they settled. As a direct result of their intervention, the Great Pyramid of Egypt was built. This was an engineering feat so mysterious that it cannot be repeated even today. Many other wonders of the ancient world came into being as a result of the same influence.

No one knows for certain where Atlantis was located or if it really existed, but modern researchers have variously situated it near Bermuda, in the mid-Atlantic, in the Mediterranean, Antarctica and Cuba.

Astrologically, Neptune is associated with artistic expression, especially dancing and poetry – and also with illusion. The planet can encourage fine creativity, but at the same time mislead the unwary into the dead end of illusory activities such as gambling or obsessive daydreaming.

Pisces is ruled by Neptune. Pisceans, the dreamy, artistic, indecisive and sometimes even deceitful sign, reflect Neptune's curious power. There is an element of insubstantial promises about Neptune, like wishes in fairy stories. They may come true, to the letter, but in a cruelly deceptive way.

Neptune has no sacred day but, by association with the Moon, which rules the sea, Monday may be considered a suitable candidate.

Poseidon, Greek god of the sea

PLUTO

First seen by Clyde Tombaugh in 1930, the existence of the tiny planet Pluto had been deduced mathematically by the 19th-century American astronomer, Percival Lowell. It is only about 3000 miles (4800 kilometres) across and 3600 million miles (5800 million kilometres) from the Sun, which it circles at a rate of once every 248 years. Its single Moon – Charon – was discovered in 1978.

Pluto was named after the ancient Graeco-Roman god Pluto who ruled the Underworld, which the souls of the dead reached in a ferry that crossed the River Styx, and from which no one ever returned. He was associated with dread, inevitability and doom. However, the Egyptian version, Osiris, who ruled the Duat (the Egyptian 'otherworld'), represented the endless cycle of death and rebirth. Man could rise from death to become, like the Pharaohs, literally a star in the night sky and follow the Sun across the sky during the day, while his soul remained on Earth to be reborn. In many ancient mythologies the Underworld was visited by courageous goddesses – such as

Ishtar and, in some stories, Isis – to rescue their beloved god-consorts. Afterwards, they returned to the world of the living. There was also Persephone, who in Greek mythology was kidnapped and taken down to the Underworld by its god, Pluto. On the orders of Zeus, she was sent back up to Earth for six months of the year. Her return was understood to mark the start of spring, and her sojourn in the Underworld typified winter.

Astrologically, Pluto is associated with the dark, unconscious mind, with secrets and karmic liabilities. With Mars, the ninth planet now co-rules Scorpio, endowing that sign with its passion for the occult (meaning 'hidden') and for plumbing the depths of the human psyche.

There is no day sacred to Pluto but, by association with Mars, Tuesday could be eligible. Saturday, the day of Saturn, is also a formidable contender.

Ishtar, one of the courageous goddesses who dared visit the Underworld in order to rescue their beloved god-consorts, and returned safely to the world of the living

THE
QUALITIES

*In addition to the influence of gender, the elements and the
planets, each sign of the zodiac is affected by having an
intrinsic quality – Cardinal, Fixed or Mutable.*

CARDINAL

Those with a strong Cardinal quality to their chart are, traditionally, supremely ambitious and perhaps somewhat ruthless in getting to the top. They are bursting with ideas and are dynamic in pursuing their goals, especially where their careers are concerned. They see themselves as achievers and winners: every day is a challenge that they willingly accept. Their sense of determination inspires others, although they themselves will continue to take the lead and initiate every new project. They can be dismissive of lesser mortals. Cardinality also represents new beginnings.

THE CARDINAL SIGNS

Aries: Arians are volcanic in their desire to get ahead and achieve great things, and will not stand for any opposition. Energetic, forceful and competitive, they rush headlong towards their goal and are not above behind-the-scenes skulduggery to get their own way.

Cancer: At first sight, this sign does not seem to fit the classic profile of Cardinality, being too unassertive and introverted. However, many Cancerians are courageous and determined fighters, although usually on behalf of others, especially their children.

Libra: Again, these indecisive and decent individuals do not appear to fit the bill of Cardinality. But many Librans use their pleasant, 'anything for a quiet life' manner in order to achieve their ambitions, for example lulling potential rivals into a false sense of security. They can be surprisingly assertive and ambitious.

Capricorn: Like the Goat of their sign, Capricornians will react with fury if anyone attempts to domineer them. There will come a point when they erupt, put their heads down – and charge! They also harbour strong, long-term ambitions, which they determinedly pursue, even though it may take them years to achieve them. Many Capricornians are not happy in a competitive situation and will do anything to end it – but only by winning.

FIXED

*Individuals born under a Fixed sign have an inherent
disposition towards tradition, convention and stability.
They hate change and often refuse to adapt to new
circumstances. These people are not happy taking the
initiative or being in situations that require a quick-fire
response. Fixed signs also tend to have conventional,
conservative opinions and find it hard to move with
the times. However, they do tend to be
reliable and down-to-earth.*

THE FIXED SIGNS

Taurus: Strong, stubborn and traditional, Taureans are the people who translate the great plans of others into solid, three-dimensional reality. They are at ease with customs that are hallowed by age, and have great respect for old-fashioned values. They are loyal, patriotic and unhappy with any challenge to the status quo.

Leo: Those born under the sign of the Lion believe that they have a natural nobility and that they are leaders of men. Their innate laziness, however, makes them disinclined to stir from any comfortable situation, be it a job, a life partnership or a particular house. They hate change for its own sake and, despite their ambition, they lack the necessary stamina to fight their rivals to the bitter end.

Scorpio: Although highly emotional, those born under this Water Sign know their own mind and react strongly, even violently, against challenges to their position. Many of their opinions were formed when young and will remain the basis for much of their adult decision-making. Often unable to adapt or see alternative points of view, Scorpians take everything very personally.

Aquarius: At first sight, this progressive, idealistic sign would seem to be the antithesis of Fixed. However, many Aquarians are remarkably set in their ways, even though those ways may seem unorthodox. For example, there are still many Aquarian hippies eking out a living in communes. They are the backbone of what might be called the New Orthodoxy, espousing anything that fits their idealism, and rejecting everything that does not.

MUTABLE

*Those born under the Mutable signs are always
on the move, either physically or mentally, forever seeking
fresh fields and pastures new. They are restless, versatile and
flexible, hating routine and any form of strict discipline. These
individuals can have butterfly minds, endlessly alighting on new
enthusiasms, fads or crazes, then dropping them just as quickly
and moving on to the next thing. Mutable people can be
unreliable and irresponsible, and are rarely self-disciplined,
although they are often extremely charming.*

THE MUTABLE SIGNS

Gemini: Creative and persuasive, Geminians personify Mutable qualities. They loathe restriction of any kind and tend to despise more solid citizens. Forever seizing on the main chance, they are quick-witted and articulate, and can be very amusing. Extremely gregarious, they are unhappy alone or in the same unchanging environment. They often lack depth.

Virgo: Excellent communicators, Virgoans make amusing and pleasant companions, revealing a sharp wit and a sense of the absurd. However, their Mutable qualities are tempered by being an Earth Sign, which restrains their flights of fancy and makes them essentially realistic. Surprisingly, perhaps, they are not completely put off by change and can adapt very well to new situations and challenges.

Sagittarius: Always on the move, always with an eye to the next project, lover or ambition, Sagittarians are very Mutable individuals. They become unhappy, sometimes to the point of becoming ill, if they are restricted or expected to conform. Sagittarians are delightful people with unbounded energy and a relentless curiosity about life, but they frequently lack the energy necessary to follow projects through to their conclusion.

Pisces: Emotional, insecure Pisceans are creative and intuitive, but often seem a little adrift in the everyday world. They seek peace, harmony and love, and can tend to have an unrealistic view of life. In some cases, this is all that gets them through, because a negative side of this sign is the ease with which Pisceans lose incentive and take refuge in escapism and illusion.

SIGNS
AND
SYMBOLS

Most people are familiar with the zodiac 'zoo' – the collection of symbols
that represent the twelve signs. They are not random images, but accurately
reflect the characteristics traditionally assigned to each sign and contain
a wealth of secret knowledge about its true nature.

ach sign of the zodiac is represented by a symbol – the twin fish for Pisces, for example. No one is sure exactly when or why the symbols were chosen, although some authorities believe they date from Sumeria or Mesopotamia, some 4000 years before Jesus Christ. The priest-astrologers of the ancient world were the first to impose recognizable patterns on the great constellations – Leo the Lion being one example.

Today, seeing such shapes in the stars may seem fanciful, but thousands of years ago imaginations were more poetic, and many myths told of magical animals, such as the dragon, which had strange powers to influence Man's everyday life.

Although the ancient Egyptians left few astrological records, they were almost unique in antiquity for worshipping archetypal, animal-headed gods. However, these strange hybrid gods – half-man, half-animal – were worshipped as aspects of one God. Contrary to the general belief that the Egyptians were idolaters, their religion was basically monotheistic. Each statue represented an aspect of the one true God. Parallels are to be found in Hinduism and in the role of the different patron saints in the Catholic Church, who 'rule' or protect various human activities and endeavours.

Since they were established, the signs have remained unchanged, although there was a movement in the Middle Ages to change the sign of Aquarius into the sign of John the Baptist – presumably because of the connection with water. If this suggestion had been taken up, we would now be about to enter the Age of John the Baptist. (See The Great Years.)

The twelve signs of the Zodiac do seem particularly apt on the whole, and accurately reflect the archetypal character of typical Sun Sign types. The great Swiss psychoanalyst Carl Gustav Jung (1875–1961) believed that, deep in our psyches, humanity shares a collective unconscious – a set of archetypal images, which, at a profound level, we all understand. The signs of the zodiac are but part of this pool of images, conveying eternal truths to our unconscious minds, whether we consciously know it or not.

ARIES

The Ram

Protector of his harem, the ram is an alert, autocratic animal who may look noble from a distance – but at closer quarters he can deliver a ferocious head-butt. Rams are strong and tough, but hardly lovable. Those pale blue eyes seem cold, bereft of feeling, yet somehow always charged with danger. Rams often seem like coiled springs: all that energy winds them up to exploding point, then they either fornicate furiously with the ewes in their flock or cause trouble elsewhere. And once they begin to attack, there is no stopping them: after all, they gave their name to that ubiquitous war-machine of the ancient and medieval worlds: the battering ram.

In ancient Egypt the Sun god Amun-Re (or Amun-Ra) was represented with a ram's head. Hundreds of statues of the god in his ram form line processional avenues at the great temple of Karnak.

The ram was seen as a symbol of fertility, and was often shown wearing a beard, standing for kingship and virility. Even queens were expected to wear false beards on ceremonial occasions to indicate their sovereignty.

Egyptian sun god, Amun-Re (Amun-Ra)

TAURUS

The Bull

The bull can be wild, raging and dangerous, or content to stand in his field, eating and watching the world go by. Think of the difference between the elegant, doomed bulls of the Spanish bullrings and the domestic British version, lumbering, dull and almost too heavy to move. Although essential to the continuation of his bloodline, the bull does not usually have the sexual voracity of the ram. The quiet, stolid air of many bulls can be misleading. Many picnickers have discovered to their cost that the overweight beast idly chewing the cud in the corner of the field has a nasty temper and can move like a train when he wants to. Once mobilized, bulls have extraordinary strength and courage. They also have a certain innate dignity.

In the ancient world the bull was venerated as a symbol of sexual potency and strength, especially in the Minoan civilization of the island of Crete, where bull-leaping was a sacred sport (see The Great Year). A sculpture of giant bulls' horns was set up at the boundary of the necropolis of Knossos, where it still stands overlooking the valley.

In Greece, the king of the gods, Zeus, once transformed himself into a bull in order to kidnap and rape Europa.

In Egypt, too, the bull was a sacred animal. In the Middle and New Kingdoms the bull was venerated as the dying-and-rising god Osiris, who was, like Jesus, born on 25 December in humble surroundings. He, too, died on a Friday and rose again three days later. The bull was also seen as the living form of the god Ptah Seker Asari, while during the latter stages of the Greek and Roman occupation of Egypt, the bull represented Serapis, another dying-and-rising god very similar to Jesus.

A sculpture of giant bull's horns stood at the boundary of the necropolis of Knossos, where bull-leaping was a sacred sport

The Egyptian god Osiris, twin of Isis

GEMINI

The Twins

The celestial twins of Gemini are the Graeco-Roman semi-divine characters, Castor and Pollux. In recent years, research has demonstrated the amazing similarity between the lives of many twins, even if they were separated at birth. Not only do they share the same mannerisms, likes and dislikes, but they also often make the same life-choices, even marrying people with the same names and on the same dates. Then, the same number of years later, they divorce them and marry new spouses, also with the same names! This almost paranormal phenomenon is by no means uncommon, suggesting either that forces other than genes are at work, or that our understanding of the material carried by genes, and the way they work, is far from complete. Conversely, however, the closest possible type of duos – Siamese twins – can show marked differences in predilections and behaviour. One may smoke while the other hates tobacco, for example. It is, therefore, fortunate that with modern surgical skills as advanced as they are today, it is possible to separate Siamese twins and so, if they survive, give them their own meaningful lives.

In the ancient world, twins were believed to have magical powers , perhaps because of their natural telepathic abilities. The twins Romulus and Remus were believed to have founded ancient Rome in 753BCE.

The name of the great Meso-American god, Quetzacoatl, means either 'feathered serpent' or 'magnificent twin'.

In ancient Egypt, there were several sets of twins in the pantheon of gods, including Geb, god of the Earth, and Nut, goddess of the Sky, and the more famous Isis and Osiris, with their darker counterparts, Nepthys and Seth.

The duality of twins represented the eternal fight between light and darkness, good and evil.

Above: *Romulus and Remus, founders of Rome, who were suckled by a she-wolf*
Left: *Nepthys, twin of Seth, and dark counterpart of Osiris*

CANCER

The Crab

The Crab is perhaps the least appropriate symbol in the zodiac. Whereas the small scuttling sea creature is a loner and scavenger, Cancerians are passionate about their families and immediate circle of friends. They can become upset and depressed if denied their company. More than any other sign, Cancerians need others in order to fulfil themselves and to satisfy their innate urge to be of service.

Crabs live half their lives in the water and half on the land, and, in a figurative sense, this is true of those born under the sign of Cancer, for they bring an intense awareness of the submerged, subconscious realm into the light of everyday reality. This, though, does not always make for an easy life. Too often, Cancerians feed off the psychic, intuitive and feminine aspect of the hidden mind and turn it into a constant demand for emotional satisfaction. However, the more well-balanced Cancerians have learned to tame this side of their character and to use their unique insights for the good of others.

Cancerians possess all the typical Water Sign's emotional intensity, which is further enhanced by being ruled by the Moon. Their moods often ebb and flow like the tides, and they frequently allow themselves to be carried away on a wave of feeling, trusting to fate that no harm will befall them.

Like the crab, those born under this sign tend to put up a protective front when their loved ones are threatened, or in order to conceal their own soft-heartedness. Some Cancerians become so frightened or embittered by life that they take to hiding behind their shells most of the time.

Of course, crabs, no matter how tiny, are liable to give nasty nips with their claws, especially if cornered, and this aptly describes the normally amenable Cancerian, who is nevertheless given to lashing out hurtfully if put on the spot.

There are no known mythological associations, but as the crab, in one form or another, was known to all ancient cultures, it may be assumed that its characteristics were generally agreed to fit those of the typical Cancerian.

Recently, there was a move to change the name of those born under this sign from Cancerians – because of the unfortunate connotations arising from the disease of the same name – to 'Moon Children', but it failed to catch on.

Cancer is ruled by the Moon and is strongly associated with feminine qualities, particularly intuitiveness. The Moon in the Tarot also represents these qualities and speaks of things that are hidden

LEO

The Lion

Lions are magnificent beasts – strong, athletic and noble. They can be excellent hunters, although it is the lionesses who usually do the lion's share of the work. Sometimes, even the King of the Jungle stoops to stealing the kills of others. They are good protectors of their pride but can be irascible, chasing off those who challenge their male supremacy. They can even kill their own offspring should they have the temerity to be demanding or too playful.

Throughout history, because lions have always represented kingship, ferocious strength and nobility, their image has often been incorporated into heraldic devices such as banners or shields. The archetypal appeal of the beast can be seen in powerful adopted names such as 'Lionheart' for King Richard I of England and 'The Lion of Judah' for emperors of Ethiopia.

In the so-called 'black art' of alchemy, which was outlawed by the Church, the lion represented the uncontrolled forces of nature in the real world.

In ancient Egyptian mythology, Sekhmet, the lioness-headed goddess, was the avenger and protector of her worshippers. The daughter of the great sun god Ra, her name meant 'powerful' or 'mightiest', and her other titles included 'Lady of the Flame', reflecting Leo's archetypal association with fire.

The story goes that Sekhmet was instructed, in the name of her father, to punish Mankind for its waywardness but once unleashed, her vengeance far outstripped his intentions and nearly destroyed the world. The only way she could be halted was by tempting her with rivers of beer – which she drank. Afterwards, she fell asleep, fortunately forgetting to annihilate Mankind. But Sekhmet had a gentler side and was very popular among those who needed courage in their endeavours.

Lioness-headed Egyptian goddess, Sekhmet

Because she answered the prayers of a certain Pharaoh, granting him triumph in battle, he raised over four hundred statues to her in Egypt. To this day, there are more statues of Sekhmet than of any other Egyptian deity, many of which are in western museums.

She is now a great favourite with New Agers.

VIRGO

The Virgin

The symbol of innocence, the Virgoan sign also, conversely, represents the time of harvest, when the seed sown was finally reaped, a symbol of fertility. This apparent contradiction derives partly from the old confusion of the word 'Virgin' with young woman – the original Greek word for the 'Virgin' Mary in the New Testament simply meant a girl – and partly from associations with pagan goddesses.

All major goddesses who were represented in human form – such as Demeter, Diana, Ceres and Isis – were believed to have three main chronological 'aspects': virgin or young woman, then mother and finally old woman or crone. These synchronized with, and were symbolized by, the New Moon, the Full Moon and the Dark of the Moon. However, unlike the Virgin Mary, whose status is unchanging, these goddesses moved fluidly from one aspect to another, thus symbolizing all aspects of womanhood. Some were worshipped in one aspect only – Isis was usually the Mother, for example – but they were understood to be rulers over all female experience, which is why they were so beloved of their women worshippers.

The Greek goddess Demeter

LIBRA

The Scales

The only inanimate object in the zodiac, the Scales represent the eternal struggle to achieve balance and justice. These days scales can be very hi-tech, usually with a single weighing pan, which does not adequately convey the essence of balance as did the old double-pan version.

The Scales have a profound association with the concept of justice – as exemplified in the statue of blind Justice holding the scales outside London's Old Bailey criminal courts. But once again, this concept originates in the mythology of ancient Egypt.

In Egyptian mythology, the soul was believed to undergo extraordinary adventures in the Underworld after leaving the body. The central event in this journey of the afterlife was the weighing of an individual's heart in the balance by the goddess Ma'at, the ruler of human and divine justice. She carefully weighed the hearts of men – which, the ancient Egyptians believed, encompassed a lesser 'soul' – against the feather of truth, which was her own symbol, as a measure of their goodness on earth and their right to enjoy eternal life with the gods.

Egyptian priest-judges always wore masks of Ma'at when pronouncing their verdicts in legal cases.

Ibis and the Egyptian goddess Ma'at, ruler of human and divine justice

SCORPIO

The Scorpion

These tiny, armoured creatures are greatly feared, yet few of them possess a sting that is serious, let alone fatal. Image is all to a Scorpian! Sometimes, however, they are so eager to attack enemies with their venom that they overreach, and actually sting themselves. This should act as a dire warning to vengeful, dark-hearted Scorpian types!

Originally, the symbol for this sign was the Phoenix, the magical bird of mythology, which was consumed in fire, only to rise from the ashes, as magnificent as ever. This is very much the positive side of Scorpio.

There are many mythological and magical associations with the Phoenix. He was intimately involved with the transformative aspects of

alchemy, and often represented the cycle of incarnation, death and rebirth. The Phoenix also, occasionally, symbolized the many dying-and-rising gods of the ancient world. These included Attis, Osiris, Tammuz, Adonis, Dionysus, Mithras and, last of all, Jesus himself. Their deaths were associated with the coming of winter, and their rebirth with the renewal of nature in the spring, and with reincarnation. Every year, there were great festivals to celebrate the death and resurrection of these gods – which were eventually appropriated by the early Church and became the Christian celebrations of Easter.

Mithras, one of the many dying-and-rising gods of mythology

SAGITTARIUS

The Archer or Centaur

The Archer was the mainstay of ancient armies. Poised, strong-armed and alert, with his eye constantly on the far-distant target, the arrows flew swiftly from his bow. Although some may have fallen short, many hit the bull's-eye – rather like the myriad ideas and ambitions of a typical Sagittarian.

Energy, virility and even a certain dream-like surrealism distinguish the symbol of the Centaur – who is often also shown with bow and arrow. The Centaurs were ubiquitous in Greek mythology, where they were often depicted as being particularly sexually voracious. For example, in the story of the rape of the Sabine women by the early Romans, it is the Centaurs who carried off the women.

Sometimes Centaurs were associated with Pan, the hooved nature god of the ancient world, whose musical pipes could lure the unwary into the deepest woods. There, they would become so disoriented that panic ensued. Indeed, this is where our word 'panic' derives from. Pan was also linked with unashamed sexuality, and his statues were often depicted with erect phallae. In ancient Egypt, he was known as Min, who was also shown as ipthyphallic.

Pan was believed to have been killed off by the coming of Christianity. One story tells how a mysterious voice could be heard moaning 'Pan is dead!' – but the modern pagan movement, both in Europe and the United States, has seen a return to his worship and a newed respect for nature.

Pan, the great Nature god

CAPRICORN

The Goat

The goat is a highly adaptive creature who can – and often does – eat just about anything. He can also live just about anywhere, even in some very hostile environments.

The goat is usually a pleasant, amenable beast, getting on well with its own kind, other animals and humans alike, and producing delightful milk. However, goats can be difficult, as any farmer who keeps them will attest. They can also be very destructive. Goats frequently appear to come from nowhere to land a very painful butt on the particularly tender areas of humans.

In Christian countries, the goat has had a bad reputation as an associate of the Devil. During the witchcraft hysteria that began in 15th- century Europe, it was believed that witches flew on their broomsticks to unholy Sabbats, or meetings with the Devil, in which their evil master appeared as a gigantic goat. This was said to represent the worship of the Goat of Mendes (or Memphis) in ancient Egypt, for which there is little or no evidence. Later, this idea was amended: the Satanist High Priest was said to wear a mask of the Goat of Mendes while presiding over filthy – that is, sexual – rites in his master's name. Modern researchers have found no evidence that such ceremonies ever took place.

Witches on their way to a Sabbat

AQUARIUS

The Water Carrier

Usually depicted as a young man pouring water from his vessel, Aquarius evokes feelings of compassion, refreshment and rest after a hard struggle. There is also the resonance of a constant flow of ideas or good fortune.

Travellers across the arid wastes of life feel their hearts lift up at the sight of the water carrier; they are refreshed and perhaps inspired by him, reinvigorated before resuming their journey. It is a potent and apposite symbol for the idealistic and humanitarian Aquarian.

In ancient times, the Egyptian goddess Isis was the water carrier: she was often depicted as holding two jars, constantly pouring a stream of life-giving water from one to the other, an image that became incorporated into the symbolism of Temperance, in the Major Arcana of the Tarot cards (and, in some packs, in the Star).

For thousands of years before the building of the Aswan Dam in 1960–4 , Egypt was totally dependent on the River Nile for its livelihood. Water was deemed to be very precious, which is why only royalty and certain priesthoods had their own pools, and why water was the central element in their sacred ritual of baptism. They had practised the rite of confession of sins and the symbolic cleansing by immersion many centuries before John the Baptist (who had his headquarters in Alexandria in upper Egypt) took it into Judaea.

John the Baptist. Moves in the Middle
Ages to rename the sign of Aquarius after him came to nothing

In the Middle Ages, there were moves to rename this sign 'John the Baptist' but they failed – perhaps because it would have been too confusing, or because his feast day, on 24 June, does not fall within the span of Aquarius.

Astrologers are uncertain about exactly when the Age of Aquarius will transpire. Some believe it has already dawned, while others believe it will not begin for another two or three hundred years. However, whenever a new Great Year arrives, its influence is always felt many years beforehand. Either way, therefore, we have already begun to feel the effects of the Age of Aquarius.

PISCES

The Fish

The symbol is two fish, sometimes apparently tied together, constantly swimming against each other and wasting their energies. Even if they are free, one is set to go one way while the other forever journeys in the opposite direction. It is an apt symbol for this often contrary, dual Water Sign.

Fish are notoriously difficult to catch – otherwise there would be no sport in fishing. They symbolize the elusive, unpredictable characteristics of those sometimes slippery customers born under the sign of Pisces.

However, fish also go deep, sometimes to the very bottom, plumbing the depths. In dreams, water always symbolizes the hidden emotions and darkest secrets of the unconscious mind, with which many Pisceans are intuitively in touch.

The fish was an early symbol of Jesus: 'fish' in Greek was made up of the same letters as his name. In the first days of Christian persecution under the Roman Empire, the sign of the fish, scrawled on walls and doors, told fellow-believers in which houses they could safely take shelter.

Many of Jesus's male disciples were originally fishermen: Simon Peter, the founder of the Christian Church and the first Pope, was affectionately known as 'the Big Fisherman' because of his unusual height. Like many of the dying-and-rising gods of his day, Jesus was known as 'the Fisher of men'. However, few today realize

Above: *Mary Magdalene, the original 'Fisher of Men'*

Left: *Jesus, whose symbol was the fish*

that this was a title that, according to the many gospels not included in the New Testament, was originally given to his close companion, Mary Magdalene, by Jesus himself.

THE SUN IN ARIES

(21 March — 20 April)

Sun Sign: ARIES

Sign: THE RAM

Ruling Planet: MARS

Gender: MASCULINE

Element: FIRE

Quality: CARDINAL

Compatibility: TAURUS

AND VIRGO

Non-compatibility: LEO,

GEMINI, LIBRA AND AQUARIUS

Sun Sign Arians are feisty, straightforward and adventurous. Blessed with abundant energy and drive, they have no time for laziness or prevarication and make excellent motivators whether in the workplace or at home. Keen-witted, they see straight to the heart of a problem, cutting away all the unnecessary detail and distractions and are much admired for being quick on the uptake. They are idealistic, eager to defend the underdog, and impulsively drawn to many campaigns for the betterment of humanity, even if they are often lost causes.

The first sign of the zodiac, Aries represents springtime, the burgeoning of new life and a great upsurge of energy and optimism. There is a childlike belief in miracles, in things coming right – perhaps at the last moment, just before disaster strikes. Often, though, this blind faith is justified. Positively aspected Arians can be very lucky. There is an attractive naivety about them, a marked lack of deviousness or pessimism, and an ability to find energy and resources inside themselves when everyone around them is burned out. If they believe in something, they will harness all that Martian zeal and go for it, without allowing themselves to worry about the consequences.

Negative Arian characteristics arise out of their driven nature. Often, they seem cold and afflicted with tunnel vision. To them, the end usually justifies the means, even if the way to the top involves methods that are questionable, even ruthless. They are childishly egocentric, extremely demanding and liable to throw violent tantrums if denied their own way. Always leaping before giving even the most cursory look around, Arians often find themselves in deep trouble. Then, they become hurt and bewildered at what they see as the blind force of fate singling them out for undeserved punishment. 'Why me? I was only trying to help!' is a typical Arian response when things fall apart because of their own miscalculation or inappropriate behaviour.

Arians are disarmingly frank, and in their eagerness to let everyone know exactly where they stand they can be very hurtful and over-blunt. They are good with words but all too often they use them as weapons and can be cuttingly sarcastic and dismissive. Profoundly self-centred, they rarely bother to see themselves as others see them and this is the hardest lesson for them to learn, often at great cost to themselves and those around them. Born under the archetypal fire sign, Arians can burn up and burn out with equal ease, destroying even their loved ones as they flame their way through life. Many people find badly aspected Arians hard to know and even harder to love, especially when they are well on their way up the ladder of success. It is then that they use anyone and every one as stepping stones.

APPEARANCE

Typical Sun Sign Arians tend to be angular, slim people in early life, although they may fill out later. They have a high colour and brown or reddish hair. Rarely graceful, though, they seem awkward and ill at ease in their bodies, with particularly sharp elbows and knees.

HEALTH

Traditional Arian areas of weakness are the eyes, head, teeth and upper jaw. Always in a tearing hurry, they often have a fast metabolism, which keeps their weight down, but the constant speed has its drawbacks, and they are prone to stress. They suffer badly from tension headaches.

Though usually far too motivated either to notice illness or give in to it, they may be suddenly felled by feverish ailments or accidents, to which they are particularly prone, due to their haste and carelessness.

Their Arian impetuousness makes them neither good patients nor natural nurses, and they rarely follow a course of medication or treatment through to the end. This, unfortunately, causes relapses or recurrences of the illness. If given a choice, they may change doctors or type of treatment in mid-stream, not because of indecision, but out of impatience. Arians are not good with pain. The slightest twinge worries them out of all proportion to its danger, but they rarely have time to be hypochondriacs. They demand quick fixes or none at all. For this reason, they tend to favour conventional medicine, deeming alternative or complementary therapies too time consuming and uncertain. Why waste time boiling up Chinese herbs or meditating when you can pop a pill?

CAREER

Arians are made for adventure, whether it takes the form of dealing with 'futures' on the money markets or hacking their way through the Amazonian rainforest. Their energy and disregard for their own safety or comfort makes Arians, both male and female, pioneers at heart, willing to put up with enormous difficulties and setbacks for the sake of reaching their goal.

As long as they can be number one, a star in their chosen field, they are generous and inspiring to work with. However, once they are questioned or crossed, their bad temper can make them difficult – even dangerous – colleagues. Well-aspected Arians are public spirited, as long as they can make tangible improvements and see results quickly. They are impatient with anything requiring diplomacy or long, drawn-out committee work. With Mars as their ruling planet, many Arians are drawn to the armed services, where they often achieve high rank and distinguish themselves under fire. They can also express this side of their nature in paramilitary organizations, the police or the Scout movement.

Arians hold strong political and religious views – at worst to the point of fanaticism. They can be either extremely right- or left-wing, or they can slip easily into the role of missionary with regard to their chosen religion. They have the dubious honour of making excellent cult leaders.

Anything involving long-term planning is anathema to Arians, and money-making is usually incidental to their ambitions. Typical Arians, who find materialism and luxury off-putting, are better at making money for others than for themselves.

They are ill at ease with boring and repetitive jobs, seeking to express themselves as individuals whenever possible. They thrive on challenges, and have an enviable capacity to shut out background noise and concentrate on the job in hand. They can be enterprising and excellent motivators of a workforce, but once they are expected to be second-in-command or knuckle down to unappealing tasks, their performance drops sharply.

They find it hard to back down or apologize, although they are usually direct in most of their dealings. However, if they are forced to say sorry, don't expect sincerity from them!

Rows will be frequent, although male Arians are quick to make up with chocolates, flowers and romantic gestures, such as a trip to the theatre or a weekend break. Always demanding, all Arians will expect, rather than give, support, although they can be motivated to save a relationship if their hearts and sexuality are really engaged. Under their pomposity and bluster, they can often be very vulnerable, and the wise partner soon realizes that they need to be encouraged and praised constantly, perhaps even 'babied' through any crisis.

Hot-headed and devil-may-care, Arians often put themselves and others in all sorts of danger. Never go exploring caves with a lone Arian. All the same, they can be charming, if irresponsible, parents. Some may even find themselves being treated like teenagers by their own children and may be the cause of despair for the more cautious and sober members of their family throughout their lives. Although they will love their spouses, parents and family devotedly, everything begins and ends with their own perspective. Arians rarely ask: 'How do you feel?' The way they approach problems in the family inevitably begins with: 'I think… I feel… ' When their sarcasm or thoughtlessness reduces their loved ones to silent fury or hurt bewilderment,

RELATIONSHIPS

Passionate and incurably romantic, both male and female Arians tend to need joyous sex and close relationships throughout their lives. This is a sign of extremes: the pendulum can swing the other way. Some Arians find sex a complete waste of time, although they tend to be in the minority. Most typical Arians find the bedroom either an adventure playground or a battlefield, and they love sexual experimentation, although their basic egocentricity can make them too demanding and selfish as lovers. Incompatibility is often more about a partner's occasional need to sleep rather than a different attitude to the sex act itself.

Arians find themselves rudderless, without the resources or people skills to put things right. Fortunately, they rarely sulk, seeking above all to get things out in the open and to let others know exactly where they stand, even if this means adding further to an already hurtful situation.

ruling planet, Venus, is the perfect counter to Martian extremism, softening a tendency to see life as a series of all-or-nothing challenges. Taureans are traditionally no-nonsense, four-square individuals who are conservative and restrained. Fortunately, they often have a secret

there is an attractive naivety about them, a lack of deviousness or pessimism and an ability to find energy and resources inside themselves when everyone around them is burned out

When romance dies or a loved one disappoints them in some way, Arians can appear to be cruelly dismissive, often reacting by completely cutting the 'culprit' out of their life, as if shutting a door on the relationship and throwing away the key. Always looking forward, to the next project or lover, they rarely indulge in nostalgia or sentiment, and they can seem to discard lovers, friends and family without a backwards glance. Any slights cast on them and their integrity will meet with raging fury followed by cold disdain. Arians are unlikely to give second chances or sit down and think about the motives or problems of other people.

admiration for more flamboyant characters, and can fall deeply in love with Arian fire. Virgoans can be considerably more organized than Arians, which is no bad thing. However, their introversion and tendency to keep their emotions under wraps can be either intriguing or, at worst, deeply irritating to the average Arian.

Although there are always notable exceptions to the rule, another Fire Sign, Leo, is far too similar in character and disposition to be a life mate for an Arian. They would constantly be fighting to be at the centre of attention. Air signs – Gemini, Libra and Aquarius – all too often succeed in fanning the Arian flames, while Cancer, Scorpio and Pisces are either too 'wet' and wimpy for Aries, or they pour too much cold water on all those magnificent, unrealistic Arian plans.

IDEAL PARTNER

Arians need support, encouragement and bringing down to earth – with a bump, if necessary – so their ideal life partner belongs to one of the Earth signs, Taurus or Virgo. Their

Compatibility in Relationships

Aries
Fire meets fire with fellow Arians, and a clash of egos may cause far too many problems for a happy life.

Taurus
Calm, dignified and stolid Taureans can give madcap Arians the status and stable home they seek.

Gemini
Geminians tend to be too flighty – and often too wily – for pioneering Arians' long-term plans.

Cancer
Home-loving Cancerians may offer stability but cause too many scenes. Sometimes, it works though.

Leo
Two volatile Fire Signs together do not make for a happy life. Some Leos are big enough to compromise.

Virgo
Orderly, down-to-earth Virgoans can ideally complement Arian fire, as long as they are not too secretive.

Libra
Gregarious and fun-loving Librans can suit Arians but the Ram's ambitions can be too self-centred.

Scorpio
Aries will be fascinated by the deep, unfathomable Scorpian but life will prove too intense for comfort.

Sagittarius
Arians and easy-going Sagittarians do get on but in the end both will go their separate ways.

Capricorn
Repressed, inhibited Goats may hero-worship Arians but this combination won't last for long.

Aquarius
Crusading Aquarians can all too often succeed in clashing with pioneering Arians for the centre of attention.

Pisces
Dreamy and emotional Pisceans will often find it hard to give Arians the emotional freedom they need.

THE ARIAN CHILD

Spontaneous and demonstrative, Arians always remain childlike, sometimes even childish. But when they are small children, they can delight and exasperate their parents more than most, being free with their affections but also particularly unruly and headstrong. They are given to foot-stamping, tears before bedtime and

Criticism and punishment need to be handled sensitively because Arians are inclined to give up if humiliated or rejected. Constructive criticism and constant encouragement, on the other hand, can produce extremely high standards of achievement. Arians always live up to others' expectations. Because of their self-centredness and adventurous spirit, they need clear guidelines for behaviour – the earlier the better. Arians have

They are given to foot-stamping, tears before bedtime and truly spectacular temper tantrums if not allowed to have their own way

truly spectacular temper tantrums if not allowed to have their own way. Nevertheless, they also have respect for authority and react very favourably to appeals to their self-esteem such as: 'Who's Mummy's brave soldier, then?' Arians are in many ways admirably independent and energetic. Foolhardy to a fault, however, they are always suffering from cuts and bruises – and more than their fair share of broken bones – so they need to be carefully supervised, especially on holidays.

a paradoxical love of rules and regulations, and once they understand what acceptable behaviour is, they will usually comply with it.

Highly competitive and combative by nature, Arians are not easy siblings to live with, although boys can become brave protectors of their little sisters. Sharing toys and treats will always be a problem, and the imminent arrival of a baby brother or sister must be discussed with the greatest sensitivity, or the sense of outrage and rejection can scar an Arian for life.

Classic Arian, Leonardo da Vinci and some of his moments of inspiration

Famous Arians

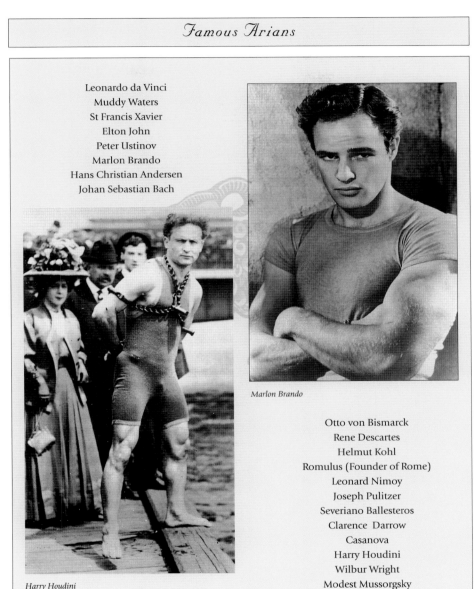

Leonardo da Vinci
Muddy Waters
St Francis Xavier
Elton John
Peter Ustinov
Marlon Brando
Hans Christian Andersen
Johan Sebastian Bach

Marlon Brando

Otto von Bismarck
Rene Descartes
Helmut Kohl
Romulus (Founder of Rome)
Leonard Nimoy
Joseph Pulitzer
Severiano Ballesteros
Clarence Darrow
Casanova
Harry Houdini
Wilbur Wright
Modest Mussorgsky

Harry Houdini

THE SUN IN TAURUS

(21 April — 21 May)

Sun Sign: TAURUS

Sign: THE BULL

Ruling Planet: VENUS

Gender: FEMININE

Element: EARTH

Quality: FIXED

Compatibility: ARIES, TAURUS

AND SCORPIO

Non-compatibility: AQUARIUS

AND SAGITTARIUS

un Sign Taureans are reliable, responsible and affectionate, with strong artistic leanings and a winning way with money. Methodical to a fault, Taureans prefer to stick to well-established plans, rather than change or adapt, and are excellent homemakers and builders of secure families. They are patient, determined and possessed of enormous reserves of strength and common sense. The 'salt of the earth' and strangers to Arian-style tantrums or impulsiveness, they are always there, towers of strength in a crisis. Taureans love routine and rarely question rules and regulations, possessing a natural inclination to respect authority and take orders. London, with its love of tradition, pomp and ceremony, is a very Taurean city. Taureans are Establishment figures through and through. For example, in one London publishers' strike, over 80 per cent of the strike-breakers were Sun Sign Taureans. Excellent seconds-in-command, they do not often aspire to be the top of their chosen profession, although there are many Taureans who are musical stars, such as Cher, Shirley Maclaine and Barbra Striesand. Natural talent in the performing arts will often take them to the top of the tree, but many Taureans in more conventional lines of work, such as banking or manufacturing, are too afraid of change to pursue the glittering prizes with any real and lasting ambition. One of their most typical characteristics is their tendency to plod through life, content with an unremarkable existence as good citizens and the builders of a stable society.

Warm-hearted and loving people, Taureans seek above all to create a happy family. Their home is always their castle, however humble it may be. They love to surround themselves with beautiful things, often doing without rather than having to settle for second-best. Frequently 'hands on' hobbyists, they are keen on decorating and home improvement, although the pace of progress may be slow. One of their most negative traits is indolence, the ability to switch off and do absolutely nothing, except perhaps eat, drink and make love.

The sensualists par excellence of the zodiac, Taureans love all forms of self-expression, except perhaps sports and self-indulgence. They turn being pampered into a serious art form. They love being touched or massaged, and can suffer real feelings of deprivation if denied the joys of love or being massaged. They are sensual eaters, who pick up food with their hands and greet every dish with an appreciative 'Mmmm'. Gourmands rather than gourmets, Taureans, nevertheless, do sometimes become food faddists, seeking out the perfect olive oil or wild mushroom with fanatical single-mindedness.

They can also become knowledgeable wine buffs. Taureans are also liable to fierce possessiveness and to making unreasonable accusations, seeing serious liaisons in the most light-hearted and innocent of banter. Jealousy can provoke sudden outbursts of fearful rage, when they charge, like a bull at a gate, in blind fits of fury. Mostly, however, Taurean negativity is expressed in dullness, stubbornness and resistance to change. Taureans can be 'Old Fogeys' at any age.

APPEARANCE

Often short to medium height and stocky, Taureans' delicate hands and feet reveal a strong artistic streak, and although archetypically broad-shouldered, they can have a marked lack of bottom. As the years go by, their lifestyle virtually guarantees increasingly generous padding. Their eyes are bright and soulful, and their voices can be musical and sexy. They move gracefully, surprisingly light on their feet, with the assurance of a dancer. However, they move slowly, in a measured fashion and at a steady pace.

HEALTH

Too much food and wine inevitably takes its toll, and Taureans are often martyrs to obesity and its associated health problems. In some cases, they can find themselves hopelessly addicted to both food and alcohol, although it will cause them great pain to admit it. Traditionally, Taureans suffer with their throat and necks, which is a grave affliction to the many professional singers in this sign.

They avoid solo sports above all, preferring team games, although many Taureans enjoy golf – that great Establishment pastime. Physically strong, they can suffer greatly from the stress caused by any of the major life changes, such as moving house or the death of a loved one, although they will find it very hard to express their emotions.

Stoical and reserved, Taureans often leave visiting the doctor until they can no longer carry on. Sometimes, this has life-threatening results. Even so, they make good patients, obeying doctor's orders and causing nursing staff no problems. They can be competent, if unimaginative, nurses themselves, and are willing to work long hours at tedious jobs without complaint. Most Taureans are content with conventional medicine, although the more bohemian types will occasionally experiment with complementary therapies such as acupuncture.

CAREER

Taureans have a wide spread of potential careers, from money matters – accounting, tax collecting and banking – to the arts, building, fashion or gardening. Intensely practical people, Sun Sign Taureans are happiest when creating something tangible and lasting, be it a house or a landscaped garden, a painting, sculpture or a piece of haute couture. A fixed Earth sign, they are good at putting down roots and above all maintaining their stability against the ravages of change. If they are trapped in uninspiring office jobs they will transfer their creative cravings to their leisure time, often keeping up several hobbies, from amateur operatics to prize-winning rose-growing.

There is no getting away from the fact, however, that Taureans are often content to sit out their entire working lives in dull-as-ditchwater jobs, never really attempting to seek promotion or change to something more demanding. Methodical and thorough, they will duck out of going the extra mile that is so attractive to bosses, and might not show enough of the initiative that marks out someone destined for success. Taureans are the career uniform policemen who rarely rise above the rank of sergeant or the publisher's personal assistant rather than a top-flight editor who snaps up best-selling authors. They are the box office manager rather than the star on stage. Having said that, however, there will be few personal crises and personality clashes in the office. Time-keeping will be flawless and absenteeism will be almost nil. Gritty, dogged and strong, Taureans will rise to tackle any major crisis, from a bomb blast to a flood – their sturdy shoulders ever ready to carry the burdens of others, both literally and figuratively speaking.

RELATIONSHIPS

Taureans like to know where they stand, so that they can carve out a distinctive role for themselves that will last, unchanging, throughout the years. In a family situation they like to know where they come in the pecking order, and although they may likely to drive non-Taurean partners mad with boredom. But, on the other hand, Taureans are very generous and hospitable entertainers, so visitors will always be made welcome. Taureans welcome any chance to show off their beautiful home and garden. Business wives born into this sign often score the highest points in entertaining

Taureans seek harmony and peace above all – 'anything for a quiet life'

fume with jealousy over a rival sibling's favoured place in their parents' affections, they will often suffer in silence, keeping their emotional burden to themselves all their lives. Taureans seek harmony and peace above all – 'anything for a quiet life' being one of their favourite sayings – but they can suffer real emotional hardship just to keep the peace. Sometimes, this results in an explosion of rage in inappropriate circumstances, puzzling those who witness it. However, this is the explosion of the long-simmering volcano, rarely having a direct link to the events of the time.

Loyal, devoted Taureans need to make real efforts to keep their relationships fresh. They possess affection, even passion, in vast amounts, but this can easily become bogged down under a welter of complacency. They may forget to speak words of love or keep themselves in attractive shape, or use those little romantic touches that make all the difference. In classic fashion, once married and settled down, Taureans tend to 'let themselves go'. Sometimes, their obsession with their home can make them disinclined to stir out of it, even to take part in family celebrations or holidays, all of which is

overseas visitors, leaving a lasting impression of culture and almost effortless hospitality.

Even when ill or out of sorts, Taureans will struggle to do what they consider to be their duty, and this makes them attentive parents – always being present at Nativity plays and PTA evenings. They will also keep their children on schedule with homework and studying for exams.

Conscientious and dutiful, they are keen to look after elderly parents and organize the best kind of sheltered accommodation if necessary. They are strong on providing for the future and can be very keen about pension schemes and insurance, and will often be insured up to the hilt for every conceivable eventuality. Though life can be unpredictable, Taureans would rather live without hassle than make a claim.

They will stubbornly cling to a way of doing things that even they admit is long outdated. This can be extremely irritating for loved ones who want to move on to more exciting territory. Taureans are suspicious, even frightened, of spontaneity, and need to be advised well in advance of any plans, even for happy social events. Surprise parties and sudden trips are not for them, and any break in their carefully maintained routine needs to be discussed and

Aries
Dashing Arians add sparkle to the life of the more prosaic Taurean. They can have long, successful relationships.

Cancer
Well-behaved, stolid, reserved Taureans can find Cancerian scenes just too much to take – but can learn to cope.

Libra
Librans, also ruled by Venus, seriously attract Taureans. Librans' outlook is too cool, though.

Capricorn
The unadventurous Goat can find happiness with a stolid Bull but sooner or later a red rag will appear.

Taurus
Fellow Taureans make for safety, convention and stability. So it can work but it won't be very exciting.

Leo
Egocentric Leos often charm Taureans but sooner or later there will be a huge, disastrous – and final – showdown.

Scorpio
Opposite sign Scorians fascinate Taureans but there may be too much murkiness for convention-bound Taureans.

Aquarius
To Taureans, unconventional Aquarians can often seem to have come from another planet. No chance!

Gemini
Taureans are often attracted to easy-going and sociable Geminians, who can be too daring for this to last.

Virgo
Earthy and very organized Virgoans attract Taurean but this combination can prove too predictable for both.

Sagittarius
All that energy and irresponsibility charm but ultimately horrify steady Taureans, who prefer pensions to penury.

Pisces
Excessively emotional, clingy Pisceans can be a very definite turn-off for salt-of-the-earth Taureans.

thoroughly thrashed out if it is to stand any chance of happening. Generally, however, Taurus is a sign remarkably free of irritating habits.

Taureans make charming company, being careful never to interrupt, make insensitive comments or become aggressive. However, if provoked into an argument about religion or politics, they may stridently defend the belief system with which they grew up, often becoming very heated. They are far happier at conventional social gatherings than anything wild and will react nervously, and with evident disapproval, if good taste is not maintained. On the rare occasions that they do make a social gaffe, they will be overcome with horror and apologize

profusely, perhaps not so much because they have hurt someone's feelings but because they have upset the status quo. Taureans of both sexes make ideal 'no strings' escorts. In most cases, the terms 'lady' and 'gentleman' fit their style perfectly.

IDEAL PARTNER

Typical, stolid Taureans who seek above all to have emotional and material stability could do a lot worse than spend their lives with another Taurean, although sparks will fly should both these obstinate natures clash. They are inclined to be faithful and carry the same values, even the same tastes, throughout life, and so make a perfect match. However, this marriage of similarities may not be the most stimulating, because the challenges they set each other will be strictly limited. With both Earth Sign sets of feet firmly on the ground, life will be safe, if a little predictable.

If Taureans want a little magic in their lives, they should go for their opposite zodiacal sign – the intense and magnetic Scorpio, whose smouldering charm often proves fascinating to the sign of the Bull. Profound and often interested in occult mysteries, Scorpians provide the antidote to bovine dullness, but their secretive nature is puzzling to the straightforward and honourable Taurean, and their esoteric interests can upset Taurean conventionality.

Arians, with their fiery energy, can also provide opposite characteristics that create a balance, even though this is often rather tense. In addition, the Ram's tendency to wander, physically and sexually, will not meet with the steady Taurean's approval, although they may secretly admire them for it.

Because of their home-loving and stoical nature, however, Taureans are the best providers of the zodiac and are second only to Cancerians as homemakers. They can, therefore, turn many of the most unpromising relationships with diverse signs of the zodiac into lasting love matches, with few real complaints.

Traditional Taureans can all too easily become worried and upset by those who mock their own values and traditions, so they should be wary of becoming too enamoured of the more rebellious sort of Aquarian – for all their many charms. Nor is the sensible Taurean likely to find much joy with happy-go-lucky Sagittarians, who are never particularly keen to discuss the household accounts or putting something away for a rainy day.

THE TAUREAN CHILD

Quiet, reserved and often timid, typical Taurean children know how to keep their views and opinions to themselves. This type is rarely naughty and perhaps even something a 'teacher's pet'. They obey every parental rule, never being too demanding. Yet, they can be stubborn and even their respect for authority can evaporate immediately if their most cherished beliefs and habits are threatened. Some Taurean children will even argue with headteachers if they are defending their right to live life at their own pace and in their own way. Sometimes the victims of bullying, they can shock their tormentors by declaring that enough is enough and turning the tables. This is when the quietly grazing bovine turns into the raging bull, and anyone and everyone in the way had better beware! Conversely, another Taurean type can become the bullies themselves, using brute force to intimidate smaller and weaker children, although they are usually too lazy to keep up a lengthy reign of terror.

As siblings, they are often fair-minded and amenable, but their lack of spontaneity and basic acquisitiveness may cause problems in the nursery. Children who are disinclined to be spontaneous and who are inclined to covet others' toys are not the best playmates. They, too, can be ragingly jealous of a new baby brother or sister – being wildly possessive of their mother's attention – although they often react favourably to being given the role of protector to the new addition to the family.

Pope John Paul II
Queen Elizabeth II
Charl Brontë
Cher
Barbra Streisand
William Shakespeare
Sigmund Freud
Emperor Hirohito
Karl Marx
Robert Oppenheimer
Eva Peron
Sergei Prokofiev
Sugar Ray Robinson
Bertrand Russell
Socrates
Rudolph Valentino
Malcolm X
Bing Crosby
Antony Trollope
Florence Nightingale

William Shakespeare

Rudolph Valentino (with co-star Vilma Banky in Son of the Sheik)

THE SUN IN GEMINI

(22 May — 21 June)

Sun Sign: GEMINI

Sign: THE TWINS

Ruling Planet: MERCURY

Gender: MASCULINE

Element: AIR

Quality: MUTABLE

Compatibility: AQUARIUS

Non-compatibility:

TAURUS, CAPRICORN

AND VIRGO

un Sign Geminians tend to be jacks of all trades and masters of none – or at least few. Quick-witted, versatile and adaptable, they love word-play and jokes, and are often extremely witty and amusing companions – the life and soul of the party. Expert communicators, they are confident public speakers with enviable timing and panache, and are excellent at networking or bringing shy or diverse people together in social or business situations. The dual sign of the zodiac, Geminians need more than one project on the go at the same time and require constant intellectual and social stimulation. Variety is not just the spice of life, it is life itself for typical Sun Sign Geminians, and they can easily become bored and restless – 'twitchy' and nervy if nothing interesting is going on, or if their mind is not being fully engaged. However, even though this is a sign noted for its sharp mind and mental fluency, it can suffer from a very short attention span and lack concentration and stamina. Geminians are inclined to do things in short, sharp bursts and display intense enthusiasm, although a day later they may have completely forgotten that

they were even interested in the subject.

Versatile and adaptable, they are quick to turn apparent disadvantages into personal successes, although long-term plans tend to bore them and routine scares them away. As for living alone, it's simply not on the agenda. A Geminian must have an audience or at least someone else to bounce ideas off – and, hopefully, someone who occasionally has the good sense to bring them down to earth with a bump. Gregarious and often actually frightened of being alone, they love constant interaction and feedback, seeking endless challenges in all areas of life.

Their major flaws are superficiality and manipulativeness. Ruled by Mercury, their quicksilver minds rarely alight on any one subject long enough to absorb the finer points. They can also be very guileful, sometimes to the point of being accomplished liars and even conmen. The tricksters of the zodiac, Geminians are constantly looking for the main chance, regardless of the cost in human terms. They are frequently cold-hearted and uneasy with the gentler emotions. You will often hear them complain of weariness during major charity campaigns sooner than any other sign of the zodiac. The fact is that Geminians are very uneasy with deep emotions, and when faced with strong feelings they tend to take refuge in flippant remarks, sarcasm or

metabolism to eat a little and often, especially energy-intensive natural foods such as bananas and dried fruit. They are particularly sensitive to the ill-effects of smoking, and should never even consider

Aquarians understand the Geminian restlessness and drive, but add their own gentleness and more profound idealism

logical analysis. Their inconsistency has given rise to the interpretation of the sign of the Twins as being 'two-faced', and there is sometimes an element of truth in that.

APPEARANCE

Wiry and bursting with nervous energy, Geminians tend to be tallish and slim, with indeterminate colour hair, which many of them dye to dramatic effect. When at rest they can appear rather mousey and insignificant, but once they are animated and enthused by life, they light up from inside and can have real star charisma. They have small, narrow hands and feet and quick, sometimes theatrical, gestures. They are Peter Pans, maintaining a youthful appearance to the end, although some of it may eventually come from the surgeon's knife.

HEALTH

Martyrs to nervous prostration, Geminians need to guard against 'burn out' and discipline themselves to get enough sleep and eat regular meals. Because they burn up so much energy, it suits their

taking it up – their lungs are delicate and are the first organs to suffer from any debility.

Sun Sign Geminians find regular exercise routines a bore, and should maintain a varied programme of sports and martial arts, which will help balance their energies and promote greater powers of concentration.

CAREER

Although many Geminians are successfully self-employed, they find working alone absolutely unacceptable because they need the motivation and feedback of a workplace – preferably as busy a one as possible. The ultimate charmers and communicators, they are particularly suited to media work, especially the ephemeral world of television and advertising copywriting, where their talent for catchphrases can really shine. Fashionable and chic, Geminians are good at creating an impressive image, which allows them to be all the more persuasive in making sales pitches. Indeed, typical Geminians are *the* salespersons of the zodiac. They enjoy challenges, but feel trapped by deadly routine or too many rules and regulations. A lack of variety can ultimately cause them enormous stress. Many are authors or journalists, often writing two books at the same time or several different articles for a variety of publications. However, don't expect too much depth or an impressive array of facts and figures. Details slow Geminians down: they would rather pay a researcher over the odds than sift their own way through a mountain of reference books. They are often skilled in speed reading and fond of quick fixes, instant answers and immediate responses, which is why they are also naturally computer literate . Surfing the Net is second nature to typical Geminians – once they are online, they can be reluctant to communicate in any other way.

Other suitable jobs for Geminians include switchboard operating, tour guiding, parliamentary lobbying, front-of-house theatre managers, theatrical agents, acting, modelling or anything that involves using personality and persuasion. They also make excellent conjurors and illusionists – sleight of hand and sleight of mind being much the same to them.

Unfortunately, Geminians make good career criminals, having the gift of the gab and the ability to lie very convincingly. Many confidence tricksters were born under the sign of the Twins, and even upright Geminian citizens can rarely resist the opportunity to embroider the truth – usually very humorously. Never forget that Geminians can charm the birds down off the trees and then sell them a used car, before persuading them to lie down in the casserole dish and cover themselves with gravy.

Bosses will often be impressed by Gemini energy and initiative, and by their easy assurance and confidence. But their fast talking and often slapdash reports, completed just before the deadline – can cause problems. But Geminians find the old-fashioned idea of 'jobs for life' too dreary for words, and often flit from one to another well before they can be shown the door.

RELATIONSHIPS

Geminians who grow up in emotionally undemonstrative families are themselves uneasy with kissing and cuddling, and can actually become distressed by others encroaching on their personal space. But they enjoy being in a lively family and seek partners with strong opinions and marked preferences – at least it's something to discuss and argue over. Talking is always the Geminian's favourite hobby, although listening has to be an acquired skill. They will stay up late into the night talking or strike up conversations with casual acquaintances. Even the normally reserved British have an easy, happy-go-lucky attitude to strangers if they are born under the sign of the Twins. Many Geminians have relatively few real friends but dozens of acquaintances, which they often insist on bringing back home for dinner or drinks, or just a chat, perhaps at an inconvenient time for the rest of the family.

Geminians are keen to make relationships work but tend to be too egocentric and outgoing to ever really know what makes their partners tick, or why they are unhappy. All too often it comes as a terrible shock when they discover the note on the mantelpiece and half the wardrobe emptied of clothes. When they moan, 'Why didn't s/he tell me they were unhappy?' our Geminian honestly has no idea what they did, because they were too busy talking to notice.

Often, Geminians content themselves with playing the field for many years before settling down, being rather proud of their image of men/girls behaving badly. Naturally afraid of commitment or any depth of emotion, the prospect of love for life terrifies them. Others throw themselves into their careers, which they use as an excuse for not having a partner or even wanting a close relationship. On the other hand, they can be effusively, even sloppily, affectionate with their pets, over whom they can become extremely protective. The uncomplicated loyalty of dogs particularly suits the Geminian temperament, whereas the lofty detachment of cats, they can find rather offputting. Traditionally, however, talking birds are the perfect Geminian pets – clever, wily, quick-

witted and with a capacity to be funny, although one sometimes suspects it is at your own expense.

Geminians have a multitude of annoying habits, which can add up to major relationship problems. Top of the list is their insistence on dropping everything for some wildcap idea that they have totally failed to think through, and which will end in misery or disaster. And it can be strangely unsettling to try to communicate with someone who does at least three different things at the same time – one of which is always talking on the telephone. (Mobile phones were invented for Geminians.) If you're looking for a nice, reliable partner who is always – literally – there for you, forget your Geminian charmer, who considers being half an hour late to be on time. (Go instead for a Taurean.)

THE GEMINIAN CHILD

Traditionally, it is often said that Geminians have unhappy childhoods, without much love or affection, and sometimes actually traumatic. Obviously, this is a very sweeping statement, which must be true of many children from other signs of the zodiac. Yet Geminians can very easily feel uneasy and out of place, especially when too young to have developed social skills. They need lots of love and encouragement, and need to be given space to be themselves, and to express their energy and creativity. Forever starting a project, hobby or enthusiasm, but rarely staying the course, Geminian children need a firm hand to get anything off the ground. Parents should encourage them to finish off each task before starting the next, although this may be a difficult task. From an early age, they should be introduced to the idea of searching around for information, using libraries and making enquiries so that they learn the value of facts and figures to give their schoolwork some depth. At school and college they will always do better in tutorials and discussion groups than in written work, and they

they naturally dislike – is necessary for everyone, even a Geminian, and so they should be gradually introduced to the idea that a lone walk along the seashore – perhaps with a dog or two – is actually pleasurable and restorative.

Geminian children may not be good sharers or team members, but their capacity for fun and being the life and soul of the party will endear them to most other youngsters, even though they may not make real friends very easily. Parents should try to ensure that they are not too flighty in their friendships.

IDEAL PARTNER

Because they often have their head in the clouds, Geminians need a planner, someone who is careful with money. Taureans are too plodding and Capricornians far too pessimistic, but typical Sun Sign Virgoans, though they can be far too analytical and organized, can do the trick if softened with other planetary influences. Perhaps, curiously, it is another air sign – Aquarius – which is ideal for them. Aquarians understand the Geminian restlessness and drive, but add their own gentleness and more profound idealism. Together they make an excellent team, and can even work happily together, either in business or for charity. Geminians need someone who is fairly thick-skinned and independent, someone who can cope with sudden changes of plan, spontaneous outbursts and the chaos that can come with trying to do a multitude of things at the same time.

may easily become distracted, more than most, by the drama group or the university magazine. Unsuited to the more ponderous subjects such as philosophy and history, Geminians excel in languages, literature, information technology, media studies and journalism. However, many will drop out in favour of more convivial pastimes, such as becoming stand-up comics or cocktail waiters in fashionable bars.

From an early age, Geminian children should be encouraged to have a great deal of sleep. They career through life at such a breakneck speed that they rapidly use up all their reserves and can become severely run down. They should be made to spend some time winding down before bedtime, to help quell their racing minds and prevent the onset of chronic insomnia, to which this sign is particularly prone. Fresh air and solitude – which

Aries
Feisty Arians may seem glamorous but underneath they are far too serious and self-focused for Geminians.

Cancer
Cancerian emotional blackmail and frequent tantrums will send Gemini fleeing. Calmer Crabs might last.

Libra
Both real charmers, Geminians and Librans can seem to have something special but they won't be soul mates.

Capricorn
The austere Goat may view easy-going and plausible Geminians with suspicion and – justifiable – cynicism.

Taurus
Taureans all too often fall for the famous Geminian charm, which will finally be too superficial for the heavyweight Bull.

Leo
High and mighty Leos can be magnificent lovers but, all too often, there will be a major personality clash.

Scorpio
Scorpians' glamour will fascinate Geminians and there may be a real sexual buzz, but tears in the end.

Aquarius
Geminians can fall for the challenge of life with a true Aquarian in a big way and find life-long happiness.

Gemini
Fellow Geminians know only too well each other's wiles – so this won't usually work for long.

Virgo
Geminians can find the more sociable Virgoans good company but they will soon tire of them.

Sagittarius
This will be a fun relationship with wild times and big plans but it won't make for a settled, cosy home.

Pisces
Geminians have little patience for the often difficult, emotionally intense and rather contradictory Pisceans.

Bob Dylan
John F. Kennedy
Marilyn Monroe
Isadora Duncan
The artist formerly known as Prince
Sir Edward Elgar
PC Faberge
Jean-Paul Sartre
Judy Garland
Che Guevara
Marquis de Sade
Anne Frank
Bob Hope

Marilyn Monroe

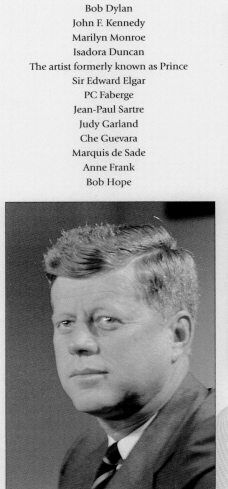

John F. Kennedy

Henry Kissinger
Paul McCartney
Cole Porter
Grigori Rasputin
Bjorn Borg
Al Jolson
Sir Arthur Conan Doyle

THE SUN IN CANCER

(22 June — 22 July)

Sun Sign: CANCER

Sign: THE CRAB

Ruling Planet: THE MOON

Gender: FEMININE

Element: WATER

Quality: CARDINAL

Compatibility: TAURUS AND

WELL-ASPECTED LEOS

Non-compatibility: CAPRICORN

AND PISCES

Sun Sign Cancerians are the most family-centred of the zodiac. Fiercely protective of their loved ones, they are nourishers and carers at heart. Loving, demonstrative and tender-hearted to the point of sentimentality, they attach great importance to anniversaries, trinkets and trips down memory lane. They are unashamedly feminine and even male Cancerians tend to be carers. Cancerians are also in tune with their true self and in touch with their intuition. They are often psychic and can be intuitively wise, but distrust cold logic and analysis: book learning for its own sake is not for them. Unlike fellow Water Sign Pisces, Cancerian dreams are rarely vague and other-wordly, focusing instead on creating images of success and happiuness for those they love. Though often without driving ambition for themselves, they yearn passionately on behalf of others. They are artistic, practical and excellent homemakers. The world outside rarely offers anything to eclipse the attraction of coming home, especially home to the family, and even lone Cancerians lavish time and money on creating their ideal.

However, those born under the sign of the Crab are great worriers, constantly fretting about the health and safety of their family and friends. As far as Cancerians are concerned, if someone is a few minutes late, something bad must have happened to them. Their constant fussing can drive others to distraction. So can their tendency to be over-emotional and sentimental, eyes brimming with tears for the slightest reason – whether real or imagined. Cancerians take offence easily, often going off in a huff. They tend to fall out with others and then keep their distance. They may not speak to those who have ruffled them, sometimes for years on end.

Cancerians are nothing if not tenacious. They hang on to a relationship, belief or cause with their crab's claws, even when it causes them pain. For them, it is enormously difficult to let go and move on. They are constantly looking back and can wallow in nostalgia, even though the past was not the Golden Age or romantic dream they seem to imagine. Cancerians are very good at creating their own myths and turning humdrum lives into fairy stories, even if it means being economical with the truth. Anyone who tries to make them face facts is answered with outrage, denial and a storm of hurt tears.

Being too emotional makes Cancerians moody, withdrawn and even secretive. Sometimes they can sulk for days, without being able to find out why. Since they are virtually telepathic, they find it hard to understand that others may not necessarily share their intuitive gifts.

Cancerians are both loving and loyal, but can be unsure of themselves and somewhat timid socially, preferrng to give someone else the limelight. They will, however, shine at providing the refreshments after the star has done his or her turn.

APPEARANCE

Cancerians are often smallish, with round 'moon' faces and a tendency to put on weight. This applies especially to women who may have what used to be described as a 'motherly figure'. Thse Earth Mother types have abundant, shiny hair, soulful eyes and are economical with their gestures. Another Cancerian type is thin and nervy, with red hair, and is more extroverted in social conditions.

Some people born under the sign of the Crab become so sour through bitterness and worry that it is reflected in the permanent downturn of their mouths, their prematurely lined faces and their cold, dissatisfied expressions. On the whole, Cancerians move as little as possible and only a real emergency will make them do swiftly.

HEALTH

Cancerians, the archetypal couch potatoes, are happiest slouching in front of the television. Exercise is generally anathema to them, but they can be encouraged to take part in family walks. Perhaps the ladies can be persuaded to join the 'family' at an all-women slimming club. Being a Water Sign, Cancerians can excel at watersports: and even the most exercise-phobic among them will willingly take the plunge if there is a swimming pool nearby.

Cancerian weaknesses include their digestive systems, where all that worry can wreak havoc, causing heartburn, colitis and ulcers. Women tend to suffer from breast problems and water retention, but both men and women become very diestressed by all illnesses, trivial as well as serious. They tend to become hypochondriacs, always visiting the doctor, on behalf of family members as well as themselves, and buying over-the-counter remedies. Many Cancerians are fascinated by holistic or alternative therapies, and can spend a fortune working their way through them. It is important to stress that those born under the sign of Cancer are not more likely than any other sign to develop the illness of the same name, but of course it is always a good idea to have regular health checks.

CAREER

Being naturally sympathetic, practical and nurturing, Cancerians make excellent nurses. They understand how unsettling illness can be, and easily relate to their patients. They are natural with children, especially tiny tots, and make memorable primary school and special needs teachers. Here their immense reserves of patience are often rewarded with remarkable progress. Their ability to sympathize with others who are in difficulties also attracts them to counselling and charity work. They can often be found working as volunteers on telephone hotlines, perhaps

as suicide or AIDS counsellors. Cancerians are also the mainstay of help for the homeless and like to make donations for far-off victims of famines. They cannot bear the idea of anyone going hungry, and are the first to react to television images of skeletal babies in the developing world. However, although excellent at 'hands-on' charity work, they can oten be far too sensitive and thin-skinned to work for any length of time in famine areas or with war victims. Most, with some notabke exceptions, simply could not take the scale of the misery, nor the sights and smell's of atrocities, of Man's inhumanity to Man.

Reliable and responsible, they make good co-workers but they can equally run their own small businesses. This is where being so organized with money helps. Cancerians also make imaginative cooks and caterers, although they prefer to see people's reactions to their dishes, rather than remaining behind the scenes in the kitchen. Because of their love of the past and tradition, you may find some Cancerians working in own lives, but Cancerian parents, especially mothers, find that hard to accept. Cosseted and over-protected, children of typical Sun Sign Cancerians can grow up timid and unadventurous or, conversely, become rebels.

Cancerians cling. Female Crabs often refuse to accept that a boyfriend doesn't love them anymore or will not even consider marriage. With an over-romanticized image of love and marriage, it is inconceivable to them that the man in their life does not also want the cottage with roses around the door and two-point-four children playing with granny in the garden. Long after any hope of reconciliation, Cancerians are still trying to revive the long-dead embers of a relationship. They seem not to realize that endless scenes of tearful entreaty succeed only in pushing their beloved further away. They also cling to old-fashiooned values, and even non-religious Cancerians still expect to be virgins on their wedding night. They may also expect their bride or groom to be equally unsullied.

Many Cancerians do not realize that they have the power to lash out and hurt others, though almost never in a physical way. When they are on the defensive – and they often are – Cancerians can hit back with very cruel words, often dredging up old secrets in order to inflict the greatest hurt. If faced with this aspect of their behaviour, they will either deny it utterly or berate themselves for being so wicked. On such occasions, it is better not to press for a rational discussion. When Cancerians are blinded by emotion, they will never see

museums and libraries, or in the antiques trade. They also make tenacious researchers, especially in tracking down genealogical data or some fact of local history. They may have problems, though, with modern technology. Some are actually technophobes, something that can hamper the progress of their chosen careers.

RELATIONSHIPS

Cancerians make rela tionships their business, but they are sometimes not as good at it as they think. They make loving parents, sensitive lovers and generally docile children. However, Cancerians tend to smother their children, suffocating them and others with their endless fussing and their inability to accept that people need their own space and freedom. Children must have their reason. Perhaps when they have calmed down, the topic can be raised in a more constructive manner. But even then it will have to be handled very sensitively. Many Cancerians can take constructive criticism, especially those whose professional training, perhaps in nursing or counselling, makes them more amenable to it. However, it is hard coming from loved ones, and often causes deep family or marital rifts. Cancerians long for an atmosphere of love and harmony to prevail in the home. However, they take every little criticism personally, and brood over it, possibly even for years, so that the hurt goes deep and is constantly fresh in their minds, while everyone else has forgotten about it.

IDEAL PARTNER

Cancerians should stay clear of typical Sun Signs who cannot cope with emotions, especially Capricornians, who tend to be wintry in the expression of their feelings. Best for them are steady, grounded types such as Taureans, who can be very happy to create a nest with these traditional home-bodies. They also understand the need to keep a firm hand on the bank balance, and this combination creates an almost ideally secure background in

Compatibility in Relationships

Aries
The fire and dash of Aries appeals but they have little time for Cancerian emotion. It might work – not for long.

Taurus
This is a perfect match: both are homemakers and respecters of family values. They will enhance each other's life.

Gemini
Self-seeking and specious Geminians can be charm itself, but they'll never be a life-long partner.

Cancer
Though they have much in common, two emotional blackmailers under the same roof can make for disaster,

Leo
Cancerians can worship Leos and make fine homes with them. With enough compromise, an excellent match.

Virgo
This combination can work, though Virgoans may be puzzled and upset by Cancerian outburts and contradictions.

Libra
Life can be easy for a while. Librans value their independence too much to hand it over to a Cancerian.

Scorpio
Flashy Scorpians may infatuate Cancerians, but the price is too high. One drama queen is enough!

Sagittarius
Cancerians want to own their beloved's body and soul – the last thing a Sagittarian will ever agree to.

Capricorn
True Goats will never understand the Cancerian's need to discuss emotion, which will frighten them off for good.

Aquarius
Home-loving Cancerians feel threatened by real crusading Aquarians who want to change their settled world.

Pisces
Both Water Signs can be tearful clingers, which is not the best recipe for lasting love or mutual respect.

which their children can grow up and fulfil their real potential.

Idealistic Aquarians and canny Virgoans can also fit the bill, although they may find Cancerian emotionality very hard to take.

Proud Leos, however, could find Cancerians supportive. Cancerians may idolize them, easily falling into their role as nurturers rather than leaders. Badly aspected Leos can be overbearing and badly aspected Cancerians snivelling martyrs, which makes a bad mix. However, most are well balanced enough to make the combination work.

THE CANCERIAN CHILD

Hypersensitive and moody, the Cancerian child will be mummy's boy or daddy's girl from the cradle. Even so, they will love both parents to distraction and live in fear of being abandoned by them or even left alone. It is important for the adopted Cancerian child to be told as early as possible about his or her background. Leaving it until they are older may cause emotional upset.

Cancerians are inherently untidy, and this is made worse by their inability to throw anything away. Hoarding is second nature to them, due partly to a grasping streak and partly to their extreme sentimentality, which invests every little item with enormous emotional significance.

This grasping side of the Cancerian nature should be nipped in the bud early in life, and sharing toys and treats should be encouraged. Discipline can be hard for parents of Cancerians

the children take everything so much to heart and can become very distressed

to maintain, especially if one or both of them are Crabs themselves, because the children take everything so much to heart and can become very distressed even when mildly ticked off. By far the best way of coping with them is by appealing directly to their love and loyalty: punishments do not need to be severe. Just sending the children to their rooms while the rest of the family enjoy an evening together can produce immediate and heartfelt response.

Many Cancerian children are placid souls and, while not especially witty, can be amusing and imaginative.

Cancerians are often timid and can develop a marked inferiority complex. Perversely, they become almost proud of this complex in later life, using it as an excuse not to take risks or improve themselves, intellectually or materially.

These children find it exceptionally hard to cope with bereavement, whether it is in the death of a pet or a family member. They will see it as a betrayal of love, an abandonment, and may easily become severely traumatized and profoundly angry with the departed. They should be encouraged to talk about their feelings.

Teenage girls born under this sign will be especially moody at the time of the Full Moon, and bursting with nervous energy when the Moon is new. Wise parents will take this into account.

Alexander the Great
Diana, Princess of Wales
Rubens
George Orwell
O. J. Simpson
Meryl Streep
Louis Mountbatten
Emmeline Pankhurst
Marcel Proust
Arnold Schwarzenegger
Julius Caesar
James Cagney
Louis Armstrong

Diana, Princess of Wales

Julius Caesar

Ginger Rogers
Jean Cocteau
King Henry VIII
Arlo Guthrie
Arthur Ashe
Nelson Rockefeller
Ernest Hemingway

THE SUN IN LEO

(23 July – 23 August)

Sun Sign: LEO

Sign: THE LION

Ruling Planet: THE SUN

Gender: MASCULINE

Element: FIRE

Quality: FIXED

Compatibility: CANCER,

AQUARIUS AND VIRGO

Non-compatibility: SCORPIO

AND GEMINI

Sun Sign Leos are powerful, ambitious, and protective – truly the kings of the jungle. Ruled by the Sun, they are outgoing and optimistic, their sunny disposition often inspiring lesser mortals to greater efforts. They are the party animals of the zodiac, dynamic and uninhibited, believing they can achieve whatever they set out to. New York is the perfect city for a Leo. As natural leaders, they love being top of the heap, their innate reserves of energy and self-belief helping them to overcome any setbacks. To Leos, integrity and dignity are as natural as breathing. Warm-hearted and often extremely generous, they love company – especially if they are the centre of attention. Their enthusiasm is contagious, especially when it comes to motivating others in more creative endeavours. Well-aspected Sun Sign Leos are intrinsically faithful partners and loyal friends, and extremely loving in a very demonstrative, expansive way. When life is good for a Leo, everyone in their circle benefits in some way.

Conversely, when Leos are crossed and their integrity or self-esteem is challenged, they can fly into towering rages – which may soon evaporate, but they can leave those at the receiving end shaken to the core. It is easy for Leos to become overbearing. Sometimes they seem to demand worship from those closest to them, without realizing that respect must be earned. Some Leos are out-and-out bullies, taking advantage of any weakness in others, while many can be domineering and unapproachable, both at work and at home. They can also be extremely dogmatic and ruthless in pursuing their particular ideology, giving no thought to the differing beliefs and lifestyles of others. Weakness or illness irritates this type and provokes them into unkindness, even cruelty. Even the lesser Leonine tyrants can be amazingly pompous, often speaking on a one-to-one basis as if addressing a formal meeting, and inevitably patronizing those they consider to be their inferiors. Badly aspected Leos are often male chauvinists or racists, in much the same way as their fellow Fire Sign, Aries. However, the Lion's bigotry arises out of a basic lack of tolerance of any threat to his or her leadership.

Even Leos who appear to be quiet and restrained have all the virtues and flaws of the typical, expansive Lion. If you want to see Leos turn from pussycat into magnificent, terrifying king of the jungle, just injure their pride or treat them with contempt. Then the seemingly docile tabby shakes out its mane and growls.

APPEARANCE

The major characteristic of the Leonine appearance is gloriously abundant hair, often reddish or tawny coloured, a true mane, wavy and untamed. Leos have 'big hair' to match their personalities. They tend to be dramatic and prone to the occasional bad day, when nothing works out and the Sun that rules them is blotted out by a haze of gloom. Slow and deliberate in speech and movement, their bearing is regal and dignified. They tend to have a direct stare, which can be unnerving, and curiously wide or upward slanting eyes, giving them an unusual and rather theatrical appearance. Their complexion is youthful, but also somewhat sallow. When suntanned, they look far more stunning than any other sign. They dress in the best of taste, but are too impatient to drag endlessly around the shops, contenting themselves with one or two good outfits, in which they know they can stop the traffic.

HEALTH

Leos tend to suffer from heart trouble: their lion hearts take so much stress, both emotional and physical, that sooner or later they will have a health scare and become very heart-conscious, though usually late in the day. Until that moment, however, they tend to indulge their love of high-fat luxury foods and good wines, as befits their innate regality. They also tend, for the same reasons, to put on weight, but rarely attempt to do anything about it for very long, although expensive health farms and intensive pampering will certainly appeal to them. They may be far too lazy to follow a regular exercise programme but by employing personal training instructors, they can be weaned off the sedentary life. Anything that requires ugly sweating in a group of lesser mortals is absolute anathema to them.

Leos also suffer from back and spine problems, made worse by their tendency to be overweight and their lack of exercise. However, they can ease their discomfort by doing regular stretching exercises and visiting the chiropractor or osteopath.

CAREER

Leos are happiest and most effective in any career where they can give orders or be the centre of attention. Being second-in-command or a humble team member is not for them, and their irritation at working – as they see it – for and with fools will not make for a happy workplace. When a Leo is upset, everyone soon knows about it. Teaching gives them the opportunity to take charge and also to express their creativity and pass on their often considerable wisdom to the next generation. Leos are often the teachers who make a lasting impression on the children in their care. They may tend to have mood swings

Even Leos without that overwhelming urge to see their name in lights need to feel that what they do is of real value, that their contribution is meaningful. Despite their desire to show off, Leos are fair-minded and meticulous in keeping agreements. They expect others to be the same.

Whatever they do, they expect their attention to be fully engaged, and to be constantly praised and given positive feedback. They can't do any job for long, especially something routine or tedious, without bursting out and opting for something that offers to fulfil their considerable potential. Never take a Leo for granted, or expect them to beaver away without any recognition. Bosses with Leo employees should be particularly careful – Leo the Lion could be after their jobs.

and can be irascible one minute, but capable of making the whole class rock with mirth at some joke or anecdote the next – all acted out with great gusto and a complete lack of inhibition. Their enthusiasms can inspire pupils for life, although they can also destroy the confidence of more timid children – such as Sun Sign Cancerians – with too much over-hearty teasing and the occasional outburst of titanic temper.

Leos have a natural bent for the theatre and the performing arts. This is why they are so much at home in the acting and singing professions, and are often excellent dancers. They are never content to take just any part that comes along, but will use these more humble occupations as a means to an end – to progress to higher things. Working with these potential stars of the show is not easy. Leos can be tiresome as one of an ensemble, and constantly seek to upstage the others – even at the expense of the show as a whole or at the expense of personal feelings. Other flamboyant Leos find fulfilment in the glamour industries of fashion, modelling and design, anything, in fact, which is luxurious and impressive and has panache.

RELATIONSHIPS

Leos make wonderfully sociable companions, amusing, urbane and expansive. They tend to have a large circle of friends, many of them close and many for life. If they can afford it (and often even if they can't) they will pick up the tab in restaurants or host lavish parties. Gregarious and charming, they rarely live alone, even if it means sharing their home with several cats and dogs, to whom they are devoted.

Leos are usually fairly easy to live with, although they do expect others to live up to their own high standards as they cannot tolerate failure. They often expect life partners to be almost as ambitious as themselves. Leos love luxury and the best of everything, and tend to be snobbish. Status means everything to certain extreme Leo types. Because of this, they may even choose to live in an area where they don't really feel at home simply because it is 'posh' or 'up-and-coming'. A Leo is usually nobody's fool, but they can make easy prey for astute estate agents with impressive properties for sale. They are not obsessively tidy and prefer a cosy home where they can relax and enjoy family life. Although they love the planning stages of interior design and home decorating, they are far too grand and lazy to get their own hands dirty. They are quite happy to pay for someone else to do the work.

Leos suffer from a certain dichotomy. Though they frequently lay on the charm thickly, they can be ruthless at the same time, a combination of the appealing and appalling. Male Leos can be surprisingly lazy, often giving up a project for the sake of holiday or changing to something else quite abruptly. The lioness, however, is almost always on the alert, whether it is for the perfect red lipstick, for the bargain of a lifetime, the dream man or the big break that leads to success. These are qualities which can disrupt a happy home, but once they are accepted as congenital in Leos, other zodiac signs are more or less able to live with them.

Though Leos are passionate and faithful lovers, they can still look elsewhere if their partners

betray them or injure their over-developed sense of pride. These partners tread on dangerous ground if they laugh at an inappropriate moment, or even try to provide comfort and understanding at difficult times in a Leo's sex life – worse still, if they show Leos up in any way, however minor. Apart from failure, what Leos hate most is boredom and pessimism. Anyone gloomy and uninspired by nature will not last the course with a typical Sun Sign Leo. They relish the chance to laugh and be sociable, and to wine and dine their loved ones. They really enjoy lavishing romantic gifts on them. In return they expect to be showered with compliments and praised to the heavens. Although they can often see through the more crude type of insincerity, flattery will get you almost anywhere with a Leo.

Leos can be difficult parents. They try very hard to enter into the child's world by playing rumbustious games and acting out bedtime stories at great length – and never mind if their partners are just longing for the little dears to go to sleep. It is in the nature of the Lion to want to be in control where children are concerned. This is why they are interfering, bossy and often extremely demanding. Unfortunately, the Leo parent can destroy the confidence of delicate flower and totally fail to understand their more introspective children, who may be very grateful for the drama lessons and birthday parties for 200 with a famous conjuror for entertainment, but would really rather stay home and read a book.

Aries
Matching fire with fire – and ego with ego – is not a good recipe for a harmonious and loving relationship.

Taurus
Steady, feet-onthe-ground Taureans can make it work with Leos but, too often, there will be a spark missing.

Gemini
Good times will be enjoyed, but difficult-to-pin-down Geminians will not provide Leo with the right home life.

Cancer
This is an enviable partnership: more well-balanced Cancerians can make a happy nest with a beloved Leo.

Leo
There can never be two kings in the same jungle. One will be forced to back off or submit. Not a happy pairing.

Virgo
More relaxed Virgoans can hit it off fairly well with expansive Leos, but most are too inhibited to try.

Libra
Librans and Leos are mutually attracted but the Scales dither too much for decisive, opinionated Leo.

Scorpio
There will be great sex and memorable times but the intensity will cause too many problems in the long term.

Sagittarius
All fire and energy, these two will wear each other out with their headlong rush at life and fierce power struggles.

Capricorn
Any initial attraction will soon wear thin due to the Goat's innate distrust of | Leonine extravagance.

Aquarius
Leos can make a go of it with big-thinking Aquarians, but they may need more support than is forthcoming.

Pisces
This combination makes for a roller-coaster partnership. The water, in this case, is more likely to put out the fire.

There is often an ambivalence in their attitude to successful partners, siblings or children. Leos can be very competitive, although many of them expect to succeed without having to fight against anything other than Fate. To take on anyone else as a competitor makes them feel stressed and threatened.

Leos – male and female – need to be wary of feelings of jealousy creeping in when they are confronted with their children's successes. They will, however, usually take some comfort in the thought that those very successes are in some way part of their own achievement as a parent.

THE IDEAL PARTNER

Leos, especially the men, can make a happy lifelong commitment to the emotional and home-loving Cancerian or the supportive, stable Taurean. There will, of course, be problems, for Leos always expect primacy and deference, and even the most martyrly Cancerian will sometimes feel slighted by this situation. Gentle, idealistic Aquarians, who may be knowledgeable astrologers and therefore forewarned, can cope better with Leo's excessive demands, although they may not always be there when needed. Aquarians are often too busy with a host of good causes to provide the kind of consistent support that Leos tend to expect from a devoted partner.

As far as Virgoans are concerned, the straightforward and usually well grounded Leos can be complementary partners, since Virgo is the sign of the obsessively organized. However, Leos

Although, at heart, Leos want to be liked, what they really crave is the near adulation of siblings, schoolfriends, parents and teachers. This they see as their unalienable right, whether or not they have earned it. Fortunately, this tendency can be positively sublimated by solo sports or the starring role in the school play, or simply by

If by any chance praise and encouragement are not forthcoming, Leo children may just give up. Their natural indolence persuades them that the fight isn't worth the trouble

are often attracted, sometimes with disastrous results, to the fascinating Scorpian or flighty Geminian. Generally, however, Leos are magnanimous and can be adaptable. As long as they are fully supported and loved, they can conduct a successful relationship with almost any sign.

THE LEO CHILD

Leo children are assertive, organized and enthusiastic, and are often independent from an early age. They are able to charm adults with their bright intellects and sunny temperaments. As long as they are given due recognition that their place in the pecking order is at the top, Leos are relatively problem-free as children. However, if their leadership is questioned or others fail to fall in with their way of doing things, they can be extremely bossy and aggressive, hitting out both physically and verbally.

being given greater responsibility and a good 'talking to' that appeals to the Leo sense of pride and honour. Most Leos, however, are naturally good citizens and may eventually seek prominent roles on their local council or become leading lights in Parent-Teacher Associations.

If by any chance praise and encouragement are not forthcoming, Leo children may just give up. Their natural indolence persuades them that the fight isn't worth the trouble. Often their achievements are in direct proportion to the high or low expectations of their teachers or their parents.

If their life is hard, deprived of treats, holidays and luxuries, Leos will feel diminished as people and personally insulted by Fate. Though little demoralizes the sunny Leo for very long, they find physical or financial hardship difficult to bear, and need extra love and support from their parents in such adverse circumstances. What gets them through is a dream, something to aim for, the light at the end of the tunnel. Many Leos succeed in life against all odds, simply because their nature demands that they must win or die.

Famous Leos

Her Majesty Queen Elizabeth the
Queen Mother
Napoleon Bonaparte
Robert Mitchum
Madonna
Robert Redford
Fidel Castro
Leonard Bernstein
Emily Brontë
Coco Chanel
Claude Debussy

Cecil B. DeMille
Robert de Niro
Mick Jagger
George Bernard Shaw
Benito Mussolini
Percy Bysshe Shelley
Sir Alexander Fleming
Dustin Hoffman
Carl G. Jung
Guy de Maupassant

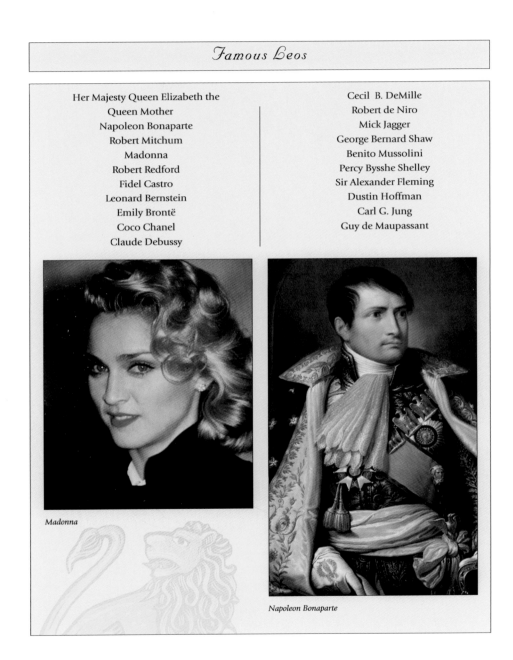

Madonna

Napoleon Bonaparte

THE SUN IN VIRGO

(24 August — 22 September)

Sun Sign: VIRGO

Sign: THE VIRGIN

Ruling Planet: MERCURY

Gender: FEMININE

Element: EARTH

Quality: MUTABLE

Compatibility: PISCES

AND SOME AQUARIANS

Non-compatibility: LEO AND

SAGITTARIUS

un Sign Virgoans are not necessarily virginal, of course, but they often have the quiet, unsophisticated air of an inexperienced person, which can be deceptive. They are meticulous, tidy and thorough. Typical Sun Sign Virgoans keep their own counsel, and although they are frequently profound thinkers, they are essentially practical, with few impossible dreams. These enormously hard-working people are the first to roll up their sleeves and get on with the job, while whimsical Geminians or hot-air Arians fail to carry through their grand plans. By contrast, it is the Virgoans who keep records and undertake research to put flesh on the bones of the ambitious projects of others. The Virgoan social style is quiet and unassuming. A typical Virgoan will never interrupt and rarely holds the floor for more than a few minutes. They listen very carefully, however, and when they do voice an opinion, it is often startlingly intelligent, cutting right through to the heart of the matter. Because Virgoans are ruled by Mercury, they are excellent at putting two and two together and seeing connections and inferences others may miss. Their memories are formidable and they can suddenly recall an essential reference from a book they read years ago. This enables them to make the connection with a current project, and the problem is solved. Virgoans are often very witty – with a dry, sometimes surrealistic, sense of humour. They have others in fits of laughter. They can also be brilliant mimics, due to their ability to note quietly every mannerism and characteristic of their subject. And Virgoan jokes linger in the mind longer than most.

Negative Virgoan traits include a capacity for endless worry, which can cloud their own lives unnecessarily. It also irritates more happy-go-lucky signs. Not only do Virgoans fret, they can also be first-class naggers, carping relentlessly about other people's failings and sloppiness. Badly aspected Virgoans can be cold, over-analytical and obsessed with detail. They can become totally bogged down with trivia, delighting in what others consider boring facts. At work, for example, Virgoans may wax lyrical about new filing systems, and they can be fussy hobbyists, collecting train numbers or matchboxes. They seem obsessed with routines. Everything must always be done in the same way, and in the same order. This type of Virgoan will eat the same food day in and day out, go to the same holiday spots year after year. They fret constantly about spending money and keep a record of every purchase in tiny, neat handwriting. Everything must be just so, or they can suffer real distress. Virgoans are great ones for inventing rules on the 'in case' principle. For example, they may insist that no one takes drinks into their study in case some gets spilled onto their computer. It makes sense, but it does not seem to occur to Virgoans that adults can take that risk. Most people enjoy a cup of coffee while working long hours at the keyboard. But this is not the extreme type of Virgoan, who hedges his or her life around with a host of such restricting rules in order to feel safe.

APPEARANCE

Virgoans have good bone structure and are often highly photogenic. They are attractive, with beautiful eyes that sparkle with intelligence, and can be vain. Their glossy, thick hair frequently rises from a 'widow's peak'. When young, they can seem prematurely old, with a wary, watchful expression. But once safely in their mid-30s, they seem to look much the same for quite a long time. It is often said

meditation would be good for them. So would going for long walks in the evening and, of course, following a careful diet. Virgoans are particularly sensitive to drugs of all types, whether they are prescribed by their doctor or are herbal concoctions, nicotine or alcohol. In such cases, it is sometimes not enough just to cut down. They may have to abstain completely for the sake of their well-being. Virgoans are notably fussy about their health, and often carry their

The natural life is best for earthy Virgoans. They need plenty of fresh air to blow away the cobwebs and rebalance their energies

that typical Sun Sign Virgoans have protruding stomachs, which can be their only rotund feature. However, some types are very angular. Sometimes the first impression they give is of slow, deliberate movements. Curiously, many Virgoans have a slightly unbalanced way of walking, perhaps with a barely perceptible limp. Once animated, though, they can leap into a higher gear, becoming very nervy and quick.

HEALTH

All that worry can play havoc with Virgoan digestions. They are often martyrs to their stomachs, and many suffer from Irritable Bowel Syndrome, which greatly embarrasses and inconveniences them. Many also suffer from food intolerances or full-blown allergies. In this case, they should seek good advice from reputable nutritionists. Usually the only answer to their health problems is to learn to unwind. Yoga or

favourite remedies, vitamins and even their own special brand of mineral water around with them.

The natural life is best for earthy Virgoans. They need plenty of fresh air to blow away the cobwebs and rebalance their energies. Many choose to be vegetarians, which suits their nervy digestions – although they must remember to include a wide variety of foods in their diet, and take extra vitamin B if necessary. Homeopathic and naturopathic remedies often suit Virgoans, and the process of tracking down the right therapies for them appeals to their love of detective work.

CAREER

Virgoans make excellent nurses because they are practical, calm, disciplined and cheerful. Their quiet confidence and efficiency can be very comforting, and their quick wit can lift their patients' flagging spirits. They make caring and effective alternative therapists, too, and are often with columns of figures and computer work. They make superb programmers and are the natural accountants of the zodiac – they can carry the details of all their clients' accounts in their heads. They can also make highly efficient tax inspectors and private detectives, as long as the work isn't too dangerous.

Dogged, analytical and intellectual, Virgoans make skilled and inspired research scientists. They rarely let their hearts rule their heads, and some types would show little sentiment towards laboratory animals.

Traditionally associated with the time of harvest, Virgoans are happy planning and cooking meals, and are often found in the catering trade.

Perhaps uncharacteristically, Virgoans, who are normally so introverted, can frequently be found in

involved in researching their subject in great depth to add to their knowledge. Virgoans also make excellent counsellors or community carers. Some love providing nourishing food for the less fortunate members of society.

They love making a contribution, and being of service to any group or corporation, to which they will be unfailingly loyal. They are, however, better as members of a team than as bosses. A Virgoan in charge can easily become tediously nit-picking and hypercritical, forever double-checking the work of others and waiting to pounce on any evidence of sloppiness. Untidiness and tardiness are anathema to strongly aspected Virgoans, and they can be completely intolerant of other ways of doing things. Like their fellow Earth Sign, Taurus, they love tradition, convention and rules and regulations for their own sake, even when these are outdated and inefficient. Virgoans like analyzing and collating and are totally at home the theatre. They appreciate the chance to cast off their inhibitions and assume another personality on stage. Many actors are actually shy and retiring people. They come to life only when they can hide behind the mask of the character they play. This suits Virgoans completely.

Virgoans have strong opinions, but sometimes hesitate to express them, and often fear attempting something new – in case it fails and they are thought stupid or incompetent. They can be excellent business partners, however, even in creative endeavours such as writing or computer graphics, where they will provide the common sense and attention to detail that may escape their more unworldly partners. They are particularly good at providing the facts and figures for a book or television documentary, while more creative colleagues translate them into words or images.

Many Virgoans are obsessive workaholics, condemning themselves to a life chained to their desk, and ignoring the world outside. Relationships, health and endless opportunities pass them by as they live in constant tunnel vision, totally absorbed in their work. Conversely, there is a type of extremely slothful, unmotivated Virgoan, whose self-worth is too low for them to attempt anything without a crippling fear of failure – so they just do nothing and drift through life.

RELATIONSHIPS

Though they are reliable, responsible, eminently sensible and can be happy in a stable relationship, Virgoans are often very difficult to live with. These fussy, critical people can make life a misery for more relaxed souls by constant complaints about tidiness or anything else.

Conversely, there is a very untidy and chaotic Virgoan, who happily lives in apparent chaos, though they usually know, roughly, where the important things are. Curiously, even this type has an element of Virgoan neatness about them – despite the litter. This type is happiest living the single life, with a small circle of like-minded friends who drop in from time to time for a chat. They love surfing the net, which satisfies their craving for accumulating facts and having a vicarious social life at the same time – and all without moving from their chairs.

If they marry, many Virgoans do so more than once, perhaps because they have to learn the hard way all about sharing and tolerance, and because they easily tire of the routine of living with one person. They can be tense in close relationships, which can badly upset their sex lives, and makes it hard for them to become truly intimate with those they love. Some Virgoans prefer others to take the lead sexually, although they soon show an aptitude for experimentation and excitement in bed.

Virgoans can be irritable with those around them, particularly those who are more physical or devil-may-care. They tend to bring their work home, which does not make for jolly family evenings. However, they take their family responsibilities seriously and can be solicitous for the welfare of wives and families. Although careful with money, they can be generous, and usually remember birthdays and anniversaries. Some extreme Virgoans, however, are penny-pinching types who would put the

Aries
Quick-fire Arians have a certain allure for more timid Virgoans but prove too combustible in the long term.

Taurus
Both being Earth Signs, they understand each other well, but life can lack that all-important spark.

Gemini
They will enjoy each other's company but frivolous and flighty Geminians can frighten Virgoans away.

Cancer
Loving, sympathetic Cancerians can hit it off with sensible Virgoans, but they will cause too many scenes.

Leo
Virgoans may love to bask in reflected Leonine glory, but can find Leo's overbearing manner ultimately offputting.

Virgo
Though safe, this can be a deeply dull combination. Two Virgoans will rarely have a sparkling love life.

Libra
Romantic, sensitive Librans can make amenable partners for Virgoans, but they may lack the staying power.

Scorpio
Though attracted sexually, straightforward Virgoans are scared off by the Scorpian's sharp tongue.

Sagittarius
True Virgoans are often horrified by Sagittarian fecklessness and their capacity to live in the moment.

Capricorn
Virgoans appreciate the Goat's measured approach to life and love, but even they need more adventurousness.

Aquarius
Virgoans often admire Aquarians greatly, but their lifestyles are too divergent for lasting bonds to develop.

Pisces
Something about loving, needy Pisceans can bring out the best in the more supportive, well-grounded Virgoan.

---

grasping sort of Cancerians to shame, and they may live bleak lives and cause misery to those around them. This extreme type may also invent strange ground rules for those living under the same roof; and they will force them to obey, no matter how inconvenient it may be. This form of control mania arises out of fear of disorder.

Virgoans may find parenthood difficult. The demonstrative motherhood of Cancerians, or the robust fathering of a solid Taurean are not for them. Virgoans find expressing emotion hard, and are often too absorbed in their world of facts, figures and fussing to give much of their time to their youngsters.

It is only when children are capable of rational thought that Virgoan parents truly come into their own, helping their children to learn the rules of life. Later, when the children are on the verge of independence and young adulthood, Virgoan parents are more than happy to help with finances, find a suitable mortgage, explain the intricacies of pensions and insurance schemes and scrutinize the small print of any financial or contractual agreement. They can make far better grandparents than parents. By that time of life, they may well have learned to relax and to enjoy the spontaneity of having very young children around them.

IDEAL PARTNER

Virgoans can find most close relationships something of a trial. But if near opposites attract, they will go for deep, dark Scorpians, whose intensity adds colour to their more plodding lives, and whose sexuality can encourage them to lose their inhibitions. Gentle Pisceans, with their soft emotions, can make Virgoans realize that they can relax and enjoy home life, although both can be their own worst enemies at times. Some types of Aquarian also bring out the best in Virgo, and madcap Arians can bring a totally different energy into their lives. Here, the relationship may be too fiery to survive, but it will be fun while it lasts. Leos, with their love of display, can help Virgoans to discover the joy and laughter they find so elusive. And though Leonine extravagance can seriously worry some Virgoans, the more relaxed of their type can fare well enough with Leo.

Like fellow Venusians of the bovine sort, gentle Virgoans can be disconcerted by banner-waving Aquarians; although they may enjoy deep discussions with them about more serious issues. And again – as with Taureans – the energy and innocence of a Sagittarian may be initially appealing, but the Sagittarian lifestyle is ultimately too unpredictable for steady Virgo.

THE VIRGOAN CHILD

Always fretting and worrying, Virgoan children need to have their self-esteem constantly reinforced. They need to be told they can succeed, and encouraged to be adventurous. Otherwise, they will simply become increasingly timorous and insecure. They need to have their expectations notched up, to be told time and time again that it is a good idea to aim for the top, to have dreams and goals and to fight for them. Equally, however, goal-setting should be realistic, or they will see through it and never make any attempt at rising to the challenge. The best thing to do is to encourage them to go for gold in their chosen field, or a subject that is close to Virgoan hearts, rather than forcing them to compete in unappealing subjects. This might include taking part in the school play, or joining a team sport – they can also be extremely loyal team supporters – or helping in an administrative capacity with special interest clubs or charities.

Virgoans are neat, tidy children on the whole. They may not present the most creative or promising work, but it will always be legible and clean. They do have a lazy streak, though, but prefer to be kept busy at some clearly defined task where they can see they are making progress. They like being told what to do, rather than taking the initiative; although they should be actively encouraged to think for themselves, perhaps through puzzles and quiz games. They are better at slow, steady course-work and do not usually shine when it comes to sitting examinations.

They can often be found deeply absorbed in the local library, while more boisterous children are kicking a ball around. Because they tend to be tidy, do their homework on time and dislike danger, upheaval or anything that disrupts the normal routine, others may think of them as prigs. Sometimes they are, but in reality they just like a quiet life – making small steps for man, rather than giant leaps for mankind.

Queen Elizabeth I
Greta Garbo
Peter Sellers
Jesse James
B.B. King
Agatha Christie
Sean Connery
Stephen King
Prince Albert
Yasser Arafat
Lauren Bacall

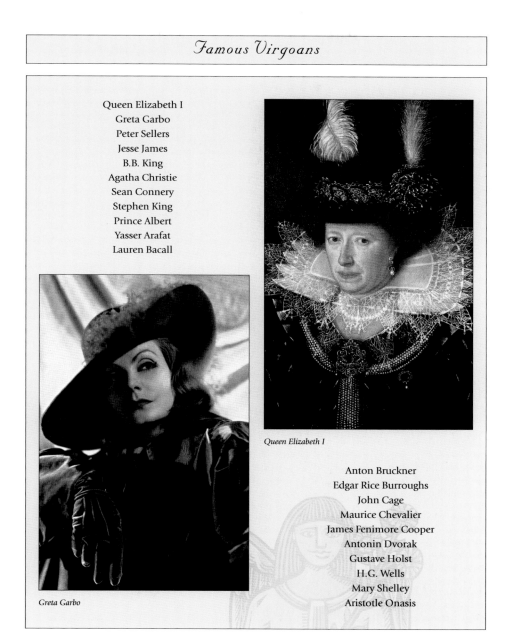

Queen Elizabeth I

Anton Bruckner
Edgar Rice Burroughs
John Cage
Maurice Chevalier
James Fenimore Cooper
Antonin Dvorak
Gustave Holst
H.G. Wells
Mary Shelley
Aristotle Onasis

Greta Garbo

THE SUN IN LIBRA

(23 September — 23 October)

Sun Sign: LIBRA

Sign: THE SCALES

Ruling Planet: VENUS

Gender: MASCULINE

Element: AIR

Quality: CARDINAL

Compatibility: SAGITTARIUS, AQUARIUS AND TAURUS

Non-compatibility: SCORPIO, CANCER AND PISCES

un Sign Librans make peace and harmony a priority in any situation in which they find themselves.

Normal arbiters and diplomats, they are constantly seeking balance, as exemplified by their sign of the Scales.

Librans are pleasant and companionable, friendly, sunny souls whose ready smile and firm handshake makes them popular and trusted members of society. They are open and unsuspicious, attractive and confident. Librans are hard workers, and their search for balance also enables them to play hard as well. They often indulge in several hobbies to offset the demands of their careers.

Librans are both personable and smart, and attractive in appearance. Even those odd Librans who are not over-concerned about choosing the right shade of dress or the most noseworthy aftershave, are still clean and presentable. They like to be surrounded by a certain amount of order and tidiness, although they are not fanatical about it; in fact, anything overdone or 'over the top' is alien to the Libran temperament. The axiom 'Everything in moderation' was probably invented by a Libran, who may occasionally go wild, but whose first concerns the morning after the night efore are to apologize for any bad behaviour and then to set about working off the excesses in the gym.

Conversely, though, Librans are famous for their hesitation, dithering and inability to make decisions. Sometimes this image is justified, but mostly Librans are simply cautious, preferring to wait and weight up their options before committing themselves to an idea, belief or relationships. On the other hand, they can be gullible and credulous, falling for ridiculous schemes, even in extreme cases becoming members of somewhat sinister cults, simply because it is not in their nature to question the motives of others, believing them to be just as open as themselves. 'What you see is what you get' is true of most Librans, although their friendliness may be more superficial than it appears. They can give the impression of being totally fascinated by your company, only to have difficulty remembering who you are a couple of weeks later.

Librans are undemanding and 'laid back', often to the point of appearing to lack all ambition or drive, but how influential this trait is depends very much on their chart as a whole. True, they are usually happy to take orders and be part of a team, but they have a strong head for business, and can reveal a surprisingly steely streak if their livelihood is threatened. Most need the security of a regular job and a happy home, seeking always to find partners who will balance their own nature. Librans are wildly romantic, though, and sometimes pursue their dreams rather than settle for what they have.

Librans can be unsettling: they are often inconsistent, even contradictory characters. Although they hate rudeness, they can be disconcertingly brash and blunt. Though extremely restless, they don't often express it in a physical way. With such charming people as Librans, it is easy to forget what the symbolism of the Scales implies: balance is transitory, and imbalance, if only slight, is in facct the usual state of affairs. Librans find that life is a constant effort to make the two sides level, and make sense of its inherent duality.

APPEARANCE

Sun Sign Librans are rarely homely or ugly. Usually they are handsome or pretty and both sexes can have charming dimples. They have sweet, open faces with laughing eyes and a devastating smile. Sometimes people fall in love

occasional allergy can bring them out in itchy rashes, especially on the face and upper chest.

Librans should learn to pace themselves and do nothing to excess. They should compensate for a trip to the wine bar by working out or going for a long walk in the country. Librans need to drink plenty of water to flush out the toxins from

Sometimes people fall in love with them at first sight, believing, often wrongly, that the Libran smile-to-end-smiles was just for them

with them at first sight, believing, often wrongly, that the LIbran smile-to-end-smiles was just for them. Librans tend to be rounded, though not often plump, rather than angular or skinny. Even overweight Librans have an aura of Venusian charm and beauty. Their hair waves or curls, and is professionally coiffured in the latest, chic style. Even the pooer Libran has an eye for classy outfits, perhaps finding them in thrift shops or at the back of a friend's wardrobe, whence they are charmed into their own. They have an innate sense of style, adding a personal touch to classic suits or evening clothes that everyone is sure to remember.

their kidneys, and cut down on salty foods, which tend to cncourage water retention and high blood pressure. They also need to counterbalance their bouts of frantic activity with yoga, meditation or aromatherapy for the sake of their minds, bodies and spirits. Indeed, Librans need to recognize more than most that humans are more than just physical bodies. For this reason, holistic therapies work very well for them, and spritual exercises are important for their total well-being.

CAREER

Gregarious, amenable Librans dislike working alone, but equally, they are not fond of suffering under a rod of iron. They like light-hearted offices with a relaxed atmosphere, lots of banter and fun, and appreciate being left to themselves to work at their own pace. Their surroundings are important: gloomy or ugly buildings adversely affect their mental and physical well-being, while touches of style and luxury bring out the best in them. Careers in glamorous industries often

HEALTH

With their roller-coaster emtions, Librans tend to suffer from nervous stomachs and, quite possibly, ulcers. They tend to over-indulge in food and wine, and that can lead to kidney and bladder problems. Stress also results in classic Libran headaches and migraines. Rich food and the other. Librans may be thoroughgoing law students, but once they have to present a strong argument as defence or prosecuting counsel, they may be lost. for the same reason, Libran jurors can show a tendency to defer verdicts.

Librans make excellent listeners and are good at giving well-thought-out advice. They love dealing with the public and are ideal fo rcustomer services and public relations, and as personal assistants. Many Librans are not particularly ambitious on their own behalf, but they are proud to be associated with successful or famous people and organizations.

Though usually equable, Librans can sometimes sulk, and it is not unknown for them to be argumentative. They will assert that blac is white, but never allow others to get away with sweeping statements. Librans can, in fact, be almost as nitpicking as Virgoans when the mood takes them. They are logical, have a healthy regard for facts and figures and are rarely airy-fairy and vague, all of which makes them perfect civil sevants, planners and designers.

RELATIONSHIPS

Librans often think they are much better at handling relationships than they actually are. They see themselves as so urbane, pleasant and approachable that it comes as a shock when angagements are broken or friendships and marriages fail. Often they are the last people to notice that their partners are flirting with someone else, or the first to miss the hints of upset in a close friendship. Librans can sail through life, unaware of the looming iceberg or that the name of their ship is Titanic.

Those born under the sign of the Scales may be moody and liable to extreme ups and downs,

appeal to Sun Sign Librans – fashion, theatre, television and modelling all provide ideal opportunities for stylish self-expression.

Librans make good diplomats, professional mediators and counsellors, but can easily become distressed by too much naked aggression. They often find it a terrible shock to discover that there is such a thing as real evil in the world.

Librans are superb at comparing and contrasting, seeing all round a problem or situation and all sides of an argument, which can make them escellent, objective researchers, assessors and evaluators. But they can find it difficult to come down firmly on one side or the which can be very difficult to live with. They can be their old charming selves on a high, laughing in a crowd, but suddenly the life seems to drain out of them, leaving them mean-minded and sulky. Similarly, their energy levels can soar or plummet, sometimes within a very short space of time, facing loved ones with the problem of knowing what approach to take. They may become too exhaused to go out on a long-awaited special date, and if it's their turn to walk the dog, they might well duck out of it. Yet how can anyone complain about Librans when they can't help working so hard? The Libran attitude is surprise if others feel let down, abandoned or lonely, when they see themselves as essentially such decent people.

Loneliness is something a Libran finds almost impossible to cope with. Even when leading a

carefree single life, perhaps playing the field, they surround themselves with a cheery crowd, the more the merrier, and barely have a might at home alone. They can keep up a hectic social life for several nights in a row, then suddenly collapse in a heap or cosy up with a good book, the television and supper on a tray. Some Librans manage to keep their social and home lives completely separate, never inviting their friends round but always meeting them in restaurants, bars and clubs – but this is an extreme type.

The overriding purpse of the single Libran is to find his or her soulmate – which they do, repeatedly! Always romantic and whole-hearted, they love the chase, the chocolates and rose, even writing poetry and arranging expensive surprises. They make romance their business, and many a heart flutters in return. Librans really know how to flatter, and will appear to be giving their entire attention to someone – even going so far as to focus their entire lives on their loved one. In many cases, though, they are fooling themselves as well as the object of their passion. Librans tend above all to be in love with the idea of love, rather than with a real

Compatibility in Relationships

Aries
They may have fun while dating but living together soon shows that self-centred Arians are too much for Librans.

Cancer
Initial attraction may not last: Librans are too uncomfortable with typical Cancerian outbursts.

Libra
Dating and sex will be fun but with two Librans together nothing will ever b e settled too readily.

Capricorn
Librans' love of wining and dining may upset Capricornian respect for nest-eggs. They have some basic differences.

Taurus
Librans can fall for beautiful and placid Taureans. This is often a lasting match made in heaven.

Leo
Librans often feel flattered by magnanimous Leonine attention, but the gloss soon wears off.

Scorpio
Straightforward Librans find Machiavellian Scorpians hard to understand but easy to fall into bed with.

Aquarius
Librans can easily become acolytes of driven Aquarians, but find them too intense for loving life partnerships.

Gemini
In many ways Geminians and Librans are too similar, but the Twins' guiles can ultimately prove unappealing.

Virgo
Socially, these signs may hit it off, but cracks soon appear in the raltionship because of Virgoan intuition.

Sagittarius
With one bound they will be free. Sagittarians offer Librans the adventure and daring they crave.

Pisces
Truly difficult Pisceans make life hell for easy-going Librans, although they can get on well at first.

---

person. Once committed, though, they have no difficulty rekindling those early rapturous feelings with candlelit dinners and romantic early nights in bed.

It is no use expecting Sun Sign Librans to be too sympathetic, despite their charm and apparent warmth. Anyone who pours out their hearts to them will find themselves asked how they contributed to their problems, and what grief they caused the others in the story. It can be a terrible let-down to find the gorgeous, charming Libran suddenly not taking your side. In family relationships, this can often seem little short of betrayal, when what is expected is partisanship and loyalty. This can sometimes seem like lack of

courage, and male Librans can sometimes be seen, rightly or wrongly, as wimps.

Many Librans are, however, kind and co-operative at home, although stress and uncertainty can make them bad-tempered. They will go out of their way to make the home a haven, where peach and harmony can prevail; but when, inevitably, teenage children begin to rebel, they find it hard to cope, and may over-react and worry excessively. Librans love fairness and as long as they are treated equally, life with them is easy. Their rule is 'Do as you would be done by'. They are keen to have a wide variety of friends, possibly from different ethnic and religious backgrounds. Librans thrive on diversity, respecting the right of the individual, and really hate racism, sexism and any other form of prejudice. They are, at heart, politically and spiritually idealistic.

When faced with any unpleasantness, Librans react either by sticking their head in the sand and pretending it isn't happening, or by trying to smooth things over. Sometimes, however, they can be surprisingly tough, really laying it on the line with offenders and demanding that they make positive changes to their behaviour.

As parents, Librans tend to be kind and imaginative, but not always deeply involved or even particularly sensitive. They can be too superficial and flippant for many children, especially Cancerians, Pisceans and some Scorpians. Nevertheless, they will always make an effort to be sociable with their frineds, and will fill the house wuth laughter, fun and boisterous family pets.

IDEAL PARTNER

Romantic Librans can get along with almost anyone, from any zodiacal sign – at least to begin with. They tend to like the enthusiasm and unpredictability of Aquarians, whose love of causes (lost or otherwise) may well add the depth that librans often feel they lack in their life, although they can find the more extreme and over-opinionated of Aquarians a bit of a turn-off. Peace-loving, gentle Taureans can bring out a Libran's more romantic streak, and many contented marriages between the two signs do last. Happy, adventurous and optimistic

Sagittarians tend to bring out the best in Librans, although Librans can find all that remorseless energy too demanding, and may need to get away from time to time, just to restore their delicate, internal balance.

Librans are also fascinated with the glamour and sophistication of sultry Scorpians, although they may find Scorpians' strange moods perplexing and intimidating. Paradoxically, many Librans should stay away from the more intensely emotional – and occasionally explosive – kind of Scorpian. The more clinging Water signs, Cancerians and Pisces, can make too many emotional demands and scenes for Librans who, above all, seek peace and harmony.

THE LIBRAN CHILD

Children born under the sign of the Scales will try very hard to fit in and be accepted, and are keen to wear the latest kidswear and own the best ccomputers. Charming and lively, they appeal to their peers and adults alike, and rarely have serious behavioural problems or learning difficulties. Because they are bright and intelligent, Librans often find schoolwork easy, although they sometimes shrink from thinking too deeply about religion, philosophy or the spiritual side of life. They seek approval above all: anything that marks them out as being different is viewed with suspicion, although they can be induced to join unusual groups and societies.

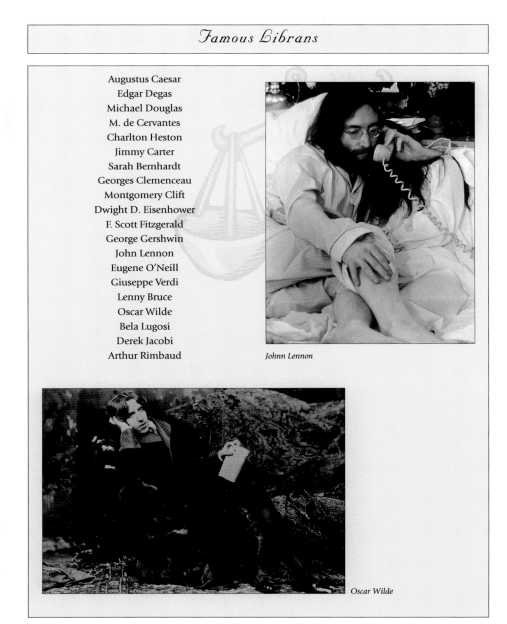

Augustus Caesar
Edgar Degas
Michael Douglas
M. de Cervantes
Charlton Heston
Jimmy Carter
Sarah Bernhardt
Georges Clemenceau
Montgomery Clift
Dwight D. Eisenhower
F. Scott Fitzgerald
George Gershwin
John Lennon
Eugene O'Neill
Giuseppe Verdi
Lenny Bruce
Oscar Wilde
Bela Lugosi
Derek Jacobi
Arthur Rimbaud

Johnn Lennon

Oscar Wilde

THE SUN IN SCORPIO

(24 October – 22 November)

Sun Sign: SCORPIO

Sign: THE SCORPION

Ruling Planet: MARS AND

PLUTO

Gender: FEMININE

Element: WATER

Quality: FIXED

Compatibility: TAURUS, VIRGO

AND LIBRA

Non-compatibility:

ARIES, LEO

AND SAGITTARIUS

Sun Sign Scorpians are energetic, passionate and exciting. They have a bad reputation among traditional astrologers, but few fortunately live up to their somewhat unsavoury image. Most content themselves with being forceful and fascinating, dramatically sweeping through the lives of others like mini-tornadoes. Of course, there are those born under the sign of the Scorpion who seem shy and retiring, but they are few and far between, and even then they will tend to harbour deep, dark secrets, for this sign is nothing if not mysterious.

Most Scorpians do have a strong sex drive, which may express itself in endless flirting or even power games. Often, though, it is sublimated in a quest for the Great Mission In Life, for finding their personal Holy Grail or plumbing the mysteries of life. Ruled by Pluto, God of the Underworld, Scorpians are concerned with esoteric matters, with the paranormal, mysticism and the afterlife, and often believe passionately in reincarnation. This is not always as negative as it may sound: Scorpians understand the concept that death is always followed by rebirth, and they can rise like the phoenix from disastrous events in their own lives to start again with enormous, positive energy. Disappointment, bereavement, bankruptcy, illness and natural disasters can depress and seem, at the time, to demolish them, but not for long. Soon they are back on their feet, building new lives for themselves and others with amazing cheerfulness and genuine joy at being given the opportunity for a fresh start.

Sun Sign Scorpians have a marked tendency to jealousy and possessiveness. Profoundly secretive by nature, they often disturb others with their air of mystery, which can sometimes seem just a little contrived. Scorpians are very theatrical, and can use every trick in the book to get noticed at social gatherings: they love to be outrageous and to shock, which they often do very successfully, just for the hell of it.

However, there is a sting in the tail with Scorpians. The full Scorpian fury can be unsettling enough – after all, their other ruler is fiery, aggressive Mars – but to be at the receiving end of their cold, penetrating sarcasm is to be upset for days. Many Scorpians train themselves to be masters of the put-down that is devastatingly witty, but very hurtful. Both male and female Scorpians can be real 'bitches'.

This is a sign of extremes, of black and white, dark and light; this is often reflected in the ups and downs of their lives. These people can be wildly successful one year and bankrupt the next, although it is a process that is likely to be repeated in a curiously predictable cycle. Similarly, they can be utterly loyal and true lovers, but great passion can rapidly turn to hatred and maybe a desire for revenge.

APPEARANCE

Once seen, rarely forgotten, Sun Sign Scorpians are always striking, whether they are stunningly beautiful or not. They have a magnetic, forceful quality which makes people stare, although they may not be sure why. Most Scorpians have a habit of staring penetratingly, and of frowning while listening to others talk. They can move slowly, as if mesmerized, although their thought processes are extremely fast. Even when dressing scruffily – and many often do – there is a certain style about them, a Bohemian air that makes all the difference. Some work at it, but many find it comes naturally. This is definitely the sign of big hats and black coats. Scorpians are also very partial to wearing leather.

HEALTH

The Scorpio motto is 'What the Hell ...' so, to them, moderation in anything is for wimps. They throw themselves into orgies of eating and drinking that would shame a Taurean, and often think that they somehow avert the day of reckoning by doing it in style, drinking only champagne, for example, or eating only the best bitter chocolate. But whatever the quality, their lifestyle will catch up with them (usually sooner rather than later) in the shape of stomach trouble, chronic constipation, gall stones, liver and kidney problems, even diabetes. A shocking health scare, however, can be an abrupt turning point for Scorpio, whose ability to live at either end of the spectrum can turn them overnight into the most zealous, proselytizing, non-smoking teetotaller or the strictest vegan. Similarly, they can go from sybaritic couch potato to marathon runner just as easily, and enjoy both lifestyles with equal gusto.

Traditionally, Scorpians are supposed to suffer from genital problems, and of course some do. But in many cases this is transposed to lower back pain, often caused by too much sitting around and weight gain in middle age.

CAREER

'The Devil finds work for idle hands' was never truer than in the case of an out-of-work Scorpian, whose enormous energy needs to be positively channelled, or they may turn to dubious ways of passing the time, for instance, playing around with the Ouija board. However, once a Scorpian is fully engaged emotionally, there are few more energetic or ambitious workers. They are keen to throw themselves into what is right for them, often working through the night without any idea of the time. It is often said that they are fanatical money-grabbers. They certainly have that potential, but mostly they see money as an outward and visible sign of their dominance in their chosen field, of dramatic success compared to lesser mortals. If their work does not appeal to them, though, they can easily be sackably sloppy and lazy, given to coming back to the office late after lunch.

Scorpians are traditionally associated with jobs that require delving and uncovering secrets, such as mining and detective work, but few actually take up such professions. However, Scorpians tend to have more interesting, even peculiar, jobs than most because of their fascination with anything deep and dark. For example, they can be criminologists or forensic scientists working on murder cases for the police, or writers of detective fiction. Many carve out successful careers in the police force. They can be drawn to 'alternative' studies, such as parapsychology, the occult, ancient Egyptian mysteries or piecing together the truth about religion. Many are passionate about conspiracy theories. Even if they have humdrum everyday jobs, Scorpians tend to follow hobbies that reflect their unusual, even bizarre, interests, and they may often find more ordinary people too boring for words.

The Scorpian need to go deep also makes them excellent hypnotherapists, psychotherapists and past-life therapists. Scorpians are at home with the unconscious mind, and are less fearful than most people of discovering its dark secrets. They can also find ingenious ways of coping with them. Some Scorpians make powerful psychics or mediums.

Not surprisingly, Scorpians can be rather disruptive in the workplace. They take every little criticism so personally and react with such black and brooding moods, perhaps even flying into dramatic rages, that other, more timid souls will steer clear of them, even when teamwork suffers. They see everything – status, pay and perks – as a reflection of their own worth: , and can make formidable rivals. If crossed, Scorpians can be very unforgiving.

They can make demanding bosses but, if their emotions are fully engaged, they can be surprisingly sympathetic and loyal to employees, taking any of their problems or setbacks as a personal challenge. Many Scorpians find life easier when self-employed, although they do like to have regular contact with others. They also need to feel that they are making their mark on the world. Too much time alone can make Scorpians very gloomy.

RELATIONSHIPS

Intense, sexual and demanding, Scorpians are not easy to live with. They are not above using sex as a form of control, although they don't indulge in emotional blackmail as much as Cancerians. Many Scorpians are much more interested in the image of sexual conquests than in the act itself.

Depending very much on other factors in the individual chart, Scorpians can throw all their energies into chasing often highly unsuitable people and will continue to pursue them when it is obvious that there really is no point any more. They won't take no for an answer, refusing to believe that anyone could reject someone as fascinating and sexy as themselves. There is another element in this scenario, however. Scorpians often believe in fate or karma, and once they've got it in their heads that the object of their affections is meant for them, they ignore every indication to the contrary. Because of their tendency to use sexuality to control others, Scorpians see seduction as a form of possession, and believe that, however reluctant the object of their desire may be, one day their view will prevail. Often, though, they are not as promiscuous as their reputation suggests and yearn to be involved in a passionate love affair that will transcend the humdrum world.

Scorpians can be very vindictive and vengeful. Never expect to walk away from a romance with a Scorpian unscathed. Not all Scorpians will necessarily bring down their full wrath upon those who have offended them – though they will fantasize about it.

They make demanding parents and can put too much pressure on their children. On the lighter side, though, they can be rather witty. Sometimes, Scorpians find it hard to give their children the necessary space to be themselves, and can be sticklers for tradition and discipline. Even so, they can learn to relax and be fun parents, so it is a good idea for them to participate in all sorts of activity with their children in order to lighten up.

Aries
Arians may bring a breath of fresh air into the claustrophobic world of the Scorpian, but they can be too demanding.

Taurus
Perhaps curiously, Scorpio's opposite sign can prove very appealing and make a long-term relationship work well.

Gemini
Flighty, wily Geminians can charm Scorpians – but not for long. In the end, they're just too shallow for Scorpio.

Cancer
Devoted Cancerians are too normal for quirky Scorpians, and their emotional highs and lows get short shrift.

Leo
Relationships will be passionate and sex exciting but Scorpians do not take kindly to Leonine attempts to dominate.

Virgo
The more sociable Virgoans can be complementary partners but not if they embody Virgoan obsessive tidiness.

Libra
Scorpians often fascinate Librans and they can enjoy very passionate sex but Scorpians are just too dark.

Scorpio
Fellow Scorpians often get on well, having the same unusual interests, but may fall out of love too easily.

Sagittarius
Scorpians find these wild-children very charming but do not go for the insecurity or lack of permanent lifestyle.

Capricorn
Capricornian repression has little appeal for sexually adventurous Scorpians and may lead to frostiness.

Aquarius
Scorpians often respect the causes espoused by Aquarians but can find them too involved in 'boring' politics.

Pisces
Both signs are complex and intense with extreme demands. Lasting and loving relationships are unlikely.

IDEAL PARTNER

Scorpians, with their love of drama, may often be attracted to their own sign for that reason alone. It rarely works out, however, because of a Scorpian's temperamental nature and all the scenes that go with it. Also, there may not be enough real love.

Underneath a Scorpian's theatrical exterior is someone who just wants to be loved and to be made to feel normal. Their polar sign of Taurus can give them just what they crave – material and emotional security. Virgoans, too, share the ability to calm Scorpians and make them relax, often winning them over with their wit and charm. Well-balanced Librans also share the capacity to humour Scorpians and see beyond the image to the real, needy person inside. Arians, Leos and Sagittarians, however, can be too caught up in themselves to take the time to understand the complex Scorpian and are more likely to compete for the limelight. Scorpian leanings towards the world of the unexplained can make them gravitate towards the more psychic Pisceans, but it rarely works out because Scorpian intensity combined with Piscean emotionality is not a good recipe for enduring love.

THE SCORPIAN CHILD

Scorpian children are natural loners, brooders and worriers. They like to sit alone pondering over very adult questions that can alarm their siblings and parents alike. They can become very religious at an early age, and although there may be nothing at all wrong with the belief system itself, they should be weaned away, gently and uncritically, into more active pursuits, and encouraged to play with other children. Yet it goes against the nature of Sun Sign Scorpians to be completely open and 'natural'. They will always have their secrets and dark passions. Sometimes it does more harm than good to try to persuade a Scorpian child to join in more boisterous pursuits. So on the principle that if you can't beat them, join them, it might be a good idea to accompany them to the Egyptian galleries in the museum and investigate the Mummies together. You could also put them in charge of the Hallowe'en festivities, which could have been invented for Scorpians. If they are at all inclined to take up an active hobby or sport, it is unlikely to be run of the mill.

When distressed or off-colour, Scorpians tend to go very quiet, retreating into their own world, to the bewilderment and hurt of their loved ones. They can bottle up all sorts of profound feelings – sometimes it comes hard even to let their parents know what they really want for their birthday present. Somehow they just can't articulate something so passionately desired, while knowing that if they say nothing, they are unlikely to get it. For their happiness and future health, they should be encouraged to open up and share at least some of their secret hopes and fears.

Although Scorpians often feel low and retreat into a gloom, this state of affairs tends to be short-lived, and they soon spring back into life. Because of their enormous reserves of energy and courage, and also their capacity to recover quickly from both mental and physical illnesses and setbacks, Scorpians are excellent people to have around in tough times. Once again, it is their underlying conviction that Fate is on their side that sees them through, and even as children, they can be surprisingly adult, suddenly snapping out of their introspection to take charge in an emergency.

Prince Charles
Theodore Roosevelt
Marie Antoinette
Richard Burton
Edward III
August Rodin
Jamie Lee Curtis
Evelyn Waugh
Charles Atlas
Albert Camus
Stephen T. Crane

Marie Antoinette

Vivien Leigh

Marie Curie
François Mitterrand
Pablo Picasso
Vivien Leigh
Erwin Rommel
Martin Luther
Cheiro (Palmist)
George Patton
Paul Joseph Goebbels

THE SUN IN SAGITTARIUS

(23 November — 21 December)

Sun Sign: SAGITTARIUS

Sign: THE ARCHER OR CENTAUR

Ruling Planet: JUPITER

Gender: MASCULINE

Element: FIRE

Quality: MUTABLE

Compatibility: AQUARIUS

AND LIBRA

Non-compatibility: CANCER,

SCORPIO AND TAURUS

Sun Sign Sagittarians are some of the most likeable folk around: open, optimistic, enthusiastic and tolerant. Their ruler Jupiter is traditionally supposed to be lucky, and this largest of all the planets in the solar system does seem to bestow very positive opportunities on Sagittarians. Possibly this is because their attitude actively invites such opportunity. Exuberant and often restless, Sagittarians are adept at inspiring and encouraging more pessimistic and cautious souls, although they can be appallingly foolhardy, getting themselves into some worrying situations. Usually, though, they get themselves out again without much trouble.

Many people born under the sign of the Archer find it hard to concnetrate for very long on any one subject unless it captures their imagination, and then they can give their whole selves to it for hours. Their keen and restless minds are always looking to the future, trying to be one jump ahead – and oftenn succeeding in being at least two. The joyful Sagittarians have an infectious joy and curiosity, and are an interesting blend of the studious – happy to sit with their books for long periods of time, totally oblivious to the outside world – and the very physical, for they are essentially outdoor types. No wonder then that many Astrologers believe Australia to be the ideal Sagittarian country.

Sagittarians are also inclined to philosophy and religion, although they rarely become bigots or fanatics. They love discussing their ideas, often late into the night, and are happy to share their home with a large number of very diverse people as well as animals, of whom they are very fond.

However, excessive Sagittarian energy can be disconcerting. People born under this sign tend to flit from job to job, lover to lover and home to home. Some may never settle, remaining life's gypsies to the very end. Most Sagittarians are natural backpackers at some point in their lives. Other people may find this restlessness disturbing, especially the more staid, security-minded materialists, such as Taurus or Virgo, whose home is their castle. They fail to understand why anyone would want to leave it. Sagittarians tend to see their home as more of a tent which they fold, metaphorically, before stealing away on their latest adventure.

Sagittarians can take this footloose-and-fancy-free attitude much too far, though. It can easily degenerate into mindless optimism and irresponsibility, and make them rely on impossible scenarious to get them out of trouble. They make compulsive gamblers, seeing Lady Luck constantly beckoning. Others may try to tell them she is merely a mirage, but to Sagittarians she is tantamountt to a religious vision.

APPEARANCE

Sagittarians come in several types, including the super-athletic. The men can have enviably wide shoulders and slim waist and hips, while the women may be bronzed and muscular. They have quick, determined mannerisms and daring, piercing eyes that are always likely to flash with laughter. While not particularly fashion conscious, Sagittarians can look trendy. Whatever their age, they favour youthful styles, but take care to add their own personal touch to each ensemble. Some Sagittarians are rather eccentric and convey bizarre first impressions.

HEALTH

With such unbounded energy, Sagittarians often fail to look before they leap and as a result, suffer quite a few bruises, pulled muscles and broken bones. What they need to do is channel and balance their mental, physical and spiritual energies. Many find yoga, Tai Chi and meditation of great benefit. Sometimes, they find themselves become teachers of these arts. Satifttarians need to geel that they are in control of their minds and bodies, and like to plan an exercise regine and diet that is right for them. Some, however, may be totally unconcerned with what they eat and drink. They will happily refuel on any old junk food, but most, especially in later years, take an

interest in healthy eating. Some can even become health-food bores. Conversely, Sagittarians can throw themselves with typical abandon into the hedonistic life, feasting rather too often on rich, fatty foods and drinking too much beer, which they lov e. However, all they normally need to change to a healthier lifestyle is sound advice from a doctor or someone else they respect.

Traditionally, the hips and thighs are problem areas for Sagittarians. Perhaps all that distinctive twisting and twirling puts a strain on them. So it is a good idea to have physiotherapy or osteopathy at the first sign of trouble.

CAREER

Sagittarians go for anything that gives free rein to their adventurous spirits. They will never persist with any job that limits them, so they don't go far in large corporations or the Civil Service, where there are too many rules and regulations, and where they find it hard to express their individuality. Similarly, dull claustrophobic offices make Sagittarians feel uncomfortable.

While rarely truly ambitious, Sagittarians like to see the fruits of their labours, and enjoy being appreciated. Sometimes they will rise to the top of their chosen profession without much effort. Making money is usually of secondary importance to Sagittarians. They are not seriously materialistic, and although they enjoy a few home comforts and the freedom which money can bring, on the whole their working lives are focused on deeper matters. Many find fulfilment in study, becoming life-long students or university teachers, or they take up bookish pursuits in ther spare time. Sagittarians make excellent publishers. They love the look and feel of books, as well as their content – and some even set up their own generally successful publishing companies. However, typical Sun Sign Sagittarians can be far too restless and disorganized to spend months, perhaps even years, actually writing abook. They would need a very efficient and diplomatic literary agent on hand to constantly supposrt and nag them. Even

then, they could miss the deadline by months.

Many Sagittarians lack staying power. They have wonderfully inspired ideas that they fully intend to turn into a concrete result, but in a very short space of time they forget all about it, become disillusioned, and turn their attention to the next tempting project. Sagittarians need to be brought down to earth gently, and can work well with the right sort of tactful, organized business partner, especially one who gives them space to be themselves.

Another area in which Sagittarians traditionally shine is religion. Many a sleepy village has been rudely awakened by the arrival of the new Sagittarian vicar, with his or her new-broom style, energy and idealism. Even when the more conventional parishioners do their best to clip the wings of these bumptious newcomers, the Sagittarians will continue t o bring a breath of fresh air into their lives, whether they like it or not. Apart from the pastoral aspect of their vocation, Sagittarians find ministering to the

Traditionally, Sagittarians makes excellent sportspeople, and many make it to the top, although they do need the strong guiding hand of a tough coach. They need to be disciplined and made to follow a regular training routine, or all that energy will be dissipated and their talent frittered away.

Sagittarians often love horses, and in fact most animals. They find great fulfilment in equestrian sports, either as keen amateurs or as professionals. In some respects, they are rather similar to these big, nervy and powerful animals, and can easily form a strong, lasting bond with them. Sagittarians are natural horse whisperers.

RELATIONSHIPS

Since Sagittarius is a Fire Sign, people born under it arehighly sexed, and have no time for prudishness or conventional attitudes.

However, they can be considerably less keen on settling down for life with one partner, and tend to take their time deciding which of their many paramours is their soulmate. Some never decide, and go blowing off through life happily solo, but always surrounded by a large circle of lovers, friends and admirers. As free spirits, Sagittarians need very understanding partners, who can cope with abrupt changes of plan. Often those born under the sign of the Centaur need to gallop off to fresh fields and pastures new, if only for a few days, to recharge their batteries. More often than not, they will want to be alone

more spiritual needs of their flock very congenial, and enjoy theological study and discussion. They tend to be very keen on ecumenical movements, comparative religion, and anything that encourages greater tolerance between different faiths or lifestyles.

Often their religious bent is combined with a desire to help their fellow man. They may be 'hands on' healers, naturopaths, osteopaths and the like, or spiritualist mediums. Some are keen psychical researchers, travelling great distances to investigate ghosts and poltergeists, and are rarely frightened by even the most dramatic cases of things that go bump in the night. Once they have fully researched the case, Sagittarians will then give powerful, inspirational talks to packed audiences and great acclaim.

Compatibility in Relationships

Aries
Aries will usually try to dominate fellow Fire Sign Sagittarius – which will only drive them further away.

Taurus
Tame, conventional Taureans often prove too stodgy for idiosyncratic and sometimes eccentric Sagittarians.

Gemini
Superficially on the same wavelength, but Geminians play too many games for innocent Sagittarians.

Cancer
Thefamous Cancerian compassion and talent for home-making is wasted on these free spirits.

Leo
The Leonine energy and verve is attractive to fiery Sagittarius, but sooner or later they will clash.

Virgo
Steady, organized and repressed, Virgoans are the complete opposite of unrealistic Sagittarians.

Libra
Librans and Sagittarians are a good match, inspiring and supporting each other. Physically very compatible.

Scorpio
Dark Scorpians often try to ensnare charming Sagittarians, but intense physicality doesn't mean enduring love.

Sagittarius
Fellow Sagittarians will get on well and fuel each other's madcap schemes. Romantic, yes. Practical, no..

Capricorn
Sagittarians find Goats hard to understand. Their caution is anathema to the untamed Sagittarian spirit.

Aquarius
This can be the perfect match. Both signs have little regard for the establishment or convention.

Pisces
Sagittarians have little time for self-indulgent scenes, so touchy Pisceans are unlikely to make good life partners.

while doing it. Restless and claustrophobic, they cannot bear any form of restriction, and often react angrily when their chosen lifestyle is challenged, or when their partner demands to accompany them on their adventures.

On the whole, Sagittarians are not good at marriage, even though there are some who seek to spend all their time with the one love of their life. Many more content themselves with being serially monogamous, perfectly faithful to wife or husband until it is time to move on.

Many Sagitarrians, on the other hand, prefer to live alone, cheerfully surrounded by the chaos of solo living, but very much at the centre of a busy social and love life. They enjoy it when friends, family and lovers drop by.

Basically, Sagittarians are good, kind people who hate unpleasantness and injustice. Any disharmony in the home or elsewhere distresses them, and often the only way they can cope with it is by running away. This tendency makes them unpredictable in relationships, and rather feckless and unreliable parents, although they can be hugely popular with children because they are very childlike themselves.

IDEAL PARTNER

Most Sagittarians prefer to have a range of partners, chosen from all signs of the zodiac, but when they do settle down, they need to spend their lives, with easy-going, tolerant but organized people who make few demands and who are not particularly jealous or possessive. This is something of a tall order, but certain Aquarians and Librans fit the bill. Those who are definitely not compatible with Sagittarians are weepy, clinging,

insecure Cancerians, dark, intense manipulative Scorpians, and reactionary, jealous Taureans.

THE SAGITTARIAN CHILD

Sun Sign Sagittarian children can be a strange mix of oddball and sporty. Inquisitive, charming, quick-witted and active, they can seem like a dream to teachers or parents, but there is an underlying insecurity and waywardness in them, which can cause problems.

They find the restrictions of school an immense bore, and can resort to playing truant simply to escape into the fresh air. Although their concentration is good when their interest is fully engaged, Sagittarian children can find it hard to focus on less congenial subjects and need a firm hand with their studies. Often they don't see the point of pursuing their education beyond the normal span of around eleven years, and yearn to travel the world, experience other lifestyles and meet as many diverse people as they can. Yet once they have had their fill of travel and discovery, Sagittarians will happily sign on for a further education course, or throw themselves into a studious hobby such as local history research.

Sagittarians can be eccentric, which marks them out from their peers. However, they can charm their way out of potential bullying and their prowess at sport is a good deterrent to anyone who thinks they must be wimps just because they like reading. Happy-go-lucky Sagittarians feel very uncomfortable with emotional intensity or cruelty, whether directed at themselves or at others. They cannot cope with the typical Cancerian possessiveness and melodrama, nor with heavy-handed brutality, whether physical or verbal.

Famous Sagittarians

Uri Geller
Steven Spielberg
George Eliot
Louisa M. Alcott
Jane Austen
Catherine of Breganza
Walt Disney
Charles Chaplin
Winston Churchill
Joseph Conrad

Benjamin Disraeli
Bruce Lee
Edith Piaf
Ludwig von Beethoven
Jimi Hendrix
William Blake
Henri Toulouse-Lautrec
Gustave Flaubert
Mark Twain
John Paul Getty

Winston Churchill

Jimi Hendrix

THE SUN IN CAPRICORN

(22 December — 20 January)

Sun Sign: CAPRICORN

Sign: THE GOAT

Ruling Planet: SATURN

Gender: FEMININE

Element: EARTH

Quality: CARDINAL

Compatibility: TAURUS

AND VIRGO

Non-compatibility:

SAGITTARIUS AND ARIES

un Sign Capricornians are disciplined, methodical, sensible and sensitive. If that makes them sound excessively cold and boring, the truth is that they can be, but often they show remarkable ambition, kindness and gentle, often self-deprecating, humour. Traditionally, their ruling planet Saturn is concerned with the tough lessons of life: illness, restriction, old age and death, but modern astrologers realize that this picture is far too gloomy. While Saturn can be a tough teacher, often repeatedly putting Capricornians through a steep learning curve, it can also galvanize them into action, to get things done, become achievers and climb to the top of their chosen profession with all its attendant status and prosperity.

Capricornians tend to be cautious by nature, sensing pitfalls and obstacles and standing back from problems. This can make them pessimistic and disinclined to move forward: inside they are saying to themselves, not 'you might fail', but 'you will fail'. Some can become so convinced that nothing good will ever happen that their unconscious mind ensures that nothing does. However, the whole point of the Saturnine influence is to present them with a series of challenges that will never actually be too difficult for them to overcome – for those who believe in karma this is actually an honour. Once Capricornians have come to understand the true nature of their path, it will be easier for them to rise above the mundane pettiness and worries that often beset them.

Sticklers for detail, and methodical to a fault, Capricornians are superb organizers, happy to deal with paperwork and the daily business of life. They

are not natural stars like Leos or Scorpians, but usually seek to oil the wheels behind the scenes and make everything run smoothly. They hate untidiness, dirt and mess, whether it is the house or is expressed as a state of mind. Of course, many more sloppy characters consider them irritating and fussy. They can seem joyless and obsessed with doing the right thing, being conventional and often reactionary, with rigid, inflexible, self-imposed rules. But when they let go and relax – even with Saturn as a ruler, this is not impossible! – they are charming, delightful companions, with a wonderfully dry sense of humour.

APPEARANCE

Many typical Sun Sign Capricornians – especially the men – look rather goatish, with prominent noses and angular features. They tend to be on the tall side and somewhat bony, with dark, straight hair. The women are often of medium height, with mousey hair and strong features, although they can have beautiful, serene expressions that give them a particularly attractive air.

Capricornians of both sexes take great care with their appearance, but hate any form of flamboyance, extravagance or eccentricity. They are neat, clean and perhaps slightly old-fashioned. Capricornian females are true ladies – a term that pleases them. They like to have their hair beautifully coiffured once, perhaps twice, a week and regularly tinted in subtle, natural-looking colours. Even young Capricornian females are wary of the latest High Street chic, and tend to stick with the more tried-and-tested styles. Capricornian men love collars, ties and formal suits. Their wardrobes usually lack ultra-casual T-shirts and jeans, and even if they wear them, they look completely wrong.

HEALTH

Capricornians think it bad form to admit to illness, and often force themselves to crawl to work even when they are suffering from really debilitating viruses. They hate what they see as weakness, and continually berate themselves for feeling off-colour. This attitude can result in serious problems going untreated – they despise people who 'bother' doctors – often making the situation much worse. Their tendency to bottle up emotions can also result in health problems in later life. Research has shown that people who express their anger, disappointment and grief are much more likely to avoid illnesses such as heart attacks – and even some forms of cancer – than those who do not let them out.

Traditionally, Capricornian problem areas are their joints, bones and teeth. There is a tendency to stiffness and arthritis, although it can be relatively mild. They need to take extra calcium, cod liver oil and evening primrose oil supplements to help their physical flexibility. They should move around more, disciplining themselves to have regular breaks, especially if working long hours at

a computer, because they have a tendency to Repetitive Strain Injury (RSI), and need to keep their hands and wrists flexible. Although they are inclined to take only conventional medicine seriously, they should at least try complementary therapies. Acupressure and aromatherapy will help to loosen them up enormously, both physically and emotionally.

They should have regular sessions with an osteopath or chiropractor and be sure to visit the dentist regularly.

CAREER

Sun Sign Capricornians are highly industrious and formidably organized, so they make superb administrators. They are happy to sit alone at their desk all day, taking, and often giving, orders by telephone, memo or in curiously formal e-mails. There is a certain haughtiness about them, a detached air that sets them apart from their chattier, more relaxed colleagues and can make them seem intimidating and aloof. However, they have no wish to be seen as one of the crowd. They frequently have their eye on the top job, and are content to work their way towards it in gradual stages. Aiming too high and too soon is likely to be disastrous for a typical Sun Sign Capricornian, although they are unlikely to try it more than once. One bad mistake in business or career, and Capricornians have learnt a lesson for life.

Traditionally associated with the Earth, Capricornians are attracted to gardening and environmental issues, and can make stalwart supporters of 'green' campaigns, either as a full-time job or a part-time interest.

Rather austere and unimaginative, they make excellent bank employees, although they are perhaps more suited to the old Dickensian days of wing collars and great dusty ledgers than today's relaxed style of 'personal bankers' and telephone transactions. They are often career Civil Servants, rising gradually through the grades to a very high position of respect and authority. Sun Sign Capricornians are very good with money matters and scrupulously honest, which makes them ideal in positions of trust.

Their self-discipline and methodical working style mean that they are happy to tackle the painstaking jobs which others avoid, and they

Compatibility in Relationships

Aries
Fiery, tempestuous Arians may be appealingly different, but this opposite sign will be too cold to attract for long.

Cancer
Cancerian emotion can drive Capricornians mad, although their compassion and loving home have certain attractions.

Libra
Librans' love of the social whirl can cause problems for the more withdrawn and hesitant type of Capricornian.

Capricorn
Two wintry Goats together may not make for much empathizing but sometimes like works with like.

Taurus
Earthy and controlled Taureans have a lot to offer the Goat, and they can bring out the passion in each other.

Leo
Capricornians admire Leonine style and dash, but are fearful of such high-profile egocentrics.

Scorpio
Intrigued by fascinating Scorpio, Capricorn may make a serious error of judgement – and live to regret it.

Aquarius
This combination can work, if only because Aquarians can get on with most people if they are prepared to compromise.

Gemini
Gregarious, persuasive Geminians can charm reserved Capricornians, but the Goat remains distrustful.

Virgo
Calm, self-contained Virgoans often make excellent partners for cautious, conventional Capricornians.

Sagittarius
Unfettered by practicalities, Sagittarians seriously upset Capricornian respect for the more traditional way of life.

Pisces
Contradictory and often unhappy Pisceans will bewilder Capricornians, who are scared by overt emotion.

may even choose unpopular careers – as tax inspectors or customs officers, for example. They see duty and law enforcement as of paramount importance, and can unfortunately become overbearing, perhaps even slightly sadistic with lesser mortals who owe tax or are not familiar with rules and regulations. Most Capricornians, however, have a kind streak, and become very hurt at the idea that they might abuse their position of power.

Capricornians tend to have very low self-worth, and see their work as a reflection of the respect they have earned. They love to be pillars of the community, and often take on time-consuming local council work, or help out in charity shops besides having a full-time job.

Redundancy hits them harder than any other Sun Sign: they take it very personally, seeing 'the sack' as their own failure, and feel they will never find another job or make their mark in life. Unemployment is always a bleak experience, but to Capricornians it represents the winter of all their hopes. Of course, many do dust themselves down and successfully start all over again, but always the threat of being unemployed haunts the typical Capricornian like a curse waiting to fall on them.

RELATIONSHIPS

Capricornians can be surprisingly passionate behind closed doors – after all, theirs is the sign of the Goat! However, they take a while to warm up, are very cautious about relating to others, and tend to be 'backward in coming forward'. Many Capricornians of both sexes can wait an unfashionably long time before losing their virginity and can be very timid with the opposite sex.

Capricornians are very rarely easy-going and can, in fact, be rather dour. They need to be encouraged to lighten up. They can be over-keen on pouring cold water on the bright ideas of more enthusiastic family members. Their ultimate accolade is more likely to be 'That's quite good' instead of heartfelt congratulations – an approach that can be discouraging, especially to young children.

Capricornians often marry relatively late in life, waiting until they can afford a comfortable home in an upmarket area. They will spend weeks peering into estate agents' windows and making calculations about how much they can afford, without ever thinking that a house must be a home and have love, as well as money, lavished on it.

Some Capricornians are constantly worried about money, scrimping and saving even though they earn a decent salary. To them, destitution is only around the corner, and Fate will hand them a place on Skid Row unless they are vigilant and count the pennies every moment of their lives. This is a manifestation of their low self-esteem: the more money they salt away, the more respectable they are in their own eyes.

Capricornians need to learn to relax and feel secure in their homes, without any threat to the status quo. They are very unhappy with emotional scenes and upheaval. They tend to carry their early hurt around with them like ice in their hearts, although they can thaw out if their partner loves them determinedly and wholeheartedly, gradually introducing them to the concept of receiving love and all good things. They must learn to accept that they are worthy of the devotion of others.

Male Capricornians tend to stiff-upper-lip reserve (even if they aren't British!), believing that dignity must be maintained at all costs, even in front of their nearest and dearest. Although this can be good for their family, who see them as towers of strength in a crisis, it is less useful for their own health. Capricornians can bottle up a huge backlog of grief and anger, often giving the appearance of cold-heartedness at the death of relatives, even of a spouse or parent. They can take refuge behind clichés such as 'Life must go on' and 'Crying won't bring them back', but inside they are bleeding. Family members should try to encourage Capricornians to discuss their feelings, whether of grief or joy.

Capricorns always try to do the right thing in life, and cannot understand those who rebel against the system, so they hardly make ideal parents of boisterous children or difficult teenagers. But they will always be very proud (in a quiet, unassuming way, of course) of their more timid, studious and sensible offspring.

IDEAL PARTNER

Capricornians need a strong, loving partner who neither whines nor clings, causes scenes or is too adventurous. Intense, dreamy Pisceans rarely fit the bill, and fellow Water Sign Cancerians are usually far too emotionally demanding. Earthy Taureans and Virgoans, who have a similar fondness for order and neatness, but possess added charm and wit, possibly make the best partners for the wintry Capricornians. It would be a mistake for a typical Goat even to consider a relationship with a happy-go-lucky Sagittarian or a wild-child Arian. Opposites may attract, but they can often destroy, too.

THE CAPRICORNIAN CHILD

Capricornians are rarely happy children. Even if their parents love them to distraction, the constant fear of losing their father or mother will seriously detract from their happiness. Capricornians are frequently far too fearful and sad, needing endless encouragement to join in the fun, get their hands dirty and have a laugh. Although naturally self-disciplined, they look to their elders and betters to give them clear ground rules for their behaviour, and can be very distressed in an easy-going, irresponsible atmosphere.

Capricornian children need to be given responsibility at an early age so that they can feel they are making a contribution. They should be praised at every opportunity in order to bolster their underdeveloped self-esteem. This is quite safe. There is no danger of Capricornians ever becoming conceited.

Sun Sign Capricornians are always old, even when young children. It is as if they carry all the problems of the world on their tiny shoulders, and they can become very introverted. They should never be bullied or teased, but always gently encouraged to make their contribution, and to make steady, rather than spectacular, success at school. It is also important that they are never compared unfavourably with any of their siblings or the flashy, natural-born achievers in their class. What they like to hear is that everything comes to

David Bowie
Louis Braille
Charles Rennie Macintosh
Muhammad Ali
Simone de Beauvoir
Bernadette, Saint of Lourdes
Al Capone
Paul Cézanne
Marlene Dietrich
Oliver Hardy
Martin Luther King

Martin Luther King

Oliver Hardy

J. Edgar Hoover
Joan of Arc
Mao Tse Tung
Isaac Newton
Michel de Nostradamus
Louis Pasteur
Edgar Allen Poe
Elvis Presley
Henri Matisse

THE SUN IN AQUARIUS

(21 January – 18 February)

Sun Sign: AQUARIUS

Sign: THE WATER CARRIER

Ruling Planet: URANUS AND

SATURN

Gender: MASCULINE

Element: AIR

Quality: FIXED

Compatibility: PISCES

AND CAPRICORN

Non-compatibility: ALMOST

NO ONE –

AT LEAST IN THEORY

Sun Sign Aquarians are friendly, idealistic, independent and humanitarian. That said, they are also the most varied set of individuals within one zodiacal group, so it is difficult to make generalizations about them. However, what is certain is that they tend to be extremely capable, kind and charitable and very forward-looking. After all, the next Great Year (see The Great Year) is the Age of Aquarius, when these people will come into their own.

Aquarians are natural New Agers, born astrologers and vegetarian eco-warriors, always eager to improve themselves and the world around them, and well aware of the spiritual side to life. They frequently hold strong political views, and often mount campaigns against some form of injustice, or join groups such as Greenpeace or Amnesty International. Usually pacifist, Sun Sign Aquarians can be relied upon to be leaders of the alternative scene and courageous challengers of Establishment values. Many of them also hold strong, but sometimes off-beat, religious or spiritual views, and are fond of philosophical debate.

The brave, free-spirited Aquarians are always true friends to the down-trodden, but find it hard to translate all that 'love and light' into close personal relationships. Aquarians may be 'New Age huggers', but they are often appallingly bad at creating a loving environment for themselves. For them, charity rarely begins at home.

Though they are good original thinkers and idiosyncratic in many ways, Sun Sign Aquarians can seem eccentric. They will, however, be mostly oblivious to the sly nudgings and criticism of others. Once they have found a lifestyle and, more importantly, a cause, to fight for, they will stick to it obdurately. They can be contrary, though, and expect others to understand their sudden changes of direction, before they settle down again on their chosen life-path.

Aquarius is an Air Sign, and those born under this sign need their personal space, both literally and figuratively. They hate limits and react very badly to being told what to do, although they can often be surprisingly dictatorial themselves.

APPEARANCE

Sun Sign Aquarians come in many different shapes and sizes, but they tend to share attractive, clean-cut looks and a proud bearing. They have open, attentive and sympathetic expressions, and a ready smile which shows off their excellent teeth to advantage. Those born under the sign of the Water Carrier tend to be slim, fairly muscular and bronzed in summer. Even those who take no exercise and eat junk food seem to be naturally at ease with their bodies and, fortunately, rarely get fat.

Many Aquarians wear unusual outfits such as happy hippy gear or floating New Age kaftans, and most would claim to be completely uninterested in something as materialistic and unspiritual as fashion. However, even those who wear thrift shop rejects somehow manage to look noble and set apart from the crowd.

HEALTH

Aquarians' lungs are particularly sensitive to cigarette smoke and air pollution, so they should be careful to avoid these wherever possible. Similarly, they can suffer from allergies more than most, and should have them checked out by a reputable naturopath.

Traditionally vulnerable to problems with their legs and ankles, Sun Sign Aquarians should take care to wear proper protective footwear when hiking, climbing or exploring caves. Another problem area is their circulation, which they should nurture with brisk exercise (especially in winter), massage, warm baths and daily supplements of gingko, cod liver oil and evening primrose oil.

CAREER

Aquarians can turn their hands very successfully to most things, since they are very determined individuals. They can turn their chosen cause into a career while remaining technically unemployed. In a perverse kind of way, some see living off state hand-outs as noble, direct action against a repressive capitalist system. Of course, this sort of Aquarian is relatively rare, but they tend to be so picturesque and newsworthy that they frequently get noticed.

Most are hard-working, perhaps even driven, in their chosen field. Many choose rather unusual or esoteric careers – astrology being one of them – and can often be found at New Age festivals, extolling the virtues of a new gadget that they have invented that will ease all aches and pains.

They are best at work that involves them in improving the lot of humanity in some way, and make excellent counsellors and advisers, social workers or charity administrators.

Traditionally, Aquarians are non-materialistic people, but this is not necessarily so. They are often rather proud individuals who enjoy social and professional status and all its perks such as large cars, comfortable houses and expensive long-haul holidays. They enjoy the freedom that comes with money and can often be wretched when it runs out. However, they're not grasping or given to signing up for pension plans and insurance policies when young, like Capricornians or Virgoans. They see life as a series of golden opportunities to make the world a happier place, and if money happens to come their way, so much the better.

Aquarians are independent and logical and their real talents frequently belie their rather unworldly image. Aquarians value education and often do very well at university or college, and they travel widely to improve their knowledge of the way others live. With this experience behind them, they are natural problem-solvers, with a strong practical streak and often a marked ability to think laterally. They are forever coming up with astonishingly simple yet elegant, solutions to apparently intractable problems that have stumped others for days, and are not afraid to roll up their sleeves to show them how it can be done.

Aquarians make good teachers and are constantly concerned about how their pupils will turn out, helping them along as best they can. They have a real sense of building the future in the here and now, and realize that the best way of building a fair and decent society is by educating the adults of tomorrow.

Despite their rather airy-fairy image, Aquarians are surprisingly adept with technology, realizing that it is the way forward. This is the key to their thinking. They rarely look back and believe that the future is all-important. For them, today's exciting developments will be tomorrow's reality. For this reason, Aquarians are often found working in futuristic careers, such as information technology and satellite and space probes or researching dolphin communication.

Aquarians have a great need to push back the frontiers of human knowledge. They see progress as the great challenge but recognize that there is a price to pay, such as the terrible human and environmental results of the Industrial Revolution. Their brave new world will be caring, compassionate and informed, and they are willing to work hard to ensure that it comes about.

RELATIONSHIPS

Aquarians are not good at close relationships, despite all their caring-and-sharing attitudes. They tend to be very wary of emotion, often misconstruing it as mere sentiment that makes irritating demands on their affections. In their minds, they belong to the world, not to one partner or family.

They need tolerance for their peculiarities, and a large measure of independence, so much so that many Aquarians choose to remain unattached, even though they enjoy having a large variety of passionate relationships. In many respects, they are happier with friends and co-crusaders than with life-partners, but in that elusive lasting relationship they can finally blossom and turn out to be very loyal.

Often, Aquarians are simply too busy rushing from one campaign to the next to stop and notice the love-light in someone else's eyes. All too often they mistake a desire for personal closeness as a willingness to carry the banners. However, no one should underestimate Sun Sign Aquarians. They are by no means obtuse, just rushed off their feet. Once they realize they are being pursued romantically, they may be amused or irritated, but are rarely won over immediately.

There is something decidedly superior about Aquarians, no matter how friendly and egalitarian they seem to be, or think they are. They have a detached, slightly quizzical air, and often assume that they are giving humanity the benefit of their expertise. This can make them seem attractively mysterious to some, but it can also be very offputting for others who do not necessarily appreciate being spoken to from on high.

Aquarians often make unusual parents, expressing themselves in slightly oddball activities. Sometimes there is a distinct element of role-reversal: they are the headstrong 'child', while their children are the ones who are comparatively prim and proper. Aquarians are always encouraging their offspring to be bold and experimental and to espouse humanitarian and ecological causes

Compatibility in Relationships

Aries
These two signs share world-saving ambitions and can have powerful sexual magnetism, but it may not last long.

Cancer
Cancerians can provide emotional support as long as they are not too clingy or excessively emotional.

Libra
Librans may fall under the Aquarian spell, but it may be hero-worship rather than love that fuels the relationship.

Capricorn
Oddly staid and cautious Capricornians can succeed in winning the love and protection of Aquarians.

Taurus
Taureans are disconcerted by Aquarian conventionality and rebellion, and will usually steer clear of it.

Leo
Leonine nobility may be appealing but their grandness cuts no ice with egalitarian Aquarians.

Scorpio
Scorpians' interest in deep, mystical subjects appeals to New Age Aquarians, but can be too dark for peace-lovers.

Aquarius
Two world-changing humanitarians must get on – or are their egos too demanding for such a union to work.

Gemini
Aquarians understand the Geminian restlessness and drive, but add their own, more profound idealism.

Virgo
Aquarians may mock safe, steady Virgoans' obsesssion with analysis and order as being too retentive.

Sagittarius
These two signs are similarly rebellious and free-spirited, but Sagittarian indiscipline may threaten the grand plan.

Pisces
Dreamy, otherworldly Pisceans can find lasting love with mystical Aquarians, who will overlook their intensity.

almost before they can walk. Sometimes Aquarian parents are so keen to free their children from the yoke of convention that they take them travelling the world or simply expose them to an unusual homelife – in a commune, for example.

Aquarian homes may be neat and bright, and superficially appear much like many other houses in their neighbourhood, but there will usually be something different about them. It may just be their large collection of crystals sparkling in every room, the patch of deliberately untended garden that is home to a variety of wildlife, or the solar panels on the roof. However, it is usually the Aquarian lifestyle that differentiates their homes from those of their neighbours. Colourful people are forever coming and going. Their garden will almost certainly be the scene of some interesting activities – Wiccan celebrations of the New Moon perhaps, or the building of a sauna.

IDEAL PARTNER

Anyone who is also an idealistic free spirit will be suitable for an Aquarian. They detest emotional blackmail so clingers such as the more badly aspected Cancerian need not apply. Sometimes they respond well to Pisceans, especially if they have a strong Aquarian aspect in their charts, and the same applies to well-grounded Capricornians. In general, though, Aquarians are so individualistic that they could – at least in theory – settle down with almost anyone. However, although the Water Carrier themselves may well be happy with a long-term commitment, the same may not be true of the other half of the relationship.

THE AQUARIAN CHILD

Children born under the sign of the Water Carrier are friendly and open and need to be free and independent from an early age. Sometimes, they can be too friendly, and need to be educated about the dangers of talking to strangers as soon as they are able to understand.

No Sun Sign Aquarian will be totally happy in a highly regimented or over-disciplined school environment. 'Progressive' schools – run, for instance, under the Montessori system – were made for Aquarians. They need to express their creativity and love of nature, and to become involved in local charities when quite young. Aquarians are superb at inventing new and effective ways of fundraising, and should be encouraged to take the lead in this at school and in the local community. Their initiative, energy and unfailing good humour are often an inspiration to others. It is also essential, early practice for all the committee work and philanthropy that they will be involved with in later life.

However, Aquarian children can be worriers, brooding not only about their own problems, whether real or imagined, but also about the state of the world. Troubling news reports can upset them for days, and the parents of Aquarians should take this into account, and treat them accordingly. They have a great need to be taken seriously and should never be mocked or teased. They genuinely appreciate heart-to-heart talks with their parents and positively thrive on family discussions, which give them the opportunity to thrash out problems and plan the way forward. They must feel, however, that their contributions are genuinely valued.

Charles Dickens
Franz Schubert
Paul Newman
Emile Zola
Christian Dior
John McEnroe
Sonny Bono
Humphrey Bogart
Eva Braun
Robert Burns
Lord Byron
Anton Chekhov
Charles Darwin
James Dean
Frederick Delius
Abraham Lincoln
Wolfgang Amadeus Mozart
Ronald Reagan
Franklin D.Roosevelt
George 'Babe' Ruth

James Dean

Aquarian genius, Charles Dickens, at work in his sleep

THE SUN IN PISCES

(19 February — 20 March)

Sun Sign: PISCES

Sign: TWO FISH

Ruling Planet: NEPTUNE

AND JUPITER

Gender: FEMININE

Element: WATER

Quality: MUTABLE

Compatibility: AQUARIUS, PISCES

AND VIRGO

Non-compatibility:

CANCER, SCORPIO

AND CAPRICORN

Sun Sign Pisceans are emotional, dreamy, insecure people with strong creative instincts. Poetic and intuitive, they often seem out of place in the everyday world. All the same, many Pisceans achieve great things. They are kind, sensitive souls, who delight in the happiness and fulfilment of others. Sometimes they go too far in this regard, for they can live their entire lives in the shadow of other, more ambitious people, and never achieve their own true potential. Born under an archetypically Feminine Water Sign, Pisceans seek above all to establish peace, harmony and love and can become terribly distressed if they fail to do so, or when others do not share their idealistic visions.

Pisceans tend to view life through rose-tinted spectacles. In some cases, this is all that gets them through, because a negative side of this sign is the ease with which Pisceans can be cast down and depressed. Once this happens, all motivation is gone and Pisceans become moody, subservient and weak-willed. Many will do anything rather than face cold, stark reality, finding refuge in escapism of one sort or another. One of their rulers, Neptune, governs illusion, and although this can manifest itself in very healthy, creative ways (see Career), it may cover some forms of addiction.

Like their sign – two fish swimming in opposite directions – Pisceans have a markedly indecisive streak. They may be afraid of offering their own opinions, although at the same time they resent it when others take command. This leads to all manner of internal tensions, sometimes erupting in crankiness. Pisceans watch more open, decisive people state their case and even if they disagree, they don't say so. Then as time passes they realize what they should have said, and how much difference it would have made. However, they manage to interpret this as the fault of others, and inwardly seethe with resentment.

Pisceans are secretive, and can be deceitful. They may lack the depth and scope of black Scorpionic vengeance, but they can still be nasty. Of course, many are delightful, open people – after all, the full picture of any one character can only be seen at all accurately when the whole chart is studied – but there is almost always an underlying feeling of not belonging, of lacking a voice, of being faceless, which manifests as resentment at the assertiveness of other people.

APPEARANCE

Pisceans tend to be of small to medium height, and quite slightly built, although they can pack on the pounds later in life if they are not careful. They often have strangely rebellious hair and spend time and money on taming it. Pisceans have delicate eyes and, if they are pale-skinned, they often need glasses. Typically, Pisceans are strong-featured, with generous mouths and a quirky, slightly twitchy smile. It is as if they are undecided whether or not to join in the fun.

Pisceans are often very chic and take an interest in stylish clothes. Both sexes are usually well-groomed and pay attention to detail. They are rarely eccentric or look out of place, and are uncomfortable with those who do. Female Pisceans often make their own clothes, favouring luxury fabrics such as silk, velvet and satin.

HEALTH

Pisceans are highly-strung, reacting badly to all manner of pollutants, whether physical ones such as dust, smog or chemicals or emotional triggers such as rows or anxiety. Even psychic 'vibes' disturb them. These things can provoke allergies, crippling headaches and a host of other ailments. To counter these adverse effects, Pisceans should seek protection – either through meditation or prayer or by strengthening themselves through hard physical exercise. Although not always naturally sporty, they should at least try to walk briskly for half an hour a day, and/or swim three times a week. (Swimming works well for a Water sign.) However, yoga is the perfect exercise: it stretches and works the muscles while at the same time calming and invigorating the soul. Traditionally, Pisceans have trouble with their feet, and if this is a problem they should visit their chiropodist regularly, and invest as much as they can afford in good, supportive shoes.

Those born under the sign of the Fishes tend to develop addictions, and should be very wary of smoking and drinking. Pisceans sometimes tend to be hypochondriacs, reaching for the medicine cabinet at the slightest twinge, while others – an increasing number – seek out various holistic therapies. Certainly, they will fare well, on the whole, with acupressure, Chinese medicine and Reiki. However, Pisceans need to realize that many, though not all, of their health problems are psychosomatic, and result from their internalized emotions. They need to find an outlet for them.

CAREER

Pisceans are almost always in touch with their unconscious minds, and once they learn to deal with this effectively, they can become very successful artists. There are many top Piscean painters and poets who obey their inner voice. Many actors who may be shy and retiring off stage positively shine once hidden behind the mask of a scripted character.

However, Pisceans are dreamy people and feel threatened by too much structure, which is why the caring professions are excellent outlets for the often repressed Piscean emotion. They make superb nurses, counsellors and therapists, finding an elusive assertiveness in speaking up for the disadvantaged and physically or mentally handicapped. However, they are not natural organizers or administrators. Often, they do not seek promotion, but are more content to take a back seat and get on with their job. They are very good team members, and can rise to occasions such as major emergencies – as long as someone else is there to tell them, clearly and decisively, what to do.

Because of their own tendency to various forms of addiction, they are especially good with the rehabilitation of addicts, finding the right mix of compassion and 'tough love' needed for the programme to succeed. They can empathize with cravings, and provide the support the addicts need to overcome their problems.

Many Pisceans find fulfilment in holistic therapies and become qualified in a wide variety

designers for the theatre, television or films. They love creating a world into which others can step and lose themselves, even if it is only for a short time. Some Pisceans are cartoonists and animators, while others invent virtual worlds through computer special effects.

Pisces is one of the dual signs, and Piscean restlessness is often assuaged by having more than one job, or by pursuing a career during the

They are particularly attracted to crystal therapy and rebirthing, and make natural dream analysts

of 'alternative' disciplines, from acupuncture to hands-on healing. They are particularly attracted to crystal therapy and rebirthing, and make natural dream analysts.

Compassionate Piscean caring also extends to the animal kingdom: many Pisceans are veterinary nurses or helpers in animal rescue centres. Many have a special empathy with distressed pets, and a sure instinct about how best to treat their ailments, often using unorthodox methods such as homeopathy. Pisceans have plenty of imagination but not too much initiative. They hate the boisterousness of courses designed to encourage team bonding and decision-making, but may, all the same, benefit from them more than most. The glamour professions also attract typical Sun Sign Pisceans, who can be both artistic and moody. They are often found as dress designers, make-up artists and sometimes models, although they are not often individualistic enough for this rather exposed profession. Since Neptune, their ruler, emphasizes illusion, Pisceans make good photographers, and can often be found as set

day, while enjoying charity work in the evenings and at weekends. Pisceans need to keep busy, or they can easily fall prey to self-doubt and depression, and become very irritable.

RELATIONSHIPS

Many Pisceans can be very loving, warm partners for life, although they are too restless to settle without the occasional change of scene. They can be quite flighty, seeking to find self-esteem in the arms of many lovers, but all too often failing to do so, even though they long to be loved.

They tend to be easily bored. It is then that they find temptation of one sort or another difficult to resist, or fly into perverse, contrary moods when they become irritated with themselves and the world around them. As a result, they may hit out at their nearest and dearest, often

Aries
Domineering and inflexible Arians find oddball and effusive Pisceans too difficult to live with.

Taurus
Pisceans' innate moodiness and contrariness can seriously annoy equable, well-grounded Taureans.

Gemini
There may be a strong initial attraction between these two signs, but party animal Geminians can seem too light.

Cancer
At worst, weepy, over-the-top Cancerians and moody Pisceans make for a nightmare domestic scenario.

Leo
Lordly Leos are very sexy and charming, but touchy Pisceans will soon back away from all that ambition.

Virgo
Pisceans can easily come to love Virgoans' charm and sense of order. This can be a lasting romance.

Libra
The last thing peace-seeking Librans need is Piscean 'baggage' and moodiness. This relationship won't last.

Scorpio
While these two signs can easily fall for each other, they are far too difficult to make the necessary compromises.

Sagittarius
Demanding Pisceans will be hurt and puzzled by the Sagittarian tendency to disappear without a word.

Capricorn
Four-square, unemotional Goats find Piscean excesses beyond belief, and won't even begin to woo them.

Aquarius
These two signs are soul mates and made for each other. Aquarian loftiness can easily overlook Piscean angst.

Pisces
A winning combination – the organizational skills of one complementing the dreaminess of the other.

---

with a deadly accuracy, instinctively knowing how best to hurt those they know well. Pisceans can usually recognize the weaknesses of others, and, if cornered, can go for them vindictively. They also do a very effective line in huge emotional scenes, although these tend to be over almost as soon as they have begun. However, the memory will continue to haunt non-Piscean witnesses for some time.

Even so, many Pisceans are truly charming, hospitable folk, who love sharing their beautiful homes with guests, family members and a menagerie of pets. They are justly proud of their home-making skills and shine primarily as

gardeners, using great imagination and artistry in the landscaping and composition of their land. Pisceans need to get out into the open air, and often love to be near to the sea. Many of them are happiest when living in seaside towns.

Romantic and tender-hearted, Pisceans can easily fall for rogues. Because charm works wonders with them, they are particularly vulnerable to confidence tricksters. If a day of reckoning comes and the flaws of their loved ones are revealed, is more than usually traumatic for a typical Sun Sign Piscean. They hate having their rose-tinted spectacles ripped off so cruelly, and can react by hitting out at those who dare to do so, before finally accepting the truth. Some, though, never do. Occasionally, Pisceans prefer to live with a lie, rather than face facts.

Pisceans are not always the best of parents, because they are vague and self-absorbed and need to live their own lives.

Of course many of the more well-balanced Pisceans make excellent parents, creating a loving, stable environment for their family.

IDEAL PARTNER

Aquarians tend to bond romantically with Pisces, although they will not easily endure too many emotional outbursts or any vindictiveness. However, the organizational abilities of Aquarians often complement Piscean dreaminess very well, resulting in a beautiful home and a spiritually aware atmosphere. Two Pisceans together will never get anything done, although their dreams may be truly exciting. However, emotions will run too high with watery Cancerians. A match with a typical Sun Sign Scorpian is out, though. The nastiness that can arise if things go wrong will be unbearable.

However, kind, earthy Virgoans can often find happiness with Pisceans, and even, in some cases, lordly Leos will magnanimously allow Pisces to live in their shadow, which may well suit both of them.

THE PISCEAN CHILD

The Piscean tendency to dreaming and absent-mindedness can get many children into trouble at school and also later in life. Parents should therefore encourage them to focus and concentrate as much as possible.

Often Piscean children live in their own fantasy world, and can slip all too easily into embroidering the truth. Some may be truly deceitful. The ground-rules should be very clear-cut: everyone here speaks the truth. These children need to understand that being straightforward is by far the best way, and that lying is an unattractive social vice.

On the other hand, it is a good idea to channel their undoubted creativity into something more acceptable, such as painting or short-story writing, in which they are often near the top of their class. All the same, they need to be taught how to separate fantasy from reality, and any tales they spin need to be taken with a pinch of salt.

It is important to establish trust between parents and Piscean children at an early age, so that there is always an atmosphere of loving support at home. These children need to feel that home is a haven, and that they have a valuable role to play there. This is vital for the development of their self-esteem, and for their future adult relationships. When they are very small, they do need strong parenting, and the knowledge that they are protected against harsh reality. These are very sensitive, sometimes weak, children, who can react very badly if mishandled at an early age.

Piscean children are not good as competitors, and may easily be overpowered by their siblings. They rarely fight for what they want, usually giving in submissively. They come to idolize a more glamorous or successful brother or sister. Parents should make it clear that they have just as much to offer, in their own way, and should always praise them for their achievements and encourage their siblings to do the same.

Michael Caine
Mikhail Gorbachev
Jean Harlow
Samuel Pepys
Glen Miller
Alexander Graham Bell
Enrico Caruso

Albert Einstein

Vaslav Nijinsky

Buffalo Bill Cody
Albert Einstein
Bobby Fischer
Yuri Gagarin
Galilei Galileo
Michelangelo
Liza Minnelli
Rupert Murdoch
Rudolph Nuryev
Vaslav Nijinsky
Pierre August Renoir
Bugsy Siegel
Elizabeth Taylor

MOON SIGNS

So far, we have seen how the Sun influences our outward manner, appearance, major personality traits, career disposition and even our health – particularly, areas of vulnerability. The Moon – the second most important body in our solar system – influences our emotions, our inner life and our inherited traits and characteristics. This section of the book provides a summary of the essential characteristics of your Sun and Moon Sign combination and a full chapter devoted to each Moon placement.

FINDING YOUR MOON SIGN

*To find out what your Moon Sign is, turn to the charts
on pages 246–253. Then, use the Sun and Moon Sign
Combinations and the relevant chapter to gain an
even deeper understanding of your true character
as influenced by the power
of the Moon.*

SUN AND MOON SIGN COMBINATIONS

*Your Sun and Moon Signs lend a guiding hand to the working of fate
in your life. They provide an outline of your essential characteristics and
help to shape the way that you will develop. Taken together, Sun and Moon Signs
provide very potent glimpses of your true character and of the kind of life that you will
create for yourself. Although nothing is written in stone, these astrological
signposts point the way to your destiny.*

SUN ARIES, MOON ARIES: Enthusiastic, motivated and quick-witted. Egocentric and impatient. They always aim for the top, seeking the glittering prizes. They can be ruthless.

SUN ARIES, MOON TAURUS: Artistic, sensuous and down to earth. Stubborn and dogmatic. They love tradition but can be fearful of change – even if it's for the better.

SUN ARIES, MOON GEMINI: Bright, articulate, persuasive. Overly sharp tongued and lacking in stamina. Excellent media people, but have erratic energy flow, so need to pace themselves.

SUN ARIES, MOON CANCER: Business-like, genial and determined. Tough facade hides vulnerability. They carry very old emotional scars and need to open up to a soulmate.

SUN ARIES, MOON LEO: Extrovert, high flyer – the natural stars of the zodiac. Insensitive to others, misses finer points. Often a huge success – thanks to the hard work and loyalty of others.

SUN ARIES, MOON VIRGO: Efficient, logical and analytical. Over-critical and fussy. Can harbour wild fantasies and surprising ambitions – which they should encourage from time to time.

SUN ARIES, MOON LIBRA: Ambitious, balanced, passionate and caring. May be over-optimistic and gullible, but their divine innocence can protect them against many unpleasant situations and people.

SUN ARIES, MOON SCORPIO: Intense, focused and motivated. Can be intimidating and too theatrical. Lots of energy and commitment, but take disappointment very hard. Even so, they bounce back.

SUN ARIES, MOON SAGITTARIUS: Motivating, encouraging, restless and daring. Insensitive and blunt. Something of the eternal child – complete with footstomping tantrums.

SUN ARIES, MOON CAPRICORN: Ambitious, determined and tough. Domineering and cold, but has a surprising capacity to hero worship others – from a safe distance and secretly.

SUN ARIES, MOON AQUARIUS: Idealistic and humanitarian. Tactless and outspoken. Vast resources of energy and resilience and many – often conflicting – goals.

SUN ARIES, MOON PISCES: Confident exterior hides timid interior. Can be something of a zealot. Seeks to wear different masks for different occasions in order to impress.

SUN TAURUS, MOON ARIES: Poised exterior hides raging inner ambition. Opinionated and dogmatic. Can feel hard done by and demand apologies where none are required, but often back down if stood up to.

SUN TAURUS, MOON TAURUS: Faithful, musical and creative. Stubborn and temperamental. Committed to maintaining old-fashioned values.

SUN TAURUS, MOON GEMINI: Articulate, witty and excitable, with good ideas. Lack stamina.

Respects and admires people with organizational skills, and those who are good with money.

SUN TAURUS, MOON CANCER: Caring, homeloving and encouraging. Less secure about own ambitions and may lack drive, but excellent at supporting others and helping them to achieve their dreams.

SUN TAURUS, MOON LEO: Loyal and colourful, dramatic and deliberate. Inflexible and opinionated. Good organizers and natural leaders, although may be inclined to laziness.

SUN TAURUS, MOON VIRGO: Meticulous, orderly and organized. Family-loving, articulate and musical. Hypercritical and often rather dull. Tend to have a hidden poetic streak, and can be a surprisingly passionate lovers.

SUN TAURUS, MOON LIBRA: Caring, compassionate and loving. Can be ambitious. Lazy and erratic, but the heart is in the right place. They seek above all to be peace-makers.

SUN TAURUS, MOON SCORPIO: Independent, strong and artistic. Inclined to take too much on. Obstinate and inclined to bottle up old regrets and disappointments. Need to open their hearts more to confidants.

SUN TAURUS, MOON SAGITTARIUS: Pious, studious, academic. Intrigued by the idea of adventure. Tend to be lazy, judgemental and dogmatic, but can indulge in flights of fancy and become rather unrealistic.

SUN TAURUS, MOON CAPRICORN: Adept in business, sensible and shrewd. Insecure in personal relationships, but secret romantics at heart. They have a desperate need to be loved and understood.

SUN TAURUS, MOON AQUARIUS: Confident, bright, free thinking, gregarious. Can lay down the law but essentially they are fairly happy-go-lucky and tolerant. Rarely nostalgic – very forward looking.

SUN TAURUS, MOON PISCES: Determined and creative, compassionate and caring. Can be gullible and naive but many see this as rather charming. They have an arty side to their personality.

SUN GEMINI, MOON ARIES: Interesting, innovative thinkers and excellent in the media. Superficial and sometimes cruel, although they may not realize how much they hurt others.

SUN GEMINI, MOON TAURUS: Patient, intelligent and persistent. Morose and emotionally insecure. Can have bursts of energy and inspiration, which quickly die down again.

SUN GEMINI, MOON GEMINI: Extremely quick-witted and amusing. Tense, glib and lacking in stamina. Can feel very isolated and lonely – even in a large crowd.

SUN GEMINI, MOON CANCER: Communicative, open and homeloving. Weak-willed and possessive – easy to influence. Can become a doormat, although rebelliousness is not unknown.

SUN GEMINI, MOON LEO: Enthusiastic, attractive and creative. Childish and egocentric. Can be very opinionated but can easily be charmed out of any inflexibility. Moody and erratic.

SUN GEMINI, MOON VIRGO: Adaptable, lateral thinker and rather intellectual. Nervy, lacking in ambition but tend to admire others who aim for the top.

SUN GEMINI, MOON LIBRA: Flirtatious, sociable and flighty. Pompous and self-congratulatory. Feel threatened by those with strong beliefs or opinions. Need to be centred and calm.

SUN GEMINI, MOON SCORPIO: Deep, possessor of dark secrets and often fascinating. Perverse, vulnerable and lonely. Love to explore the mysterious side of life. Can become hooked on the paranormal.

SUN GEMINI, MOON SAGITTARIUS: Studious, physical and adventurous. Insensitive and outspoken. Can be unrealistic and naive. Need to plan for the future.

SUN GEMINI, MOON CAPRICORN: Media type, good with words, intelligent. Emotionally uncommunicative and cold but they often cry inside. Often lonely and lost – need a soul mate.

SUN GEMINI, MOON AQUARIUS: Clever and bright, instinctively knowing. Wary of expressing emotions or becoming too deeply involved romantically and sexually. May avoid commitment.

SUN GEMINI, MOON PISCES: Extrovert, fun and very communicative. Inwardly tense and insecure, and in need of romance and sensuality. Intuitive, moody and often somewhat psychic.

SUN CANCER, MOON ARIES: Understanding, business-like and caring. Over-competitive and restless. Can easily become intense about all relationships, both business and personal. They need emotional commitment.

SUN CANCER, MOON TAURUS: Compassionate, sensual and family-centred, but with a tendency to be rather lazy, sulky and moody. Often need cheering up by friends on fun nights out.

SUN CANCER, MOON GEMINI: Genial, ambitious and quick-witted. Guileful and manipulative, often great plotters and particularly good at revenge.

SUN CANCER, MOON CANCER: Kind, sensitive, upholders of traditional values. Live in the past, are over-emotional and possessive. Can become hysterical if crossed. Have a tendency to cut their nose off to spite their face.

SUN CANCER, MOON LEO: Great integrity, passionate and loving. Dogmatic and insecure, but basically kind and compassionate. Above all – need to be understood.

SUN CANCER, MOON VIRGO: Good with illness. Businesslike, hard-working, with good – almost total – recall. Excessive worriers, mean-minded and penny-pinching, although secretly longing to be wildly extravagant.

SUN CANCER, MOON LIBRA: Ambitious, family-centred and peace-loving. Unrealistic, with little grasp of detail but can be good at seeing the overall picture. Often very charming and urbane.

SUN CANCER, MOON SCORPIO: Always after the centre stage. Very intense and sometimes psychic. Can suffer from depression and be rather secretive. Great capacity for passionate love.

SUN CANCER, MOON SAGITTARIUS: Family-loving, free-spirited and joyful. Over-optimistic, unrealistic and inclined to daydream. Often charming but feckless. Need to be somewhat more organized.

SUN CANCER, MOON CAPRICORN: Perceptive in business, ambitious and hard-working. Parsimonious and pessimistic, often seeing life in joyless terms. Can have intense, but secret, passions.

SUN CANCER, MOON AQUARIUS: Communicative, articulate and adroit. Manipulative and self-centred but can work hard for the common good. A good grasp of the long term.

SUN CANCER, MOON PISCES: Psychic, sensitive and compassionate, and a fierce champion of the underdog. Moody and fearful, and inclined to suffer from nightmares. Loving but emotionally very needy.

SUN LEO, MOON ARIES: Encouraging, enthusiastic and courageous. Domineering and callous, and given to wild tantrums if crossed. However, likely to forgive and forget fairly easily.

SUN LEO, MOON TAURUS: Traditional, placid and dependable. Can sometimes appear boring and stubborn but can occasionally surprise people by being the life and soul of the party.

SUN LEO, MOON GEMINI: Quick-witted, innovative thinkers – natural leaders. Although inclined to be sharp tongued and insensitive, and capable of lashing out without thinking, they are basically kind and well-meaning.

SUN LEO, MOON CANCER: Protective, nurturing and comforting. Over-possessive and hysterical, yet often puzzled and frightened by the emotional needs of others.

SUN LEO, MOON LEO: Successful, individual and a natural star. Domineering and unrealistic, and can ruthlessly exploit others. Charming and inspiring.

SUN LEO, MOON VIRGO: Logical, methodical, kind and decent. Sometimes petty-minded and abrupt, although this cool exterior hides a genuinely compassionate heart.

SUN LEO, MOON LIBRA: Stylish, flirtatious and successful. Egocentric with a tendency to be promiscuous and to abuse the trust of others. Surprisingly bold in coming to the rescue. Something of a hero.

SUN LEO, MOON SCORPIO: Hard-working, theatrical, colourful and witty. Melodramatic and intimidating, with a tendency to ride roughshod over the sensibilities of others. Embarrassed and contrite when this is pointed out.

SUN LEO, MOON SAGITTARIUS: Warm-hearted, enthusiastic and adventurous. Impatient, restless, too independent. Great explorers and pioneers. Able to tolerate physical discomfort and help others less fortunate than themselves.

SUN LEO, MOON CAPRICORN: Efficient, traditional and ambitious. Insecure underneath with a great need for demonstrations of affection. Can find it hard to express emotional commitment.

SUN LEO, MOON AQUARIUS: Faithful, honest, fair and idealistic. Opinionated and dogmatic. Need several different outlets for philanthropic urges. Busy and committed.

SUN LEO, MOON PISCES: Kind-hearted, psychic and caring. Easily distressed or distracted but quick to help others. Can become over-demanding in close relationships.

SUN VIRGO, MOON ARIES: Clever, versatile, adaptable and good with words. Sarcastic and hurtful but not without some grace and gentleness. Can be very amusing.

SUN VIRGO, MOON TAURUS: Solid, reliable, helpful and good with their hands. Not innovative or original thinkers, but immensely admiring of those who are. Very good supporter of family and friends.

SUN VIRGO, MOON GEMINI: Quick to speak and act, and good at research. Frightened of strong emotion and something of a cold fish outwardly, but secretly desperate to find love .

SUN VIRGO, MOON CANCER: Clever, shrewd, family-loving. Excessive worriers and very possessive. Can be hoarders, being totally convinced that civilization as we know it is about to collapse. Fond of conspiracy theories.

SUN VIRGO, MOON LEO: Honest, enthusiastic and meticulous. Insecure and sometimes unambitious, although they make efforts from time to time to better themselves. Reserved but deep.

SUN VIRGO, MOON VIRGO: Kind, reliable and organized. Petty-minded and can be penny-pinching. Terrible worriers. Good at analysis, investigation and research. Can seem over-intellectual and intimidating.

SUN VIRGO, MOON LIBRA: Diplomatic, organized and good team workers. Indecisive and hesitant but excellent at seeing all round a problem. Sociable and charming.

SUN VIRGO, MOON SCORPIO: Intense, incisive and profound thinkers. Outwardly unemotional and uncommunicative but a seething mass of hidden feelings. Often harbour lifelong – and sometimes unrequited – passions.

SUN VIRGO, MOON SAGITTARIUS: Open, amenable, gregarious and studious. Impatient and slapdash, over-eager to move on to the next project. Can be impractical and unworldly.

SUN VIRGO, MOON CAPRICORN: Serious, business-like and meticulous. Self-centred, cold and lacking spontaneity. Need to lighten up and have fun. Emotional commitment is difficult.

SUN VIRGO, MOON AQUARIUS: Independent, philosophical and studious. Insensitive to the emotional needs of others but determined to live their lives for them, whether they like it or not.

SUN VIRGO, MOON PISCES: Deep, psychic, intuitive and caring to the point of martyrdom. Doormat mentality and over-possessive, but can be very kind and understanding and extremely supportive of others.

SUN LIBRA, MOON ARIES: Excellent in emergencies, pioneering and adventurous. Lack stamina, can be self-centred and unreliable on a day-to-day basis. Often attractive and charming.

SUN LIBRA, MOON TAURUS: Creative and artistic, musical, stylish and practical. Can be lazy and erratic, but once motivated can work hard and become successful. Good homemakers.

SUN LIBRA, MOON GEMINI: Good technical mind, quick, intelligent, practical and innovative. Over-dependent on others. Glib and often speak without thinking, tearing through life in a tremendous hurry, rarely finishing anything.

SUN LIBRA, MOON CANCER: Amiable, caring, homeloving and efficient. Too selfless and over-altruistic – and easily walked over by others. Can be naive, but this innocence is very attractive.

SUN LIBRA, MOON LEO: Quick, clever and sharp-tongued. Incurably romantic and melodramatic. Love to make a splash. Can be over-extravagant and feckless. Great fun to be with.

SUN LIBRA, MOON VIRGO: Meticulous, versatile, genial and good with words. Can lack confidence and ambition but can be motivated to achieve great things.

SUN LIBRA, MOON LIBRA: Charming, stylish and gregarious. Can be slothful and unfocused, although they can certainly move very fast when chasing the object of their passion.

SUN LIBRA, MOON SCORPIO: Forceful, magnetic and sexual. Can be dominating, power-mad and 'over-the-top' but given to retreating into solitude from time to time to recharge their batteries.

SUN LIBRA, MOON SAGITTARIUS: Good with detail and logical argument. Fair and just but with a restless spirit that needs many changes of direction. Can ignore the emotional needs of others.

SUN LIBRA, MOON CAPRICORN: Tough negotiator, dedicated worker, shrewd and perceptive. Cynical and sceptical but can be a pushover in love. A great capacity for passion.

SUN LIBRA, MOON AQUARIUS: Quick-witted, intelligent and strong. A good leader. Can be interfering and arrogant with no time for the niceties of others' feelings. Good at planning.

SUN LIBRA, MOON PISCES: Intuitive, romantic and creative. Lacking in concentration and inclined to daydream. Apparently spontaneous and childlike, which many find attractive, although there is a manipulative side.

SUN SCORPIO, MOON ARIES: Intense and brave. Good leaders. Confrontational, aggressive and over-dramatic with a strong sense of destiny that drives them to become very successful.

SUN SCORPIO, MOON TAURUS: Dependable, erotic and musical. Stubborn, stolid and sometimes a little dull. However, they can be passionate and occasionally have exotic interests.

SUN SCORPIO, MOON GEMINI: Quick-witted, intuitive and a good judge of people. Cynical and world-weary, but still determined to enjoy life. Sometimes love crowds; at other times seek solitude.

SUN SCORPIO, MOON CANCER: Intuitive, magnetic and caring. Moody, suspicious – and frightened – of intimacy. Not an easy type, but once won over tends to become a lifelong friend.

SUN SCORPIO, MOON LEO: Persistent and faithful with great powers of endurance. Inflexible, dogmatic and can be hurtful. Set high standards for themselves and others.

SUN SCORPIO, MOON VIRGO: Meticulous, intelligent and dedicated. Suspicious of emotion and close relationships, but once in love it is usually for ever.

SUN SCORPIO, MOON LIBRA: Purposeful, diplomatic, career-minded and good at mediation. Uncomfortable with close family ties, often preferring to live apart from relatives. Too independent.

SUN SCORPIO, MOON SCORPIO: Passionate, dramatic, assertive and often highly motivated and successful. Intimidating and intense but can translate this intensity into extreme loyalty, either to an individual or a belief system.

SUN SCORPIO, MOON SAGITTARIUS: Funny, persistent, well grounded and good at research. Can be erratic and have unrealistic moods. Need to find a sensible pace to maintain workable energy levels.

SUN SCORPIO, MOON CAPRICORN: Serious, ambitious and determined. Lacking spontaneity and a sense of fun but often long desperately to do something surprising. Secretly seek a true soul mate.

SUN SCORPIO, MOON AQUARIUS: Determined, focused and ambitious. Dogmatic and arrogant – benevolent dictator type. Not swayed by flattery or romance, but quietly appreciative of both from time to time.

SUN SCORPIO, MOON PISCES: Altruistic, caring and artistic. Can be sarcastic and occasionally vindictive – especially if crossed in love, when they can avenge themselves with great imagination.

SUN SAGITTARIUS, MOON ARIES:
Pioneering, restless and innovative.
Impatient and impulsive, and bad with
lasting intimacy, although relationships are often
passionate while they last.

SUN SAGITTARIUS, MOON TAURUS:
Imaginative, practical, motivating and artistic.
Inclined to be self-indulgent, lazy and
undisciplined but can pull themselves
together when necessary, often producing
some very successful work.

SUN SAGITTARIUS, MOON GEMINI: Good with
words, pro-active and motivated. Impatient –
lacking stamina and persistence. Excellent at
inspiring others. Good delegators.

SUN SAGITTARIUS, MOON CANCER: Artistic,
psychic, intuitive and caring. Can be deluded and
unrealistic, with little grasp of day-to-day
practicalities. Great daydreamers.

SUN SAGITTARIUS, MOON LEO: Entertaining
and extrovert, amusing and gregarious. Often
selfish and demanding,
especially with their nearest
and dearest.

SUN SAGITTARIUS, MOON
VIRGO: Organized, thorough
and often profound. Dogmatic
and pompous, though somewhat afraid of strong
emotion, finding heart-to-hearts threatening.
Tend to hide behind a mask.

SUN SAGITTARIUS, MOON LIBRA: Forceful,
persuasive and analytical. Tend to be fashionable,
attractive and stylish – but can be a little
impatient and arrogant. Sometimes tetchy.

SUN SAGITTARIUS, MOON SCORPIO: An
efficient and sometimes inspired mind. Incisive,
dogged and profound. Good at lateral thinking.
Can be intolerant and peevish.

SUN SAGITTARIUS, MOON SAGITTARIUS: Free-
spirited, independent, pioneering and energetic.
Impatient with other lifestyles and quick to
criticize, but find it easy to forgive and forget.

SUN SAGITTARIUS, MOON CAPRICORN:
Bright, persistent and amusing company, with
great ambitions. Afraid of emotion and too ready
to condemn, with a tendency to pessimism and
lack of self-esteem.

SUN SAGITTARIUS, MOON
AQUARIUS: Unusual and
fascinating, well-read
and knowledgeable. Stubborn,
eccentric and intractable.
May preach tolerance, but can
be the most intolerant of
people.

SUN SAGITTARIUS, MOON
PISCES: Caring, spiritual and soft-
hearted. Often unrealistic, with
little or no interest in the practicalities of life.
Lacking in self-esteem and downtrodden.

SUN CAPRICORN, MOON ARIES:
Determined, intelligent, forceful and often
ruthlessly ambitious. Callous and cold.
Anyone who gets in the way of their climb to the
top should watch out.

SUN CAPRICORN, MOON TAURUS:
Dependable, artistic and down-to-earth. A good
homemaker and manager. Can be obstinate and
intolerant, hating change or upheaval.

SUN CAPRICORN, MOON GEMINI: Good with
words, and excellent at communicating generally,
seeing projects through to the end. Can be glib,
superficial and occasionally slapdash.

SUN CAPRICORN, MOON CANCER:
Faithful, family-centred, with shining
integrity. A terrible worrier, given to
sulking and brooding over what
are often imaginary problems.

SUN CAPRICORN, MOON LEO: Tough, purposeful and ambitious, though can sometimes reveal a surprisingly sympathetic streak. Sometimes secretly soft-hearted. Conversely, can be arrogant and cruel.

SUN CAPRICORN, MOON VIRGO: Business-like, serious, dependable and usually very thorough. Can be pompous and sometimes heavy-going company. Old before their time.

SUN CAPRICORN, MOON LIBRA: Good mixer and motivator, though impractical. Innovative thinker and pioneer. Sometimes gullible and a bit childish.

SUN CAPRICORN, MOON SCORPIO: Strong and determined, with a sense of personal destiny. Can be kind and caring but also sarcastic and too quick to demolish others verbally.

SUN CAPRICORN, MOON SAGITTARIUS: Focused and dedicated, stable, organized and communicative. Need to relax, have more fun and take life a lot easier. Can suffer early burn-out.

SUN CAPRICORN, MOON CAPRICORN: Hard workers, with great stamina and powers of endurance. Sympathetic and caring. Uncomfortable with emotion and far too tense. Need to take more time out.

SUN CAPRICORN, MOON AQUARIUS: Efficient, broad-minded and organized, with high standards for themselves and others. Do not suffer fools gladly and can be very intolerant towards those with different lifestyles or views.

SUN CAPRICORN, MOON PISCES: Dedicated, caring and compassionate. Often intuitive with a tendency to have significant dreams. Can be over-sensitive and easily hurt. Should put themselves first occasionally.

SUN AQUARIUS, MOON ARIES: Amusing, energetic and innovative. Often highly motivated but sometimes rather difficult and arrogant. They can sometimes come over as quirky and a little odd.

SUN AQUARIUS, MOON TAURUS: Dogged and dependable. High fliers who often have a marked artistic streak. Obstinate and grumpy, and inclined to get bogged down in the most boring of details.

SUN AQUARIUS, MOON GEMINI: Quick-witted and intelligent. Good communicators. Can be rather flippant and shallow. Occasionally insensitive to the needs and feelings of others.

SUN AQUARIUS, MOON CANCER: Caring and loving, companionable and amusing. Moody and unpredictable. Good at empathizing with others.

SUN AQUARIUS, MOON LEO: Active and busy, purposeful and frequently highly ambitious. Natural loners who are sometimes socially inept, though still keen to make a good impression.

SUN AQUARIUS, MOON VIRGO: Scholarly and intelligent. A dogged researcher. Often seen as a bit of an oddball. Rather awkward, old-fashioned and fussy. Loyal to people and causes.

SUN AQUARIUS, MOON LIBRA: Fun, extrovert, attractive and often rather charming. Can be superficial and lacking focus and stamina. Good with people and animals.

SUN AQUARIUS, MOON SCORPIO:Natural leaders, teachers or gurus. Bright and innovative, and take easily to the centre stage. Underneath the charisma lurks impatience and arrogance.

SUN AQUARIUS, MOON SAGITTARIUS: Clever, bright, impulsive and enthusiastic. Sometimes over-optimistic and unrealistic. Not good with money or planning for a rainy day.

SUN AQUARIUS, MOON CAPRICORN: Business-like and naturally protective of their family. Usually very efficient, though too serious and inclined to worry. Need to realize that life is not always hard.

SUN AQUARIUS, MOON AQUARIUS: Idealistic and broad-minded, with unusual ideas, beliefs and even lifestyle. Usually tough on themselves and others. Can lack real warmth.

SUN AQUARIUS, MOON PISCES: Intuitive, spiritual, caring and often very clever, though impractical. They can have a tendency to be too other-worldly and unfocused. They can also be naive and gullible.

SUN PISCES, MOON ARIES: Intelligent, quick-witted, purposeful and entertaining. Egocentric and occasionally manipulative and emotionally demanding. May even resort to moral blackmail.

SUN PISCES, MOON TAURUS: Musical, harmonious, kind and gregarious. Can be indolent and lacking in motivation and ambition. Easy-going.

SUN PISCES, MOON GEMINI: Quick, bright, spontaneous and amusing. Good company but tend to be anxious and emotionally insecure. All too often in love with love.

SUN PISCES, MOON CANCER: Caring, sympathetic, sensitive and helpful. Good in a crisis, though usually too dreamy and impractical, leaving decisions to others.

SUN PISCES, MOON LEO: Expansive, encouraging, artistic and compassionate. Often egocentric and arrogant. Petulant if crossed. Depressed by bad luck more than most.

SUN PISCES, MOON VIRGO: Profound, psychic and often very creative. Tend to be nervy, obsessive and somewhat weak-willed. Will seek refuge and peace when life gets too tough.

SUN PISCES, MOON LIBRA: Active, innovative, energetic and enthusiastic. Charismatic and good with people. Can inspire and motivate others, but tend to be unrealistic and lacking in stamina.

SUN PISCES, MOON SCORPIO: Compassionate, profound, psychic and often powerful in their chosen field. Unpredictable and occasionally inclined to depression.

SUN PISCES, MOON SAGITTARIUS: Restless, with itchy feet. Great travellers. Often deep and studious, with questing minds. Also unreliable and over-optimistic. Bad planners.

SUN PISCES, MOON CAPRICORN: Intuitive, creative and efficient. Very reliable and solid, with artistic leanings. Tend to be insecure and sometimes lack ambition.

SUN PISCES, MOON AQUARIUS: Open and honest, spiritual and caring. Often have very good ideas. Too otherworldly and 'fey', and inclined to gullibility. Best to keep their feet on the ground.

SUN PISCES, MOON PISCES: Spiritual and mystical, imaginative and intuitive. May have important and powerful dreams. Often lacking in ambition and motivation, and may be somewhat gullible. May suffer from erratic energy levels.

THE MOON
IN ARIES

(Ruled by Mars)

The masculine fire of Aries is certainly not quenched by the Moon's quiet calm. This Moon Sign is all action, energy and impulsiveness. The Arian tendency to rush in where angels fear to tread is enhanced by the Moon's emotionality, so here we have the great movers and shakers of the world.

Moon in Aries people tend to be personally affronted by social injustice. They will rarely pass by a homeless beggar without giving him something and they are characteristically fired up to change any situation for the better. They want the world to be a better place right now, and can become very upset when faced with intractable problems and the slow pace of change. Characteristically, these people find it almost impossible to understand opposing views, or even to comprehend that others have a right to express them. They simply cannot see that it is possible to think differently, and so they rarely pause to consider the feelings of others in their headlong rush to get things done – *their* way.

official at work or high-ranking government official. They love tackling problems themselves, and are surprisingly good at it. However, they can be delegators, if somewhat impatient ones.

These people tend to be good with money, too, although from time to time their *joie de vivre* can lead them into unwise spending sprees. They tend to be full of marvellous money-making schemes that may or may not produce results, but even when they fail disastrously, they bounce back with another one.

Lunar Arians are very quick thinking. They have charm, wit and an infectious optimism that may not always be justified. They tend to be unrealistic and to go charging off on madcap schemes that everyone else realizes are non-starters. Nobody, though, dares to say so. Lunar Arians see life on an epic scale and rarely notice the irritating details, such as having no capital, or the danger that can lie in the small print.

These people have original minds and can be very creative if given enough freedom to express

> *Lunar Arians want the world to be a better place right now, and can become very upset when faced with intractable problems and the slow pace of change*

Lunar Arians never let the grass grow under their feet. They are not procrastinators. They deal with everything immediately, sometimes without too much thought, but always with great energy and verve. They zoom towards their goals with superb self-motivation and courage. They will stand up to anyone, even the most intimidating

themselves. They hate restriction and their tempers can explode if they are crossed or frustrated in their ambitions. However, a genuine crisis will bring out the best in them. Their natural courage and qualities of leadership will come to the fore, enabling them to save the day.

Lunar Arians give the impression of being like a coiled spring. There is an underlying tension in them that all too often manifests itself in tantrums or outbursts of one sort or another. It is, though, a very creative tension, which produces some impressive ideas.

They are never secretive or deceitful, preferring to be loud and outspoken rather than hold back their opinions. They also appreciate this sort of straightforwardness in others. They can be shocked by revelations of plotting, intrigue or deception, and simply do not understand why some people need a secret agenda. Honesty and integrity are central to the character of Lunar Arians.

These people have such unbounded energy and enthusiasm that they have a talent for motivating other less-inspired souls, although they will easily throw caution to the winds. They always have their eyes on the distant horizon, which can be thrilling to others, and their faith in the future and in their own potential can do wonders to bring renewed vigour to a tired project.

Lunar Arians are warm-hearted and more sympathetic and broad-minded than their Sun Sign counterparts. They are tolerant of other colours and creeds, seeing humanity as one large team that needs to pull together to get things done. They are impatient with red tape, prejudice and pessimism.

RELATIONSHIPS

Lunar Arians have no time for whiners and whingers. They react best to practical problems, leaving others to deal with the emotional trauma. This can make relationships difficult for this type. Their constant need to get up and go often masks a fear of emotional commitment. They also crave newness and excitement, which is fine in the early stages of romantic pursuit, but it can cause serious rifts later on. It is essential for Lunar Arians to keep the flame of passion alive. Sometimes, however, they may unconsciously seek partners who are steady homebodies in order to compensate for their own fiery temperament. Then, they will expect their home to be a haven from the slings and arrows of fortune, however outrageous.

They are unhappy with competition, which they often take personally, and find equally strong partners impossible to live with. Many choose weaker, more malleable types, often younger and less experienced than themselves. There is a large dose of masculinity in both sexes, which manifests in women as a tendency to dominate their partners and take the initiative sexually. Lunar Arians need a highly charged sex life and will not tolerate a relationship that declines into mere companionship, although they do have a strong need for friendship with a life partner. They are energetic lovers but are rarely too intense. They do enjoy fun and laughter in the bedroom. However, when things go wrong, they are disinclined to seek advice for failing relationships. To them, when it's over, it's over. Lunar Aries types have high standards, sometimes impossibly so. They expect to be given unconditional love and support in all their madcap schemes, while also demanding their unequivocal independence. Any hint that their partners will permit anything less than total freedom is immediately interpreted as being too demanding. If they feel threatened, their endless fault-finding can become unbearable.

Although Lunar Arians can be happy homemakers, more often than not they leave domesticity to others. They can endure all manner of inconveniences better than most, and often simply do not notice their environment. Many see their home as a base from which they emerge in a blaze of glory to take on the world. Lunar Arians tend to be aloof parents, eager to get the best education they can afford for their offspring, but not so keen to spend quality time with them on a daily basis.

Lunar Arian parents are often hurtfully dismissive of timid or slow children, and should make efforts to see life from their perspective from time to time. Lunar Arians tend to have had problems with their own parents, particularly Arian fathers, who matched their explosive temper and personal ambitions against their children's. Often this erupted into naked rivalry, with the child constantly being compared unfavourably to the father at the same age, their achievements belittled, sometimes scathingly. Sometimes the Arian Moon child is so overawed by their father that they try to emulate him. Every failure to do so is then seen as a tragedy and another nail in the coffin of their own development as mature individuals.

As for their mothers, they may be demanding. These mothers are often too engrossed in their own lives and too busy trying to make their mark to take much notice of their children. Arian Moon children often have childhood experiences that echo those of their mothers, so they spend their whole lives trying to escape from this fate. Yet often great leaders and achievers come out of this tense atmosphere. They may not be too happy at showing their emotions, but they are successful both intellectually and in their careers.

CAREER

If a Lunar Arian is born into a family that is proud of their line of business, which they pass on from generation to generation, it can often be very difficult for this individual to break free of the established pattern. This will almost inevitably cause great problems within the family if they do.

Lunar Arians tend to be artistic and creative, and even if they fail to fulfil this potential many communicators and are especially adept with modern technology. They can also make excellent teachers – although their tendency to bully may ruin many a child's school days. Lunar Arians like

> *Lunar Arians tend to be artistic and creative, and even if they fail to fulfil this potential many continue to have the burning ambition to learn the piano or take up art*

continue to have the burning ambition to learn the piano or take up art, but somehow never get round to it and always wish they had. Even so, with their restless ambition, they need to be the best at everything they do. Producing second-rate paintings or sitting basic piano examinations when they are adults does not appeal to them. If they can't be the best, they don't even want to try.

If they escape the family business, these people seek a career that constantly challenges them. They hate routine or having to defer to someone else, so self-employment is often the answer for them. They can also make good, strong team leaders or fair-minded employers, keen to promote equality in the workforce, but they can be impatient with slow or indecisive workers, and can react angrily to those who challenge their views. It is not unknown for Lunar Arian bosses to become real bullies. They simply can't work with people for whom they have no respect. Unfortunately, because they tend to have a massive ego, they usually think that most people fall into that category.

The careers that bolster that ego are the most appealing to Lunar Arians – anything from advertising copy-writing to rising rapidly through the ranks in the army. They tend to be good

to be the centre of attention and they will tackle anything that sets them apart as leaders or stars. In the performing arts they do best as dancers.

All Lunar Arians need a firm hand, or they become ridiculously unrealistic, so in any career where a manager or agent is necessary, they should be on their guard against too much flattery or being cushioned from reality. In fact, they prefer straight talking from those who help them run their careers and can become very angry with time-wasters.

HEALTH

On the whole, these people are healthy and energetic, although they are prone to accidents. Traditionally, the Moon governs chronic conditions, which, in the case of Aries, are generally those affecting the ear, nose and throat areas.

THE MOON
IN TAURUS

(Ruled by Venus)

The femininity of Venusian Taurus is accentuated here by that of the Moon, which adds extra depth to an already highly-developed sensuality. Traditionally, the Moon is described as being 'exalted' in Taurus, which means that Lunar Taureans are emotionally stable and physically strong. These people are happy with their place on Earth, and, even if their lives are difficult, they will endure the vagaries of their lot without any complaint.

Lunar Taureans find great enjoyment in the good things of life, whether it is wining and dining, dancing cheek to cheek in the moonlight or making love. However, they are not naturally assertive, and prefer to go with the flow rather than make things happen. They are conservative and admire the status quo. The placement of the Moon at their birth means that they feel personally threatened by upheavals and can

assertive, but, if their lifestyle and all they hold dear is challenged, they will muster all their considerable strength to preserve it.

RELATIONSHIPS

Moon in Taurus people are among the least promiscuous of all the zodiac. They are solid, dependable types who see relationships as life commitments and are wary of jumping in head first without any thought for the future. They do have occasional lapses, though. They are not nature's bedhoppers and tend to look askance at those who are. But nor do they merely give their hearts: Lunar Taureans see in every serious relationship – and what other

Lunar Taureans find great enjoyment in the good things of life, whether it is wining and dining, dancing cheek to cheek in the moonlight or making love

become very distressed by any kind of change, disturbance or argument. These people are noted not only for their stability in a changing world, but also for their resistance to the new. In some cases this tendency can be so marked that it almost seems pathological. They will keep faith with a way of life that has long been outmoded. In fact, they are proud to do so and will defend it to the last. Lunar Taureans may not be naturally

sort do they ever have? – the potential for building a family, with all that it entails.

From the first date, they are unconsciously testing their partner for life-long faithfulness and loyalty. This is why those with the Moon in this position are often described as being jealous and possessive. They are constantly alert for what they see as signs of unsuitability in their future husband or wife and, once married, they are retreat hurt. They might even brood for years after because these people are tenacious about everything, including hanging on to their old emotions, which they tend to bottle up. Their scars go deep, and they may even develop a perverse pride in fretting over a hurt, much later in life.

However, Lunar Taureans will doggedly accept many situations that are less than perfect and stick with them rather than face the consequences of upheaval. Despite their extreme possessiveness, or maybe because of it, they live in uncongenial surroundings and make do with less than fulfilling careers. They can, however, be real pests towards those they live with, constantly demanding that partners uphold the same impossibly high standards as they set themselves.

Socially, Lunar Taureans may be stolid and unimaginative, but they make sensual, erotic lovers and can be a revelation in bed. They love luxurious fabrics, which may make the bed a symphony of silks and satins – even if the rest of the house is decorated in fairly unimaginative, but impeccably good, taste.

It takes a lot for Lunar Taureans to admit that there is a problem with the love of their life. Some never do, even though everyone else has recognized the difficulty for some time. Though always willing to take the rough with the smooth, Lunar Taureans are completely shattered by the break-up of a relationship, particularly if it is a longstanding marriage. They tend to find discussing their feelings extremely difficult, although they can force themselves to seek advice that may help the relationship to work again. They find it very hard to

forever testing the strength of the most important relationship in their lives.

When challenged in love, Lunar Taureans can become very distressed. Having an essentially feminine attitude, they tend not to fight, but accept the inevitable, and need enormous amounts of love and support from family and friends in messy divorces.

Lunar Taurean women may see themselves as boring, with mundane lives, and seek to counterbalance this by being attracted to exciting rogues. The road to the altar is littered with the corpses of Lunar Taurean dreams, both male and female.

Confidence tricksters, wife batterers and assorted ne'er-do-wells can often make the Lunar Taurean heart flutter as long as they are glamorous, witty and perhaps a little flashy. Dark, saturnine Scorpians, all-too plausible Geminians, slippery Pisceans and rabble-rousing Aquarians can make Lunar Taureans go weak at the knees, forget their natural good taste and discernment, and make complete fools of themselves. They have been warned.

Yet, when they eventually find true love, responsible, reliable and practical Lunar Taureans make excellent providers for their families. They are good homemakers. They always have their insurance and pension plans in order, plus a little tucked away – earning interest – for a rainy day. They may never make a fortune, but even in times of economic stringency they usually manage to do well enough.

These solid citizens can be extremely dull, and many of their more fiery or airy children cause friction by openly rebelling against their conservatism. Lunar Taurean parents long to understand their children, whom they adore in their own, reserved way, but they are genuinely hurt and bewildered when all that they personally hold dear is challenged.

The incoming Age of Aquarius will be tough for most people, with its futuristic technology, social unrest and radical new attitudes, but it will be the ultimate test for Lunar Taureans.

These people are of the Earth and make excellent tillers of the soil, landscapers and gardeners with very high standards. They love looking out across their land and being lords of all they survey. They are also very happy to help others with their own gardens, perhaps in a professional capacity.

The Four of Wands from the Tarot represents country life, repose, concord, good fortune and peace of mind – truly quintessential Taurean aspirations

Lunar Taureans love the open air: trudging through the woods on a crisp autumn afternoon, then home to tea and cakes by the fire is bliss to them. Many aspire to the lifestyle of the landed gentry or aristocratic families, where lots of dogs go along for country pursuits, followed by hearty meals with fine wine. They enjoy hunting, shooting and fishing, which can cause big problems if their relatives or children are into animal rights. Of course, not all Lunar Taureans aspire to this lifestyle, but it is a rare one who, from time to time, fails to hanker after life in a large country house surrounded by acres of land.

CAREER

This is a very practical Moon placement, meaning that these people are best at creating solid things, providing food and shelter, making furniture or coping with administrative duties. Anything that requires a good, steady pace and pays well will suit the Lunar Taurean temperament, although many such people will also be attracted to the performing arts. This may find expression in hobbies. It was once said that, being such a feminine position, the caring professions are ideal for Lunar Taureans, although this seems no longer to be the case. After all, it is unfashionable for many women to be overtly 'feminine' these days. Even so, it is unlikely that Lunar Taureans will actively seek to join the Army or other similar organizations unless there is a considerable amount of Mars in the rest of their chart.

Lunar Taureans make excellent beauticians, dress designers and craftspeople, because they have an instinctive eye for harmony of line, shape and colour. They can also be good architects and appreciate being able to see the fruits of their imagination taking real shape as buildings that will last – the ideal Lunar Taurean achievement!

Many Lunar Taureans have had to give up the idea of realizing their greatest ambitions, often because of restrictive parents or gender-specific conditioning when young. Consequently, some find it hard to motivate themselves in adulthood. They just cannot push themselves forward and seek promotion, often being quite content to sit back and let others win the glittering prizes or take the praise. Lunar Taureans are not given to seeing themselves at the top, which is why so few of them ever reach it. However, in many cases, this is the only reason they fail to become notable achievers. They are hard workers, pay attention to all-important details and are scrupulously honest and fair. Many are extremely talented. However, besides a lack of self-esteem, this is not a lucky Moon position. These people have to work hard to get anywhere in life: they are not likely to be jackpot

Lottery winners, or to enjoy similar strokes of unexpected luck.

LUNAR TAUREAN CHILDREN

Lunar Taureans often felt they had to keep their thoughts and feelings to themselves as children, and this tendency spills over into adulthood. They can become awkward if pushed into expressing themselves or may suddenly lash out in volcanic explosions of temper. Taureans are known for their stoicism, but also for their bullish rages if pushed to the very edge, and Lunar Taureans are no exception. They feel things deeply, even though they find it almost impossible to say so. Unfortunately, they usually manage to rage at inappropriate moments, bewildering and frightening those around them, especially the youngsters.

HEALTH

Lunar Taureans are generally physically robust, but stress can adversely affect their traditionally weak areas, such as the throat and thyroid, especially in winter. With their sensual love of food, alcohol and all the fine things in life, there is a tendency to put on weight. Fortunately, this can be mitigated by their distaste for poor self-presentation. Lunar Taureans love to have an appealing image, to be slender and chic, so they may well force themselves to work off their overindulgence at the gym.

THE MOON IN GEMINI

(Ruled by Mercury)

Lunar Geminians are nervy, changeable and witty, and make natural communicators. There is also a profound underlying restlessness in this Moon placement, as if they feel their skin doesn't fit. An inner conflict often drives them to achieve great things but can also provoke bursts of extreme irritability and bouts of depression.

people and – to devastating effect, too. Both males and females can be 'bitchy' and sarcastic, and some revel in the power their superior fluency gives them over others.

However, the Moon gives added depth to this sign: these people can be profound thinkers who – as long as their full interest is engaged – can spend hours grappling with abstruse

> *Lunar Geminians are also natural writers, journalists and radio and television presenters. They were made for the media, and the media was made for them*

This Moon Sign cares passionately about promoting themselves and their ego: these people package themselves like a commercial commodity, planning every stage of their climb to the top. They are calculating and shrewd, using their considerable charm as a major weapon against the competition.

As a mutable sign, Lunar Geminians are rarely still for very long. They can become bored very easily, although their attention span can differ widely depending on the level of their interest in the subject in question. Some of them find it hard to focus on any topic for any length of time, constantly waxing enthusiastic about the next task, and never finishing the last one.

Words are their natural medium. Lunar Geminians can talk for hours and are never far from a telephone. They tend to be witty, finding humour in puns and wordplay, and may be good at crosswords and anagrams. The negative aspect of this love affair with words is that they can use them as weapons against slower or less articulate

philosophical problems. They make excellent teachers at all educational levels, really caring that their pupils understand the subjects they teach. Lunar Geminians are also natural writers, journalists and radio and television presenters. They were made for the media, and the media was made for them.

Lunar Geminians are very keen on travel – the influence of speedy Mercury – and can often be found in the air travel

Temperance from the Tarot perfectly reflects the Geminian tendency to moderation and restraint. Reversed the card signifies excess and imbalance – the flip side of Gemini

industry or in the car trade. They are also superb salespeople.

Lunar Geminians have very conflicting attitudes to money. They can spend money like water on clothes, cars, aids to grooming and on being seen in all the fashionable places. Yet there is, paradoxically, often an underlying cautious streak that means excess is followed by parsimony.

Not generally as scatter-brained as many Sun Sign Geminians, they appreciate order and logic, although they are not happy taking a back seat, endlessly poring over facts and figures. They derive great pleasure and job satisfaction from being 'up front', demonstrating the new ideas to the workforce, representing the company abroad

or taking the microphone at a big sales show.

Lunar Geminians love change and can drive themselves furiously hard in pursuit of their goals. They can be obsessive and workaholic, ignoring all the warning signs as their system becomes overloaded with stress and lack of rest. They constantly push themselves too hard. They can be so eager not to miss any opportunity to better themselves that they reap the sorry harvest of this lifestyle quite abruptly, when their exhausted minds and bodies simply cannot go on any longer. They are not naturally robust, but constantly seek to prove to themselves and others how hard they can work, how little sleep they need and how they can get by without holidays or proper meals.

Lunar Geminians, therefore, need to pace themselves. They should learn calming techniques such as yoga and meditation and should try to take up some exercise to work off all that nervous energy. Swimming is good for them, and so is fast walking or rebounding on a trampoline.

They are prone to changeable moods, falling from lofty 'highs' to deepest lows. Then, they retreat from the world and feel that fate has been

RELATIONSHIPS

In relationships, Moon Sign Geminians can be irritable, very often feeling trapped and held against their will. Many take a long time to commit themselves emotionally. Some never settle down at all. They prefer to 'marry' their careers and make their mark in

Moon Sign Geminians have more depth and sensitivity. They may look trendy but their interests go well beyond the fashionable

extremely unkind to let them become so despondent. However, these dark nights of the soul can ultimately be very creative and positive, somehow allowing them to dredge up from the depths of their unconscious minds the elusive answer to their current predicament. Often they pull themselves out of their anguish into a new and exciting world.

Lunar Geminians are very keen to create a memorable first impression. They spend time and money on their image, and they can be startlingly chic and trendy. But while Sun Sign Geminians may go for up-to-date clothes, designer homes, cars, mobile phones and laptop computers, Moon Sign Geminians have more depth and sensitivity. They may look trendy but their interests go well beyond the fashionable. Sometimes, a Lunar Geminian can be very much in the world though not always totally of it. Some have unusual intellectual hobbies or interests, including unorthodox religious beliefs.

more spectacular fashion than 'just' being someone's Mum or Dad. However, this can be a strange sign. The Moon's femininity and Gemini's masculinity often produces the right mix with enviable success.

Lunar Geminians are tactile and outgoing. They may appear flirtatious and sexual, but the truth is that many of them prefer to think and talk about sex rather than do it. There is often a lack of real

Lunar Geminians can spend money like water on clothes, cars, aids to grooming and on being seen in all the fashionable places

underlying libido and the honest warmth needed for the full expression of physical love. These individuals tend to shy away from putting emotions into words. Sometimes, it is enough for them to know that they are desired. The knowledge alone provides a kind of stable basis for them, both socially and emotionally. They have no real desire to make a relationship out of the first flickerings of attraction. It is easy to flatter a Lunar Geminian simply by flirting.

However, those who do enjoy sex are easily bored with the usual routine and may rapidly progress to something they consider more entertaining, just to spice things up a little bit.

This is a Peter Pan sign, full of children who never grow up, something that can make Lunar Geminians excellent parents but rather tiresome siblings. They move restlessly from one activity to another, thinking up games and bedtime stories until even the most energetic small children get tired. Lunar Geminians are very good at the practical side of parenting too: they spend money on their offspring, ensuring that they have everything other children have, and more. They also spend quality time with them if they can.

However, many of these people are too busy, working on several projects at once: working late at the office, taking work home, fixing up dinner parties, talking on the phone, spending time at the gym and shopping. Often, when they do come home their non-Gemini partner has put the children to bed hours before. Even weekends are such a mad rush that the time can slip by without 'quality time' ever arriving.

Lunar Geminians are often so keen to sell themselves and their ideas that they sometimes resort to embroidering the truth because they are inclined to see the truth as a commodity like anything else – to be dressed up or down, depending on the circumstances.

HEALTH

Healthwise, apart from the tendency to overtax their nervous energy discussed previously, these individuals are traditionally prone to auto-immune diseases and have problems with their lungs, hands and arms. In addition, all that rushing about may make them prone to accidents.

THE MOON
IN CANCER

(Ruled by the Moon)

Lunar Cancerians are plagued by their extreme sensitivity and so are those around them. They are sympathetic, kind, compassionate people who care deeply about their loved ones, the underdog and everyone else with a genuine hard luck story. They react strongly to any hint of unhappiness, instantly becoming the valiant protector and carer, although often at great cost to their own peace of mind, for Lunar Cancerians are obsessive worriers.

Life is a roller coaster of emotions for these people. Responding from the heart, not the head,

for just a moment, their fears will all come true.

Lunar Cancerians are sensitive to good or bad atmosphere. Simply by entering a room they can tell what kind of person lives there, or even lived there many years before. Of course, this kind of psychic awareness is a very much a mixed blessing. On the one hand, it enables Lunar Cancerians to know, or at least strongly suspect, the truth behind the public mask that most other people show the world. On the other hand, this ability may involve too many unpleasant insights to make for a comfortable social life. Lunar

Lunar Cancerians are sympathetic, kind, compassionate people who care deeply about their loved ones, the underdog and everyone else with a genuine hard luck story

is typical of them in most situations. It is said that their moods change as often as the tides. Since they are ruled by the Moon that idea is especially apt, but some change even more frequently than that. Every new development provokes an emotional reaction, especially in Lunar Cancerian children or those who are not fortunate enough to have strong mental discipline.

Lunar Cancerians are great, but unrepentant, worriers. Some seem to make an occupation out of fretting about others. This can often be a rather unattractive trait if carried to extremes. They worry that their loved ones may suffer accidents or that some other fearful fate will befall them. It is almost a superstition: they feel that in some way worrying prevents bad things from happening, and if they relax and drop their guard

Cancerians are also very much in tune with children and some animals, although their tendency to be sentimental can prevent them from understanding them completely.

Unfortunately, Lunar Cancerians can be inveterate sulkers and expect to be cajoled out of their moods. They also have the disconcerting tendency to burst into tears – that is, mostly, but not exclusively, female Lunar Cancerians – and throw things around. Fortunately, the outbursts do tend to be short-lived.

When sentiment rules, as it often does here, nostalgia in never far behind. If Sun Sign Cancerians hoard every last photograph and memento, then those with the Moon in Cancer are much worse. They have collections of bus tickets and beer mats going back twenty years, and cannot bear to be parted from them. Deeper still, however, is their tendency to hoard people, or rather their memories of them. They will not let go, and can wave the fairy wand of wish-fulfilment over reality until it becomes something else entirely. For example, women whose fathers were drunken abusers can really believe they were loving protectors. Men who truly hated their deprived childhood will declare later, hand on heart, that it was the happiest time of their lives. Some Lunar Cancerians, however, are keen to create harmony and seek a peaceful atmosphere above all. They can also tend to complain about less-than-perfect surroundings, but as long as there is a degree of emotional stability, they will actually endure a great deal of inconvenience and discomfort.

RELATIONSHIPS

Men and women of this Moon placement have a strong desire to create a nest and they are willing to roll up their sleeves and tackle the hard work of creating it themselves. They will, however, expect those around them to acknowledge their efforts and be grateful.

Lunar Cancerians are great martyrs and will nurture grievances for many years. They may become extremely bitter about some trivial argument that happened in childhood and carry it into adult life. However, they do try to put matters right between warring factions, even if sometimes their diplomatic skills are hampered by their own hypersensitivity.

Lunar Cancerians are in touch with their senses and make extremely good lovers. These people really know how to blend a heightened sense of

scenes. But in there somewhere is the capacity to hit out and hurt – or at least give a nasty nip with those overgrown Crab's pincers.

CAREER

Traditionally, Lunar Cancerians work best as carers, in hospitals, hospices and with the mentally and physically disabled. They are particularly good as nursery nurses, although their tender loving care is also very effective at the other end of the age spectrum, in geriatric nursing. They are also good counsellors, though they need to be thoroughly trained to override their tendency to overempathize with the clients.

Lunar Cancerians are not especially ambitious and are best in supporting roles, sometimes literally, for they can be surprisingly good actors,

Lunar Cancerians are not especially ambitious and are best in supporting roles, sometimes literally, for they can be surprisingly good actors

the erotic with the expression of true love, which can be an explosive and memorable mix in the bedroom. By nature they are loyal – often to a fault – and so tend to make and keep partners for life, because of their sheer dedication to making the relationship work.

However, unfaithful lovers should take note: they may think they can ride roughshod over poor, clinging Lunar Cancerians, but they may be in for an unpleasant surprise. True, any evidence of infidelity will come as a terrible shock to their delicate system, resulting in violently emotional

possibly because their natural reserve can be sublimated by playing at being someone else.

They make excellent teachers and genuinely care for the all-round welfare of their pupils. They are also interested in their subsequent careers and family lives. They have a real sense of contributing to history, even if only in a small way, and often their nostalgic tendency manifests itself in passing on a vivid awareness of the past to the children in their class.

They can be practical – using their hands creatively is the perfect way for them to forget their

*They really know how to blend a heightened sense
of the erotic with the expression of true love*

worries – and can find success as decorators, interior designers or carpenters. They love making things for the home and often have hobbies such as tapestry making, pottery or decorative metalworking.

They can easily abandon or suppress their own ambitions in order to support those of their loved ones. They take a real pride in the achievements of others, especially those close to home, but can become huge bores about it, constantly showing photographs of their children to virtual strangers and going on at length about how their husbands or wives have been promoted at work.

However, whether seeking advancement for themselves or basking in the glory of others, Lunar Cancerians need financial security. There is nothing devil-may-care about them, nothing of the Sagittarian backpacker or the Geminian tendency to flit quite happily from job to job. Security is imperative for Cancerians, both Solar and Lunar. Their emotional happiness often rests on freedom from financial worry.

LUNAR CANCERIAN CHILDREN

Lunar Cancerians are often very insecure as children, and may pass this tendency on to the next generation. Often there is a genuine reason for this fear of the future and distrust of the present. Material deprivation or the break-up of their parents' marriage are two examples. However, in many cases it is simply part of the intrinsic baggage of this Lunar placement.

These people believe that they will become social pariahs if made redundant. In their mind, starvation and destitution are not far behind in their fears, so that periods of unemployment seem like nothing less than the end of life as they have known it.

Lunar Cancerians can be very mean-minded, both in money terms and – perhaps surprisingly – in emotional terms as well. They can scrimp and save compulsively, even when there really is no urgent need to do so. At such times, they may bewilder and hurt others with their frankly cheap and uninspired gifts. They can also show a marked lack of empathy with those they dislike, and can cut them out of their lives only to brood over it afterwards. This can upset children greatly, especially those born under more generous-minded signs, who tend to forgive, forget and move on much more easily.

HEALTH

Women with this Lunar placement may suffer more than most with menstrual, menopausal and hormonal problems because of the influence of their ruler, the Moon. Similarly, they may incline to water retention and should drink at least six large glasses of mineral or filtered water a day in order to keep their water balance healthy. In later life they may react badly to Hormone Replacement Treatment (HRT). Alternative or nutritional therapies could prove more helpful.

Traditionally, this Lunar placement is quite robust physically, although it has a tendency towards breast, chest and stomach problems. However, the extreme emotional sensitivity of these individuals can result in a whole host of psychosomatic ailments such as blinding headaches, stomach upsets, insomnia and weakened auto-immune system.

Lunar Cancerians should seek advice in order to sort out their emotional problems, especially at times of greatest stress, such as bereavement. If they try to soldier on by themselves, their health is in danger of breaking down altogether.

THE MOON IN LEO

(Ruled by the Sun)

oon Sign Leos are generous, noble, encouraging and optimistic. They are natural leaders who exude energy and drive, and are often protective towards more timid mortals. They have an innate sense of style and love beautiful, chic and successful people. They are the leaders of the pack, and can genuinely care for those they feel are in some way inferior to them.

They set remarkably high standards for themselves and others, which can lead to all manner of problems. Although endlessly willing to give others the benefit of the doubt, whenever they feel let down, they react with shock, disbelief and dismay. Lunar Leos expect the best but rarely get it. However, what horrifies them the most are their own failings. They tend to have a very elevated image of themselves as the most moral and ethical people. If the image slips and they experience the less noble emotions such as jealousy, pessimism, envy, infidelity or even downright dishonesty, they become very depressed and angry at themselves and everyone around them.

Lunar Leos love display. They will always aim to look expensively fashionable, even if their clothes came from a thrift shop, and they like to be surrounded by people with similar style. They can feel mortally offended by those who look dirty or sloppy. They fail to understand people who choose alternative lifestyles, for – being a fixed sign – Lunar Leos are very proud of maintaining the status quo and have little time for rebels or eccentrics.

However, even though they like society itself to be stable and unchanging, they hate routine and sameness in their personal lives. Fired up by their

RELATIONSHIPS

Lunar leos are very romantic and generous and love to wine and dine, going to great lengths to flatter their partner and make them feel very special. In return, they expect loyalty, support and understanding, besides a fair amount of ego-bolstering.

Lunar Leos will go to almost any lengths for those they love or want to protect, but they can

Fired up by their ruler, the Sun, they burst with restless energy, constantly prowling around looking for new experiences and challenges

ruler, the Sun, they burst with restless energy, constantly prowling around looking for new experiences and challenges. Frustration makes them irritable, even aggressive towards others, and they can pounce on tiny mistakes as if they were major blunders.

Leos long for excitement, a longing intensified by the influence of the Moon. They long for the sexual thrill which power gives them, and may seek situations where they can show off their mastery – in relationships, in their careers or in dangerous sports. If there is any chance that a specific course of action will make them powerful, they will follow it, even if it means they have to live very near the edge of danger. Lunar Leos rarely lack courage, although their judgment may be in doubt.

become extremely hurt and angry if their generosity is rejected. To them, ingratitude is a cardinal sin, and they do like to be thanked often and effusively. Sometimes, in fact, their insistence on gratitude can effectively take the shine off the original gift.

They are warm and passionate lovers, and adore the idea of romantic involvement. Sometimes, their own capacity for infidelity takes them by surprise. However, their inner restlessness gives them a wandering eye, a hankering after new and exciting experiences and an inner conviction that this is no more than their due. They can put up with a less-than-perfect relationship for a surprisingly long time, often because they feel it is the decent thing to do, but suddenly they will tire of it and begin again with a new partner.

*Leos are natural leaders, exuding energy and drive,
and are often protective towards more timid mortals*

Lunar Leos can be irritatingly superior and aloof. Many of them believe they have a God-given sovereignty over the rest of humanity and believe they always know best. This can be very annoying, but in an intimate relationship it could prove critical. Few loved ones find this attitude truly attractive, and it can wreck many a promising relationship before it has a chance to begin.

For the same reason, Lunar

CAREER

Despite this, Leos often find young people stimulating company, and become teachers or sports instructors, where their natural qualities of leadership are most appreciated. They are good in a crisis and are often hero-worshipped by the youngsters in their care, who see them as extremely glamorous role models.

Whatever career they choose, Lunar Leos like to be stars. Naturally ambitious, Lunar Leos forge ahead along their particular path to the top, rarely giving the sensibilities of others a thought.

> *Despite this, Leos often find young people stimulating company, and become teachers or sports instructors, where their natural qualities of leadership are most appreciated*

Leos can be overbearing parents and difficult siblings, although often their innate charm and generosity will help restore their popularity. Although they can be irritable with slow or introverted children, or rebellious teenagers, they will – at least in theory – always defend the right of these youngsters to live the way they choose. Lunar Leos are not always at ease in discussions about emotions, which can often upset youngsters who are struggling to explain themselves. Fortunately, Leos usually – if belatedly – know the value of affection.

Lunar Leos can tend to put their children under constant pressure to be great achievers and to repress their natural emotions, which they see as 'weak'.

Whatever the route, they make excellent employers, and can be surprisingly understanding towards those who work for them.

Lunar Leos love power and can even sublimate their own need for conquest by immersing themselves in a greater enterprise. For this reason, they are excellent career soldiers but are not content with lower ranks. There is, though, another sort of power that fascinates Lunar, though not all Solar, Leos and that is the world of the paranormal. It is said that many of the great magi, who belonged to the priestly caste of ancient Persia (Iran), were Lunar Leos, and it is easy to see how their power of ritual magic earned respect and a certain amount of awe. Of course, there are also dire warnings

For Leos, the World and all that's in it is theirs for the taking

and cautionary tales about dabbling in magic.

However, magic, apart from stage magic, is rarely a career. It is more of a hobby-cum-religion. Because they love the good things in life, Lunar Leos are attracted by the hotel trade, where they can revel in the bonhomie, although they are considerably less happy working behind the scenes where no-one notices them. They are the television chefs with a string of bestselling cookbooks to their names rather than the service station cooks.

However, Lunar Leos can be all style and little substance, and although they think they have stamina and work very hard, this often proves less than true. Their style is very erratic and depends on immediate rewards, which they always expect.

It is said that Lunar Leos are shyer than Sun Sign Leos, but often not all that much. They may seem slightly less flashy and be deeper thinkers, but they share the same inner drive and self-regard. A basic personality that revolves around self and the promotion of self means that everything Lunar Leos do is driven by the need for

personal fulfilment. Of course, egocentricity can take many forms and it is not always anti-social since it can be a potent motive in making the world a better place. Many Lunar Leos are zealous charity workers who espouse humanitarian causes with the same energy that their more self-centred co-signs usually reserve for promoting themselves. The Lunar Leo will see the cause as an extension of themselves, and cut swathes through those who stand in their way.

They love above all to see action, and hate stifling committee work with its endless discussion and formalities. Grand though they may be, their lunar sensitivity makes them formidable champions of the underdog, and they can move very swiftly if they see injustice being meted out to the socially deprived.

HEALTH

The flamboyant lifestyle of Lunar Leos often has an adverse effect on their waistlines, so they need to work off the excess poundage by taking some form of aerobic exercise on a daily basis. Kick boxing is particularly good, though putting on the boxing gloves and doing ten rounds with a punchbag will let off their massive build-up of steam.

In later life Lunar Leos can suffer from heart problems. Unfortunately, they will automatically choose cream-laden sauces and juicy steaks over healthier fare every time. Of course, it would be terribly disappointing for a Leo to have to give up all such treats, so a compromise lifestyle may well be the best solution. They could eat healthily for five or six days every week, then indulge themselves in a social setting at the weekend.

Psychosomatic ailments in Lunar Leos tend to centre on back problems, usually when they feel without emotional support.

THE MOON
IN VIRGO

(Ruled by Mercury)

Sociable, dutiful, logical and clear-headed, Moon Sign Virgoans are the commentators of life. They operate from the shadows, rarely seeking the spotlight like a Leo but analyzing and observing, noting everything and, for the moment, saying little. Yet there is an essential paradox in both Solar and Lunar Virgoans. They have all the makings of dullness, and, of course, some of them are. But many of them are very witty and charming, with idiosyncratic and even exciting views about life. Some can be downright eccentric, which certainly contradicts the concise terms. They love reducing ideas to the bare essentials, and are fond of any kind of word games from Scrabble to anagrams. Whereas a Geminian might spout words just to hear the sound of his or her own voice, a Lunar Virgoan would rather be quiet and pick their moment to speak. Then, they can deliver a funny or astute one-liner in quiet, deadpan tones.

Trustworthy and reliable par excellence, Lunar Virgoans are stalwart friends and colleagues, with a naturally strong personal code of ethics. They go to great lengths to keep their word, even if it means suffering as a result. They cannot

Trustworthy and reliable par excellence, Lunar Virgoans are stalwart friends and colleagues, with a naturally strong personal code of ethics. They go to great lengths to keep their word

traditional image of the middle-of-the-road, somewhat down-to-earth Virgoans.

They are by nature self-effacing, although if and when they decide they want to shine, they do so memorably and with great panache. This is rare, though. Most of the time Lunar Virgoans are content to take a back seat and concern themselves with the daily minutiae of life. They are keen on details: for example, travel arrangements must be to the letter.

Mercury, their ruling planet, makes them excellent communicators; although they tend not to be high-flying television presenters or top salespeople. Their mode of communication is to present even the most difficult contractual, legal, financial or philosophical concepts in clear,

understand those who break their promises or, worse, never intended to keep them in the first place. In many ways, Virgoan standards are even higher than Leo's. Leos can often fool themselves into thinking they are behaving decently, when in fact they are doing no such thing. However, Virgoans carefully and coolly analyze their own motives as well as those of other people.

Traditionally, Lunar Virgoans are tidy, orderly people with a marked penchant for cubby-holing and categorizing everything. In fact, they may be just as untidy in their surroundings as wild-child Sagittarius, but their thought processes are almost inevitably neat and tidy. In their minds there is a logical flow of ideas from A to Z, and their memories can be phenomenal. They may not be notable stars or leaders but they are second to none in their ability to think laterally, and can often solve problems through sheer ingenuity.

RELATIONSHIPS

Emotionally, Virgoans are often said to be cold fish, but this is rarely the case beyond a superficial level. Their reserve can give the impression that they are passionless, but like still waters, their feelings actually run very deep. It may take them an unusually long time to commit to a relationship, and even then they will be tentative at first. Once they have declared themselves, they are truly dedicated to life-time love.

The problem is that Lunar Virgoans have an inner conflict where expressing emotion is concerned. They want to be romantic and passionate and, in fact, many of them are accomplished poets. But, somehow, in life itself, it just won't come out right. Some have major problems with emotions and sex, finding the whole business overrated – even though their instincts are much the same as anyone else's. Many actually become celibate, even within relationships. They find that the early sexual passion has fizzled out, never to be rekindled, even though their devotion remains just as strong. Many Lunar Virgoans tend to adore from a distance, putting the object of their affections on a pedestal or unconsciously choosing inaccessible people, such as film or rock stars, on whom to lavish their frustrated adoration.

of sulking and nasty, mean-minded nit-picking. They can become very critical, lashing out with scathing remarks and cutting comments. They can even match Scorpio with their verbal attacks. And when the 'No more Mr Nice Guy' mood is upon them, they rarely regret their outbursts. In many respects they feel, sometimes rightly, that others take their good nature for granted, walk all over their finer feelings, never give them due credit or return favours. It takes just one last straw and the barbed comments burst out – not as explosions of fiery temper as with a Leo, or a headlong charge of anger like Taureans, but

Emotionally, Virgoans are often said to be cold fish . . . Their reserve can give the impression that they are passionless, but like still waters, their feelings actually run very deep

Many Virgoans sublimate their sexual energy in work or a more general social round, or both. They are often in great demand as friends because of their ready wit, intelligence and rock-like reliability. However, it can come as something of a shock when their friends discover that they have their failings, too.

Virgoans can easily descend from their Olympian heights of good humour and easy fellowship into black depression, lengthy bouts

usually in a much more controlled way. And it is all the more deadly for that.

Like many naturally reserved people, Virgoans often feel secretly hard-done by. They are intelligent enough to realize that others are stealing their thunder, but too introverted and modest to put up a fight for what is theirs by right. They also believe, with uncharacteristic irrationality, that others should somehow realize how they feel, even though even their body language characteristically gives little away.

Lunar Virgoans can be good homemakers, preferring solid, lasting homes and furniture to flashy, expensive decor. They can be minimalistic, with a taste for bare white walls and plain furnishings. Conversely, they may live in incredible chaos. Ultimately, as long as they can find what they want, they are happy.

CAREER

They are not particularly keen on moneymaking, although certain aspects of banking and accounting appeal to their logical nature. They usually have pension schemes and insurance cover arranged even while relatively young. Typically, they will be savers rather than splurgers, but once again, they can surprise with sudden sprees and irresponsible extravagances.

Lunar Virgoans are brilliant natural researchers, particularly in the science and technology field, and are notably skilled with

them deeply, but at some basic level are often afraid to express it. Fortunately, they can learn to do so within a loving, stable and faithful relationship.

HEALTH

Lunar Virgoans are often obsessed with health – their own and that of others – and make good doctors and efficient nurses. They can also choose careers in the alternative health field and make good homeopaths, naturopaths and nutritionists. They are always trying to push back the boundaries of human knowledge through study and research.

Lunar Virgoans tend to worry about the state of their health, both inner and outer. They often take their temperature, check their tongue in the mirror or pop pills for real or imaginary ailments.

Lunar Virgoans often take their temperature, check their tongue in the mirror or pop pills for real or imaginary ailments

computers. They love all forms of study and information, from the books in libraries to sifting through e-mail. They also enjoy committee work and the intricacies of office politics. They are superb librarians, archaeologists, theologians, historians, political analysts and systems analysts. Many work in laboratories. They are also good at practical skills, such as driving, computing and even the more mundane filing.

Virgoans can be very uncomfortable around children, especially toddlers, who need lots of spontaneous love and affection. They may love

They can get quite dictatorial on the subject, constantly lecturing others on what to eat and what not to eat, regaling everyone with the latest medical research. Their bookshelves are full of diet and vitamin books; although exercise videos may be absent or, at least, underused. Their kitchens will contain jars of vitamin pills and the latest food fads. None of this, however, can avert health problems if they are going to arise anyway. Lunar Virgoans can suffer from nervous ailments such as upset stomachs, to which they are particularly prone.

However, they need to find a balance between excessive worry about their health and a complete lack of interest in it. Perhaps the best course of action is to have regular health checks, maintain a well-balanced diet, avoid doing anything to excess and, above all, try to be happy, which, for them, is more easily said than done. Happiness for Lunar Virgoans is often elusive simply because they think too much about what can go wrong.

THE MOON IN LIBRA

(Ruled by Venus)

*M*oon Sign Librans are charming, urbane and creative. They seek both harmony and excitement – which can lead to a certain amount of inner tension and contrariness in their behaviour patterns. They also pride themselves on their skills as mediators and diplomats. Libra is a cardinal sign, which adds vibrancy and stamina to the slower, more intuitive characteristics of the Moon in this zodiacal position. Even so, many Lunar Librans find the early stages of a project considerably easier than the latter. Seeing it through to the end can often be truly challenging for them. They are rather lazy and, although they may have more than their fair share of leadership qualities, often prefer to take a back seat and let others take the responsibility.

Lunar Librans are naturally stylish. They love fashion, haute couture and chic

Lunar Librans often find themselves in the role of peacemakers, which they fulfil admirably. They can see all round a problem and are unusually perceptive about its underlying causes. However, they are able to maintain a fair and objective viewpoint. All the same, under that impartial exterior lies the ability to speak passionately on deeply-held views and to hatch plots against those who put obstacles in their path. If the beliefs of Lunar Librans are challenged too strongly, their famed even-handedness will suddenly evaporate.

They become excited by innovative ideas. They may go a long way towards accepting them, but inevitably the time comes when they stop and question them. Many people make the mistake of thinking Librans, both Solar and Lunar, are all too gullible. This is not so, as they frequently discover to their cost. There is a strong undercurrent of cynicism and a desire for independence beneath all that Libran charm.

Lunar Librans are naturally stylish. They love fashion, haute couture and chic. When young and impressionable, they may even judge others on their dress sense and superficial image. Many Librans secretly despise those who fail to 'make an effort', choosing to have nothing to do with unfashionable or scruffily dressed people.

They love the challenge of travel, and often take off on their own, knowing they will soon make new friends wherever they go. The very thought of new horizons and fresh fields keeps them going when stuck at home or in a routine, and they are usually planning their next holiday or weekend break while still unpacking from their last. They tend to be self-sufficient. They have no problem with being alone, but usually choose to spend more time with others and enjoy parties.

Lunar Librans appreciate glamour and luxury, and can be dedicated homelovers if their environment is calm, tasteful and welcoming. They enjoy entertaining, but will need to set themselves apart from other people from time to time in order to recharge their batteries.

They have very quick minds and can swiftly see straight to the heart of the matter, although it may take them a while to make up their minds about it. The symbol of the Scales, after all, is concerned with weighing up the pros and cons. Librans bore easily and certainly don't suffer fools gladly. Lunar Librans can be very outspoken and sharply critical, despite their open and welcoming smiles.

RELATIONSHIPS

Moon Sign Librans are often in love with love and throw themselves wholeheartedly into the excitement of the chase. They cool off, though, once a relationship is established and everyday reality intrudes. They can be very fussy and even tactless with their loved ones, which is rather uncharacteristic of them. They will criticize them for their bad taste, poor dress sense or even, worst of all, 'unacceptable' weight gain. They love to be seen with good-looking people and feel personally insulted if their wives or husbands 'let themselves go' or fail to match up to their attractive joint image.

However, Lunar Librans are adept lovers, very tactile and sensual, and can be very uninhibited in bed. They do need gentleness and love, though, and can rapidly become ill at ease in any relationship based on deception or one which exists just for sex alone. They will try to fool themselves, however, that they are happy with the situation. The Libran search for harmony can go very deep, and anything that may rock the boat can seriously upset their equilibrium.

Although Lunar Librans tend to be hypercritical and fussy, they are not always as difficult to live with as this might suggest. On the household, even if it means compromising their own position. However, this certainly does not mean that they are pushovers, merely that they need to keep their own environment peaceful and free of 'bad vibes'.

In many ways, Lunar

even in male Lunar Librans there is a strongly developed gentleness, which can be very attractive to those in need, and can add a caring dimension to most relationships

contrary, they can be very loving domestic partners. They are excellent in a crisis and can be relied upon to be caring when others are ill; although, if the problem drags on, their sympathy may begin to wane! They love rising to a challenge and can be very practical in their approach to problems – helping with transport, catering, shopping and entertaining the children. Lunar Librans tend to be good with children and animals, although this will vary depending on the rest of their chart. Anyone who is weak or defenceless wins their attention and they can be formidable champions of the underdog.

Moon Sign Librans cannot abide a tense atmosphere and will go out of their way to smooth over ruffled feathers in the Librans can be martinets, even though they hide behind great urbanity and apparent altruism. They can even be rather interfering and nosy. They love gossip and tittle-tattle and use the information to spread their influence beyond their immediate circle.

They can often be secret manipulators and exploiters, although this can be mitigated by their compulsively soft hearts. All the same, if they feel that someone deserves it, they will be quite happy to weave a web of intrigue around them.

However, even in male Lunar Librans there is a strongly developed gentleness, which can be very attractive to those in need, and can add a caring dimension to most relationships. Young Lunar Librans characteristically long for the freedom of adulthood, when they feel they can stamp their own personalities on the world and develop their own tastes. They often chafe at the regimentation of school, where scholastic achievement, and not their personal qualities, are the order of the day.

As parents, Lunar Librans are tolerant, open-minded and demonstrative. However, because they hate untidiness and love harmony, they are less inclined to be tolerant of unruly teenagers.

CAREER

This Moon placement encourages careers in some form of negotiation or mediation – perhaps in trade unions or local government, international charities or the diplomatic corps. A just cause brings out a certain steeliness in Lunar Librans, and their famed humour can successfully defuse many a potentially explosive situation.

They are also good at 'fronting' organizations, making excellent public relations officers for large corporations and presenting an admirable image for their employers. In many ways they make excellent representatives. Sometimes, though, their motivation may falter, and they need to be given a strong party line to follow; they are not keen on making major decisions or thinking on their feet. For that reason, they are not usually senior executive material; although their hard work and personal qualities may take them very close to the top of their chosen career. Besides, their love of luxury will drive them to make as much money as possible – if they can do so without ruining their social life!

They are also artistic, good at selling, marketing, architecture and at ease with technology such as computer graphics

and desktop publishing. Modern technology, in fact, fascinates them so much that they may spend hours entertaining themselves with computers.

Many Lunar Librans are engineers. They also adore speed, and love flying and driving. However, although they enjoy tinkering with engines, the heavy repair work is usually left to someone else.

Few Lunar Librans become workaholics, although they may occasionally come very close to it. They need to work, and can do a great deal in short, sharp bursts – but rarely overdo it for extended periods at a time. Unemployment or the suspicion that their work is not fully appreciated can make them extremely depressed. They feel that how they earn a living is an extension of their own deepest self, which is a serious – and potentially very damaging – misconception.

HEALTH

Lunar Librans, whose lungs are very sensitive, generally suffer from respiratory illness. This means that smoking involves greater risk for them than for most people. Similarly, they should avoid polluted atmospheres and always keep the home and office fresh.

Being acutely aware of disharmony in the environment, they should balance its energies through the application of *feng shui*.

THE MOON
IN SCORPIO

(Ruled by Pluto & Mars)

*M*oon Sign Scorpians are competitive, intense, sexually inclined and compelling. They seek all sorts of excitement, while at the same time appreciating a stable, calm sort of life. There is usually an element of the contradictory and perverse in these people, which adds to their unfathomability and even to their sex appeal.

This is a potent placement – for good or evil. It is the sign of great reformers, cult leaders and magi, people who inspire others at a very profound level and who rarely do anything without deep personal motivation.

Often very hard to understand, Lunar Scorpians tend to hide their true feelings. This can go on for years, until some last straw ignites a truly memorable outburst. Scorpians are nervy and intense and hide a great well of sensitivity under their somewhat hard exterior. Everyday problems can be very distressing for them.

Many Scorpians – both Solar and Lunar – have 'leaky auras', losing energy form their vital core on a daily basis. They should learn how to retain it through meditation and other spiritual exercises. In fact, most Lunar Scorpians are already interested in such matters, for this is a very psychic placement and many of these people are occultists, psychical researchers or are, in some other way, involved with New Ager practices or the paranormal.

Traditionally, Lunar Scorpians are drawn to magic. They enjoy the feeling of personal power it gives them, and the thrill of coming into contact with unseen forces. Of course, this is by no means always a good thing, for at the very least they could be wasting their time and deluding themselves. At worst, they could open themselves up to the nasty influence of malign spirits. However, Scorpians are survivors if nothing else, and rarely fall prey for very long to the darker spirits.

This is a potent Moon placement – for good or evil. It is the sign of great reformers, cult leaders and magi, people who inspire others at a very profound level

It is easy for Lunar Scorpians to become depressed and retreat into a world of their own; but that world may be a somewhat dark and threatening place. Many of them are outwardly very gregarious, apparently loving the social round; but occasionally they will need to break off and spend time by themselves to recoup their energies.

The positive side of their psychic awareness is a well-honed intuition about insincere and exploitative people, and an ability to guard against those with hidden agendas. Lunar Scorpians love slightly dark, dangerous types and can get into trouble because of it. Yet somewhere under all that hankering after a life lived on the edge is a robust sense of self-preservation.

These people have the enviable ability to bounce back after personal disaster. Although they may become very depressed and low for long periods, it is rarely forever. They will suddenly rise up from all the gloom again in a new, more positive frame of mind. Many see life as a series of tests of strength, and may even unconsciously manipulate people and events to create the challenges that keep their wits sharp, while at the same time bemoaning their fate.

This placement means that Lunar Scorpians are perhaps more caring than the Solar kind, and they are attached to home and family in an almost Cancerian way. They are keenly aware of the needs of others and can operate very skilfully behind the scenes to ensure they are met. They are also fiercely proective, going to great lengths to help those less fortunate, or simply less aware, than they are. Many see their intuition as a special gift, and waste no time using it altruistically.

RELATIONSHIPS

The Moon in Water Signs always make for great emotionality. Moon Sign Scorpians have great difficulty when it comes to expressing their feelings. They can be only too eager to unburden themselves to others, but somewhat less willing to be at the receiving end of emotional angst. They can be markedly demanding and possessive, but rapidly distance themselves from those they regard as 'clingers'.

Sexually, Lunar Scorpians are intense and very active. They have a taste for the unusual, even the dangerous, in the bedroom. However, they also need to be loved and valued as people, and it may be that they will seek to have at keast two different relationships running parallel with one another to fulfil their opposing needs.

As with every other aspect of life, Lunar Scorpians like an element of danger in their relationships. They will also provoke inflammatry situations at home – rows and 'scenes' – just to keep the edge of danger nicely sharpened. Even so, they can be surprisingly sympathetic and affectionate, empathizing with the feelings of their loved ones; although this will depend on their mood and should never be taken for granted! They are very sensitive and, if approached in the right way, can easily be persuaded to see another's point of view. They are easily hurt if accused of being in any way unjust or uncaring, and will turn over a new leaf immediately – if not permanently. They are keen to reform and become better people.

Many Lunar Scorpians may not have enjoyed their childhood, and may even have felt it was a bit of battleground. But Scorpians are survivors and will rise like the phoenix from the ashes of even the most arduous or trying situation. However, Scorpians may be left with repressed anger and frustration and should be wary of a tendency, at an unconscious level, to provoke emotional scenes, in order to feed their need to be heard. As parents themselves, Lunar Scorpians can be unpredictable and moody. But many of them are loving, dutiful parents whose love of drama and dressing up can provide great entertainment for their children.

CAREER

Lunar Scorpians are naturally good with ideas in concrete form, as in sculpture or architecture. They are excellent engineers or graphic designers, and can be real wizards with computer-generated special effects. They can also be found in the fashion and entertainment industries. Many work in medicine, as surgeons or forensic sicentis.

A sign of extremes, Scorpians can experience great ups and downs in a career. Apparent disaster such as redundancy, bankruptcy or disablng illness may strike, only to be followed by another turn of the Wheel of Fortune ushering in a golden time of prosperity, health and happiness.

They will suddenly rise up from all the gloom again in a new, more positive frame of mind

Often this roller-coaster is unconsciously engineered by the Lunar Scorpian as a test of strength. Scorpians are true believers in fate and love to pit their wits against it. Although they can, and almost always do, bounce back from the brink of total disaster with staggering regularity, they often take less resilient people down with them – and leave them there. They should realize how unfair it is to involve others in their games of Russian roulette with Destiny.

The Wheel of Fortune represents fortune, success, luck, happiness and opportunity. Despite frequent setbacks, illness and even disaster, the life of a Scorpion – more than any other sign of the zodiac – is characterized by such happy reversals of fortune.

HEALTH

Traditionally, women with this Moon placement have exceptionally heavy periods. Both sexes tend to have problems with their reproductive organs. It is a good idea to have regular specialist check-ups and – of course – always to practise safe sex.

Lunar Scorpians can be great worriers about their health but fail to act for some time, letting their symptoms worsen. They must be brave and visit a health professional at the first sign of a problem. Even if they have only imagined that they have some kind of serious ailment, it is far better to be safe than sorry. They simply cannot afford to take chances with their health.

Lunar Scorpians have enormous nervous energy and need to work off their frustrations through healthy exercise. The problem is that this is hardly a sporty Moon placement, so perhaps they could simply settle for brisk walks and regular visits to the local swimming pool.

THE MOON
IN SAGITTARIUS

(Ruled by Jupiter)

*M*oon Sign Sagittarians are courageous, intellectually inquisitive, studious and very free spirited. They love their independence, which they guard very jealously, and cannot abide being trapped or regimented. Highly adaptable, Lunar Sagittarians are made for action and are innately gregarious, with a wide circle of admiring friends.

They have clear minds and are able to cut through unnecessary detail to the central issue, communicating its ins and outs to others in easy-to-understand terms. They hate fuss of any sort, preferring things to be clear-cut and direct; they particularly dislike pomposity.

In their love lives, Lunar Sagittarians are keen for new experiences and hate to be tied down, either physically or intellectually. Energetic and optimistic, they really believe that the grass is always greener on the other side, but even when, disappointingly, it turns out not to be so, they readjust their sights and press on.

These are not power-hungry people, nor are

Justice – the card of fairness, rightness and probity. These are essential, motivating characteristics of Lunar Sagittarians, who passionately despise bigotry and injustice

Lunar Sagittarians hate bigotry and prejudice of any sort, and can throw themselves

Moon Sign Sagittarians are, to some degree, less outgoing than their Solar counterparts; but they still possess the same basic desire to like – and be liked by – everyone they meet

they money-mad or particularly fond of competition. They cannot be bothered to claw their way to the top. If they have their own space and enough to pay the bills, buy a few books and CDs and travel the world in modest style, they are content enough.

energetically into helping those in trouble. They are firm believers in justice and fair play, but they can also can be oblivious to the feelings of those who stand in their way. Sometimes, though, their best intentions take a rather strident form, alienating the very people they are eager to help.

Traditionally, this Moon placement has few serious faults, but can live very much in a world of its own, always optimistic that things will turn out all right in the end. Sometimes it does, but their Sagittarian lack of foresight can occasionally hurt others, even their own family.

Similarly, they can bank – only too literally – on uncertain plans and insubstantial projects, seeing the future as rosy to a ridiculous degree. Even regular dousings with very cold reality often fail to make them see sense.

Moon Sign Sagittarians are, to some degree, less outgoing than their Solar counterparts, but they still possess the same basic desire to like and be liked by everyone they meet. However, they tend to withdraw into their own quiet room from time to time and spend many hours reading or daydreaming, just to centre themselves. Often, too much of their time is spent in a flurry of activity, so their instinct is to go to ground to build up their energies once more. Sometimes they will disappear for many hours at a stretch, perhaps studying intensely or going for long recreational walks.

Lunar Sagittarians can easily become carried away by the sound of their own voice and forget the sensitivities of others. Many are too blunt and most can be very tactless. Yet, in general, they are kind, compassionate people who never intend to hurt those around them.

They are good in a crisis – almost enjoying them sometimes – and can be extremely practical their partners have feelings and needs of their own. Too often, Sagittarians merely pay lip service to this concept.

On a day-to-day basis they are easy to live with. They are tidy and clean about the house and quite willing to do their share of the chores, even if

These people make energetic and inspiring teachers, although they will often rebel against too strict a regime

if they have to be. Although they can be rather lazy about the house, once they start the work they actually like putting up shelves and mending the gutter. Itchy feet aside, once they settle down in their own home, they will take pride in it, and decorate and furnish it in a solid, tasteful, unostentatious style.

RELATIONSHIPS

Lunar Sagittarians may find problems with close relationships. They tend to make a distinction between sexual passion and the gentler sort of unconditional love – although their partners may not see it in quite the same way. Obviously, this is not the recipe for long-lasting love, and many Lunar Sagittarians have several relationships going at once. In a one-to-one situation, they may feel their partners are trying to trap them or take away their independence.

Lunar Sagittarians are often more attracted to the idea of sexual encounters than to the act itself. The problem is that

they do need reminding from time to time. They will not accept nagging or dogmatic demands, however, and emotional blackmail is anathema to them.

Lunar Sagittarians can have filthy tempers. All that inner fire and energy can suddenly explode in a volcanic eruption of fury and a spate of highly colourful abuse. It can come as a real shock to those at the receiving end. However, the fire usually fizzles out and is forgotten, at least by Sagittarians – although others may remain shaken for some time afterwards.

They often talk big, persuading themselves and others that they are high-fliers, but do nothing to make their dreams become reality. Their innate charm (which can be overdone) is their biggest asset. At its most negatively aspected, this Moon placement creates fantasists. However, their tall tales are not deliberate manip-ulations – they often believe them themselves.

Lunar Sagittarians can have filthy tempers. All that inner fire and energy can suddenly explode in a volcanic eruption of fury

As parents, Lunar Sagittarians love their children, but find it hard to be good disciplinarians or help them keep their feet on the ground. Both Lunar and Solar Sagittarians tend to be like overgrown children themselves, which at least makes for some interesting games but not much guidance. They are not very good with the boring or downright unpleasant aspects of parenthood and can be rather forgetful about mealtimes and other routine demands of daily life.

CAREER

These people make energetic and inspiring teachers, although they will often rebel against too strict a regime in much the same way as their pupils.

They enjoy working in the entertainment industry, although many with this Moon placement may be too shy to work in front of the microphone or camera, preferring to stay behind the scenes. Many make excellent tour guides or seasonal workers and are usually happiest when self-employed or signing up for short contracts. They like to feel in control of their working lives and able to get up and go at a moment's notice. Many Lunar Sagittarians are excellent television researchers, moving from programme to programme as each series ends, enjoying the change of pace and subject.

Any kind of selling is attractive to this type, but the hurly-burly of market trading is not for them. They prefer to work in comfortable, classy surroundings with interesting people, and dislike chaotic working conditions.

Over-optimism can lead them to make some very unwise career moves and, possibly, tempt them into gambling more than is advisable. The problem is that few Lunar Sagittarians ever truly learn from their mistakes.

HEALTH

Lunar Sagittarians use up a great deal of energy through nothing more than simply conducting their daily life. But they need some form of structured exercise, such as team games, to keep them mentally and physically on track. They are good swimmers and also tend to be adept at surfing.

Traditionally, Lunar Sagittarians suffer from problems connected with their legs and hips, although this may be a symptom of general wear and tear. Being so active, they are constantly putting a strain on various parts of their bodies, and the legs bear much of it.

Other problem areas include the veins, and varicose veins can be a real bugbear in later life. So as not to encourage this painful condition, they should train themselves not to cross legs or ankles when sitting and to eat plenty of fibre to prevent overfull intestines putting pressure on the veins.

Sagittarians should get into the habit of taking regular naps during the day to keep up their energy, and should avoid sugar and caffeine, which throw their blood sugar levels out of balance.

THE MOON
IN CAPRICORN

(Ruled by Saturn)

oon Sign Capricornians are serious, dependable and controlled. Very practical people, they do not shirk responsibility and have great foresight and powers of endurance. Sensitive and refined by nature, they may seem slightly old-fashioned and out of place in the modern world, but they can adapt surprisingly well to new situations.

They tend to be reserved and somewhat shy when young, but gradually develop an outward sophistication. This, though, is often merely a device for keeping the outside world at arm's length. They have beautiful manners and great respect for the old traditions of country and home.

Lunar Capricornians tend to plan their future when others are still more interested in

shoulders – and the chance to develop spiritually well beyond the usual opportunities granted to most people. Significantly, it is usually a flighty Geminian or a ludicrously over-optimistic Sagittarian who accuses them of being so unexciting, so perhaps that criticism should be taken with a pinch of salt.

RELATIONSHIPS

Under their wise, cautious image, Lunar Capricornians hide a great deal of sensitivity – more so than their Sun Sign counterparts. However, they learn early in life to keep their feelings under control – perhaps to obscure them with their bright and charming manner. They are very uncomfortable with any kind of

Many Lunar Capricornians endure totally incompatible relationships simply because it would not, in their eyes, be honourable to break them off

playground games, and can seem rather serious and studious. Their solemn ruler Saturn bestows very mixed blessings: they are expected to take life seriously right from the cradle.

Capricornians, both Solar and Lunar, have acquired an unfair reputation as boring and pessimistic people plagued with bad luck and all sorts of restrictions. In fact, this is not the case. Saturn gives them a great deal of wisdom – which can bestow somewhat old heads on young

emotional scene, though deep down inside they may be crying out in sympathy. Outwardly they can appear cold, but this is rarely – truly – the case at all.

They are slow to give their hearts, even in friendship, but once committed to a relationship will honour it through thick and thin. Many Lunar Capricornians endure totally incompatible relationships simply because it would not, in their eyes, be honourable to break them off.

Because they are inhibited and over-controlled, they usually find sex and demonstrations of affection very difficult to cope with. Love and sex are inextricably entwined for these people, and marriage is for life.

They need patience and understanding to bring out the best in them sexually, but they can be great romantics under that aloof exterior and respond enthusiastically to a more experienced partner.

Being an Earth Sign, they love romantic walks in the country and the scent of flowers, and will rarely miss an anniversary or birthday – although these cautious types don't like surprise parties.

Once they have found their life partner, they are happy to settle down, since now they have acquired a safe environment in which they can truly express themselves. It is important to them to have security, both emotional and financial, and the thought of having it taken away from them is too much to bear. They worry about financial collapse, even if it is the least likely disaster to befall them, and hardly dare admit that they do ponder from time to time about how they could cope with divorce or the death of their loved one.

However, the opposite side of this obsessive worrying means that they understand the need which others also possess to be centred and safe, and are wonderful providers and protectors. Where Lunar Cancerians can be seen as the archetypal mothers, Lunar Capricornians are classic fathers. Women with this Lunar placement will also have a great urge to defend their nearest and dearest against the world.

However, they do need their own protectors against the insensitivity of the outside world. Their ideal partner is a strong, warm and understanding person with an independent mind and a well established career. They don't understand rebels or those who choose a more bohemian lifestyle, although they may entertain a

sneaking admiration for them. Anyone who lives from hand to mouth can seem very heroic and exciting to them, but not desirable.

As parents, Lunar Capricornians can often be too severe when handling sensitive or unorthodox children. Somewhat repressed themselves, they need to be encouraged to let go and have fun. Often this skips a generation, making them somewhat stiff parents but wonderful and adored grandparents. They like children to be orderly and disciplined, which may sometimes seem like a contradiction in terms, but they love their offspring dearly even if they fail to empathize with them.

Lunar Capricornians hurt easily, and nurse the scars of secret humiliations for years, often forever. They bottle up their feelings, believing that 'it's not done' to cry at funerals or punch the air with joy in moments of triumph.

Decency, self-control and hard work are their watchwords. Many Lunar Capricornians have a delightfully dry sense of humour, often at their own expense, and can reveal surprising insights and great depth of thought.

Lunar Capricornians are naturally inclined to relaxing. They love taking even short breaks, varying the location and types of holiday with a sense of adventure. However, even if they claim they have no problem with solo vacations, this is rarely true. Most do not cope well alone, and need a bright and energetic companion to lift their spirits and share their adventures.

CAREER

Moon Sign Capricornians are disciplined and reliable, and they need to work hard to feel valued as people. They are particularly badly affected by setbacks, disappointments and bad often enjoy jobs in insurance or accountancy.

Lunar Capricornians can become very tetchy and fussy. They hate sloppiness of any sort, and have a natural regard for routine and order, although the armed forces suit their solar counterparts rather more. These people are basically too easily humiliated to enjoy the boisterous cut-and-thrust of the military life, although the regimentation has many attractions for them.

They like to see the results of their labours and are good at what others consider tedious office work. It is important to Lunar Capricornians to feel they make a concrete contribution. With minds so well equipped to deal with detail, they make adept engineers and architects – although perhaps not the most imaginative around. They like tradition and stability in whatever they do.

Lunar Capricornians hate being rushed. The mad chaos of a busy newspaper office or live television studio is not for them. They appreciate being able to settle down to their tasks in their

The Tower from the Tarot, which signifies disaster waiting around the corner, has particular significance for Capricornians, who – unlike Scorpians, who bounce back effortlessly from catastrophe – are more than usually adversely affected by setbacks and disappointments. In fact, they may never truly recover.

Lunar Capricornians hate being rushed. The mad chaos of a busy newspaper office or live television studio is not for them. They appreciate being able to settle down to their tasks in their own time

news of any kind, and can see redundancy and unemployment as true catastrophes. If this happens, they may never totally recover in their deepest psyches, even if they go on to achieve great things in their future careers. Business and the financial world are attractive to them and they

own time, working through them slowly and methodically, then checking and double-checking their own work. Many Lunar Capricornians are happiest when working with a partner in their own company, and will enjoy working out the tax returns and keeping the accounts.

However, it is not a good idea to treat the loyal, efficient Lunar Capricornian like a doormat. As with all Earth Signs, it takes a great deal to make them angry; but once they are, stand well back. When Capricornians blow, they can be coldly furious, dredging up old scores and being bitterly sarcastic and downright nasty. The hurt of decades can finally surface in a shower of insults and innuendo that may or may not be connected with the issue in question. Even with their great respect for authority, this venom can be aimed at their superiors in the workplace. Of course, they will bitterly regret any such outburst and will very probably offer to resign. Such an offer will probably not be accepted because many Lunar Capricornians are simply too good at their jobs.

HEALTH

Lunar Capricornians live long and are fairly robust. They can suffer from skin disorders, rheumatism and stress ailments such as upset stomachs and headaches. Bottling up emotions can have serious repercussions for their health, especially in later life, taking the form of heart problems and even some types of cancer.

It is important for Lunar Capricornians to learn to express their feelings and work off their tension through some form of exercise. This is especially true because they can dwell on things that have gone wrong in life, blaming themselves and feeling shame where others would only see bad luck.

Although they usually manage to keep quite trim and are not given to excesses in food and drink, many have no interest in their diets and can exist for years on sub-standard food. They should educate themselves about healthy eating, and begin a regime that includes fruit and vegetables and plenty of vitamins.

Their loved ones would do well to encourage them to enjoy mealtimes a little more, which will do wonders for their all-round health and happiness.

THE MOON
IN AQUARIUS

(Ruled by Uranus & Saturn)

oon Sign Aquarians are cool, broad-minded, humanitarian and optimistic. They are idealists with high personal standards, exemplars of integrity and honesty, and their strongly developed sense of independence means that they rarely become a burden to others, either financially or emotionally.

They are unusual in their tastes, embracing a wide social spectrum where their friends are concerned. They have no time for any form of prejudice or bigotry. However, Lunar Aquarians are often emotionally detached. They can give the impression of not really caring deep down about

individuals, although their commitment to large groups such as charities or environmental organizations is second to none.

Forward-looking and optimistic, they embrace the future with enthusiasm. They can be slow to learn the lessons of history, though – often a major mistake. They also have a tendency to be too eager to abandon old ways of doing things, and the traditions that have become hallowed by age; and they can be very insensitive to those who still uphold them.

Lunar Aquarians are extremely gregarious and may seem very open and universally friendly. There is a steely watchfulness about them, though, that can be disconcerting. It is as if they are constantly holding back some secret part of themselves while being eager to give the impression of total openness. What you see is not necessarily all you get with this Moon placement.

They hate to appear weak or needy, and will suffer in silence rather than ask for help. They feel that they are the guardians of society and should be the ones who look after the rest of us, rather than the other way around. In many ways there is a quiet arrogance about Lunar Aquarians which can become very irritating. It is an almost subliminal aloofness that speaks volumes about their inner attitude. Not surprisingly, Lunar Aquarians rarely lack self-esteem.

This strong sense of inner worth can lead to some spectacular risk-taking; although few possess the often childish over-optimism of a Sagittarian or the blithe boastfulness of a Geminian. Lunar Aquarians tend to take calculated risks virtually every day of their lives, acting from an inner core of belief in their own destiny and the essential rightness of their actions.

Taken to extremes, this Lunar placement encourages a rather cool, unemotional attitude towards other people that is masked by a tendency to interfere and intrude. This is the sign of the bossy charity worker who organizes everyone, regardless of their actual needs.

Energetic and highly motivated, these people love to be in control, whether in their home life or at work. Many of them extend their sphere of influence into hobby groups or charities and will work long hours on their behalf, although they are rarely content to take a minor role.

On the whole, however, Lunar Aquarians are easy-going, congenial folk who attract a wide range of friends and lovers. Sexually, they can be romantic, passionate and – being a Fixed sign – very loyal, even to partners who repeatedly let them down. Some Lunar Aquarians have such an impossible dream of their ideal love that they spend their entire lives alone, waiting in vain for them to come along. Even then, though, they will not be particularly unhappy. Aquarians, both Solar and Lunar, rarely sulk or brood, being far too busy with a hundred and one plans and schemes.

When they finally give their hearts, though, they do so willingly and are happy to settle down – although their home may be somewhat eccentric in some way.

President Kennedy in 1963. The more personal planets they have in Aquarius, the more pronounced this tendency will be.

Most Lunar Aquarians, however, have a certain emotional objectivity which prevents them from

It is essential for Lunar Aquarians to find a life partner who shares the same interests. Aquarians desperately need to find their own niche in life and stay there

They don't mind chaos as long as it is their sort of chaos! Some barely notice their surroundings and need a partner who is more centred and meticulous about the mundane chores of daily life. Others, however, are orderly and houseproud, imposing their own taste very quickly on a shared home and being happy to help with the housework, the decorating and the financial upkeep.

Many Lunar Aquarians have no regard whatsoever for orthodoxy or tradition. They tend to espouse bizarre beliefs and alternative lifestyles, and can be rather gullible about the more unusual New Age fads. Their homes tend to sparkle with large collections of crystals, wind chimes and Aboriginal and Native American artefacts. Their bookshelves are crammed with tomes on extreme political, religious, mystical or sociological beliefs.

They may be fruitarian, vegetarian or, possibly, vegan. They tend to believe conspiracy theories, especially those alleging governmental involvement in famous assassinations, such as that of

going too far, and a well-developed logic that enables them to see through some of the wilder theories. There is a feeling that many Aquarians embrace eccentric ideas or belief systems simply because they feel they are the way of the future. This seems logical to them, for they never want to miss out on the latest ideas or the next big opportunity for social and self-development.

RELATIONSHIPS

It is essential for Lunar Aquarians to find a life partner who shares the same interests. Aquarians desperately need to find their own niche in life and stay there, and anyone who is uncomfortable with that or has completely different views will not last the course. Some Lunar Aquarians enter into a relationship with high hopes of it making the world a better place – only to discover later on that their loved one has no interest in that, but has other concerns. However, being essentially loyal and devoted, Lunar Aquarians will make every effort to blank out the truth of the situation, because they don't enjoy having to begin again with someone else. They hate underhand dealings and dislike the idea of illicit affairs, even though their hearts and the demands of their sexuality may point them in that direction.

The irony is that Lunar Aquarians can easily become bored within a relationship, despite their protestations of life-long love, and may simply fall into other relationships without making any particular effort. Although they have no intention of hurting anyone, their essential self-centredness can harden their hearts when they are faced with a romantic break-up. Aquarians operate from the premise that they know what is best and have the only valid interpretation of events; others had better do things their way or get out.

On the whole, however, these people are kind and compassionate parents who encourage their children to express themselves, bring their friends home and turn a blind eye to the inevitable mess.

Lunar Aquarians tend to have big egos no matter how soft, gentle and understanding they may seem. For once, the Moon has the effect of diminishing emotionality, and this can help create some very cool customers indeed.

AQUARIAN CHILDREN

As children they are unusual, self-possessed and probably of above-average intelligence. They have a practical streak, which makes them natural leaders and organizers from an early age; although paradoxically they can be rather shy in some social situations. They are independent children with strongly-developed opinions, and they show remarkable self-discipline. They are funny and have an easy charm but are also stubborn and intolerant of the opinions of others.

They can be delightful parents themselves, appreciating the problems of childhood and the teenage years, and showing great sympathy towards youngsters who are disabled or different in any way. However, they may be over-eager to impose their view of the world on their offspring who may dare to think differently.

CAREER

The patient and devoted Lunar Aquarians are suited to careers in education, perhaps with children with special needs. They love the principle of learning and are often attracted to higher education, perhaps becoming a university lecturer or graduate research student.

Being a Fixed Sign, Lunar Aquarians are naturally determined and see projects through to the finish. They have no time for empty talk or procrastination. This innate self discipline makes them ideal team leaders, and although they can be inept and reluctant delegators, they do well working for themselves. Lunar Aquarians can be very irritable with those whose work is not up to the same high standard as their own, treating them with withering sarcasm.

HEALTH

Traditionally, where health is concerned, the legs and ankles are problem areas, manifesting themselves as ailments connected with veins and ulcers. Lunar Aquarians tend to suffer from food intolerances and allergies – from seasonal hay fever to violent reactions to dust mites, chemicals and household pets. It is a good idea for them to have themselves checked for food intolerances or allergies with a reputable nutritionist.

They are rarely overweight – in fact, Lunar Aquarians tend to despise obesity. However, they can easily adopt a diet that is far too restricted for good health. Perhaps they should realize that food is not always a major political or moral issue, and that meals can be relaxed, fun occasions.

THE MOON
IN PISCES

(Ruled by Neptune & Jupiter)

oon Sign Pisceans are emotional, kind, creative and psychic. They instinctively reach out to others, and may even sacrifice their own well-being in order to help and support those around them. Soft-hearted and vulnerable, this Moon placement cannot bear disharmony or 'bad vibes', and works hard to eliminate all upsets – real, potential or imagined!

These are very artistic people who enjoy poetry, dancing and painting. They can be surprisingly ambitious in these fields, even though they are naturally disinclined to push themselves forward in most other areas of life. They have a profound awareness of balance and harmony, and their creative

work tends to reflect a striving for peace. They hate ugliness in any form. Living in an unpleasant environment can make them feel quite ill.

Lunar Pisceans are the psychics of the zodiac, picking up information about people and places at a profound, often inexplicable, level. They instinctively know that life is more complex than is suggested by the evidence of our five senses and, with their well-honed spiritual antennae, feel the curious ebb and flow of unseen energies.

Many of them are committed to religious or mystical belief systems and ponder deeply over the great questions of life and death. They may read widely about the afterlife and reincarnation and have a strong personal belief in a continued existence after bodily death.

This colours their whole attitude to life, and gives them a firm base on which to build their personal development.

Cancerian comes close. They constantly fret about their nearest and dearest, but also spend valuable time worrying about the state of the world, seeing

These people love their friends almost as much as they love family, and would go to the ends of the Earth for them if they felt it was necessary

In fact, this underlying conviction is a very good thing. Lunar Pisceans tend to be buffeted this way and that by the demands of others, and they rarely stand up for themselves or insist on their own rights. Naturally supportive and caring, they can easily sublimate their own needs and desires by looking after others. This can escalate to a very unhealthy degree: many become uncomplaining, downtrodden martyrs who harbour secret resentments for years.

Traditionally, Lunar Pisceans are extremely moody, unpredictable, irritable and often sulky. But in reality they are so sensitive and easily hurt that they are often merely taking time out to recover. An unguarded or unwise word, even a mild joke at their expense, will go deep and continue to rankle in their sensitive souls for a long time.

Other people come first to a Lunar Piscean, which is not always a good thing. They can be rather bossy and smothering, interfering in the lives of others when they would do better to leave well enough alone. Often they see all ills as their problem, and are constantly weighed down with the sorrows of the world.

Lunar Pisceans are also the olympian worriers of the zodiac – not even the most motherly

global warming and the possibility of collision with meteorites as not only imminent, but also intensely personal problems. Unfortunately, by their very nature these particular problems are intractable, adding to the burden of Lunar Piscean worry.

RELATIONSHIPS

These people love their friends almost as much as they love family, and would go to the ends of the Earth for them if they felt it was necessary. They are loyal and supportive, rarely letting relationships grow cold through lack of contact, and are usually extremely dependable in a crisis. For their friends there will always be a shoulder to cry on, a hot meal and a sofa to sleep on. And this is despite the fact that Lunar Pisceans types often find that people take advantage of their good nature, using and exploiting their soft-heartedness with no regard for their needs.

*Many of them are committed to religious or
mystical belief systems and ponder deeply over the
great questions of life and death*

Lunar Pisceans are rarely content to live alone. They see their own worth in terms of how much they are loved by others, not understanding that they themselves need to love just as much, if not more. But if the reality of love never quite matches up to their romantic expectations, they are happy to make believe, living in a world of illusion – perhaps even seriously deluding themselves. The presence of their co-ruler Neptune encourages escapism, which can become a serious threat to their mental well-being. A safe way of channelling this trait is in creative pursuits, where imagination can take a concrete form without any danger to the psyche.

They are intensely loyal to their life partners and may be happy to put their own ambitions on hold while their partners struggle to get to the top. This is not always desirable, though, and can eventually make for a tense home atmosphere of resentment and rivalry.

Sexually, Lunar Pisceans are eager, sensuous and imaginative. They enjoy erotic caresses and know how to wed deep feelings of love with shows of intense passion, all to the great delight of their partners.

Lunar Pisceans usually have lovely, comfortable homes, tastefully and often luxuriously furnished. Minimalism or austere chic is not for them. They like a home to look tidy and clean but definitely lived in. They see it as a haven for their friends, neighbours and lame dogs. Many Lunar Piscean homes have had the *feng shui* overhaul to achieve the maximum harmony possible, and the resulting relaxed, welcoming atmosphere is balm to the soul of everyone who enters.

These people detest being ridiculed or humiliated. Their self-esteem is low enough as it is, but criticism reduces it even further, and they are vulnerable for a very long time afterwards. Even well-meant constructive criticism is a deeply personal slight, a rejection of their whole selves. Their feelings are easily hurt, which is why some people with this Moon placement hide behind a tough exterior. Seeming hard, even indifferent to everything that fate can throw at them, conceals the hurt inside.

LUNAR PISCEAN CHILDREN

Pisceans often fear rejection – especially in the context of intimate relationships. Young Lunar Pisceans tend not to have a happy time, and often have difficulty facing the grim facts of life when confronted with them at an early age. If a parent or sibling should become gravely ill or die, the resulting insecurity lays down a pattern of desperation and desire to be loved that typifies this sign in later life.

Sometimes fragile children, they seek compensation for life's hard knocks by becoming teacher's pet, burying their heads in books or in an elaborate fantasy world. Daydreaming can become a way of life for unhappy Lunar Pisceans.

With their own children, they are loving and warm, but may communicate their own sense of worthlessness to them. They need to build up their children's self-esteem and confidence, a process that may help with their own self-image.

Their tendency to be fussy and over-protective can be counter-productive, however, alienating the people they love and for whom they want only the best.

CAREER

Glamorous and creative work appeals to Lunar Pisceans more than mundane routine in offices, shops or factories. They are good with their hands and make excellent dress designers, florists and craftspeople of all kinds. They also make good, imaginative cooks and excel at preparing more unusual and exotic foreign dishes. Because they are fond of detail, they can be very well suited to the complex worlds of computer graphics and engineering.

Many people with this Moon placement are natural dancers, or can earn a decent living as professionals or teachers. Most Pisceans, either Solar or Lunar, love music in all its forms and are happy to surround themselves with it, both at work and home. Some may play an instrument professionally.

An increasing number of Lunar Pisceans are attempting to earn a living by harnessing their psychic powers, perhaps as mediums, channellers or tarot card readers. Most have a passionate interest in the paranormal, mystical and unexplained, and can often be found freezing on night-long 'ghost watches' at haunted houses, or on the tops of hills searching the skies for UFOs. They feel part of the great unseen cosmic dance and want to understand it.

These are meaningful dreamers, whose lives are full of astonishing coincidences. They are very superstitious and tend to interpret weird events as omens. Having a strongly developed intuition, they can be very successful clairvoyants.

However, there is a certain danger in becoming too obsessed with the unseen world and not properly connecting to this one. Problems can arise, too, from Pisceans deluding themselves about the extent of their powers. Where possible, budding psychics should have disciplined training of the kind available in development circles for mediums.

HEALTH

Since they are so hypersensitive, Lunar Pisceans should take care not to overtax their rather limited strength and lay themselves open to unwanted influences that can drain their vital energy. They need to get plenty of fresh air and exercise and eat properly at regular intervals. They could top up blood sugar levels by nibbling at dried fruit every hour or so, and should avoid caffeine and sugar, which actually depletes energy after the initial 'rush'.

Traditionally, they tend to suffer from blood disorders, respiratory problems and heart trouble in later life. They also face a host of psycho-somatic ailments and allergies. This is not a physically robust sign, and those born under it should learn to take great care of themselves.

MOON CHARTS

In the charts below, the position of the Moon is shown at midnight on alternate days. To find your Moon Sign, find the day of your birthday or the day before if you were born on an even-numbered day. The sign given for that day is your Moon Sign, and the figure next to it indicates the number of degrees of that sign (the maximum number of degrees for any one sign is 29). The number of degrees indicates the greater or lesser extent to which you are influenced by that sign. Unless you were born on or just after midnight, you will have to add half a degree per hour to find the number of degrees for your sign. If your counting takes you beyond 29 degrees, then you move on to the next sign of the Zodiac. For example, if you were born just after midnight on 19 June 1961, then your sign would be 1Vi (one degree of Virgo as given in chart for 1961 on page 249). If you were born at 10.00am, then you would add five degrees (half a degree for each hour after midnight), which gives you 6Vi – six degrees of Virgo. If you were born at midnight on 20 June 1961, then add 12 degrees, which gives you 13Vi. If you were born at 8.00am on 20 June, you would add 16 degrees, which gives you 17Vi.

If you were born on 17 May 1962 at or just after midnight, your sign would be 25Li (25 degrees of Libra as given in the chart for 1962 on page 249). If you were born at noon on the 17th, then you would add six degrees, which completes the cycle for Libra (25 plus four gives the maximum number of degrees of 29) and pushes you two degrees into the next sign, giving you 2Sc – two degrees of Scorpio. If you were born eight hours later at 8.00pm on the 17th, you would add a further four degrees to arrive at 6Sc – six degrees of Scorpio. Adding a further half degree for every subsequent hour up to midnight on the 19th would bring you to 20Sc, which, as you can see, is the figure already given for this day in the chart for 1962.

These figure are based on Greenwich Mean Time/Universal Time (UT). If you were born in another time zone, then take into account the number of hours that it is ahead of, or behind, UT, and add or subtract another half degree per hour. For example, New York is five hours ahead of UT, so anyone born in New York should add another 2.5 degrees. Someone born in Bangalore, India, should subtract 2.5 degrees because Bangalore is five hours behind UT.

Finally, for an absolutely accurate placement, it is best to consult an astrologer and provide him or her with precise details of the time and place of your birth.

1930

	Jan	Feb	Mar	Apr	May	Jun	Jul	Aug	Sep	Oct	Nov	Dec
1	20Cp	5Pi	14Pi	1Ta	7Ge	0Le	0Vi	1Sc	19Sg	22Cp	6Pi	8Ar
3	14Aq	19Pi	9Ar	27Ta	5Cn	29Le	8Li	27Sc	13Cp	16Aq	0Ar	2Ta
5	8Pi	24Ar	4Ta	25Ge	4Le	27Vi	4Sc	22Sg	7Aq	10Pi	24Ar	27Ta
7	2Ar	20Ta	0Ge	23Cn	2Vi	24Li	0Sg	16Cp	1Pi	4Ar	20Ta	26Ge
9	28Ar	18Ge	28Ge	22Le	0Li	20Sc	25Sg	10Aq	25Pi	28Ar	17Ge	27Cn
11	25Ta	18Cn	27Cn	20Vi	28Li	16Sg	19Cp	4Pi	19Ar	24Ta	14Cn	24Le
13	24Ge	18Le	18Le	19Li	24Sc	11Cp	14Aq	28Pi	14Ta	20Ge	13Le	22Vi
15	25Cn	18Vi	18Vi	16Sc	20Sg	5Aq	7Pi	22Ar	10Ge	18Cn	11Vi	20Li
17	25Le	17Li	17Li	12Sg	14Cp	28Aq	1Ar	17Ta	7Cn	16Le	9Li	17Sc
19	24Vi	13Sc	21Sc	7Cp	8Aq	22Pi	25Ar	14Ge	6Le	14Vi	7Sc	13Sg
21	22Li	8Sg	16Sg	1Aq	2Pi	17Ar	21Ta	12Cn	6Vi	14Li	5Sg	12Cp
23	17Sc	2Cp	11Cp	24Aq	26Pi	13Ta	19Ge	12Le	6Li	13Sc	4Cp	4Aq
25	12Sg	26Cp	4Aq	19Pi	22Ar	11Ge	19Cn	13Vi	5Sc	10Sg	26Cp	28Aq
27	6Cp	20Aq	28Aq	14Ar	18Ta	10Cn	19Le	12Li	2Sg	6Cp	20Aq	21Pi
29	29Cp		23Pi	10Ta	17Ge	10Le	19Vi	10Sc	28Sg	0Aq	14Pi	15Ar
31	23Aq		18Ar		16Cn		18Li	6Sg		24Aq		10Ta

1931

	Jan	Feb	Mar	Apr	May	Jun	Jul	Aug	Sep	Oct	Nov	Dec
1	23Ta	13Cn	21Cn	14Vi	23Li	14Sg	19Cp	5Pi	19Ta	22Ta	9Cn	11Le
3	20Ge	12Le	20Le	14Li	22Sc	11Cp	15Aq	29Pi	13Ta	16Ge	5Le	13Vi
5	19Cn	13Vi	21Vi	14Sc	20Sg	8Aq	9Pi	23Ar	7Ge	10Le	2Vi	13Li
7	19Le	12Li	21Li	12Sg	16Cp	1Pi	3Ar	17Ta	3Cn	9Le	2Li	11Sc
9	18Vi	10Sc	20Sc	8Cp	11Aq	25Pi	26Ar	12Ge	1Le	8Vi	2Sc	10Sg
11	17Li	7Sg	16Sg	3Aq	5Pi	18Ar	21Ta	9Cn	0Vi	8Li	2Sg	8Cp
13	14Sc	2Cp	12Cp	27Aq	29Pi	13Ta	17Ge	7Le	0Li	8Sc	1Cp	5Aq
15	10Sg	27Cp	6Aq	20Pi	22Ar	9Ge	14Cn	7Vi	0Sc	8Sg	27Cp	0Pi
17	5Cp	21Aq	0Pi	14Ar	17Ta	5Cn	13Le	6Li	29Sc	5Cp	21Aq	24Pi
19	0Aq	15Pi	23Pi	8Ta	13Ge	3Le	12Vi	5Sc	26Sg	1Aq	16Pi	18Ar
21	24Aq	8Ar	17Ar	2Ge	11Cn	2Vi	11Li	3Sg	21Cp	25Aq	10Ar	12Ta
23	18Pi	2Ta	11Ta	29Ge	9Le	1Li	9Sc	0Cp	17Aq	20Pi	4Ta	6Ge
25	11Ar	27Ta	5Ge	26Cn	8Vi	0Sc	7Sg	27Cp	11Pi	14Ar	28Ta	2Cn
27	6Ta	23Ge	2Cn	24Le	8Li	28Sc	3Cp	20Aq	4Ar	7Ta	23Ge	29Cn
29	2Ge		0Le	23Vi	7Sc	25Sg	29Cp	14Pi	28Ar	1Ge	20Cn	29Le
31	28Ge		29Le		7Sg		23Aq	7Ar		26Ge		24Vi

1932

	Jan	Feb	Mar	Apr	May	Jun	Jul	Aug	Sep	Oct	Nov	Dec
1	8Li	1Sg	26Sg	15Aq	18Pi	2Ta	5Ge	21Cn	10Vi	18Li	12Sg	20Cp
3	6Sc	29Sg	22Cp	9Pi	12Ar	26Ta	1Cn	19Le	9Li	15Sc	11Cp	17Aq
5	5Sg	25Cp	17Aq	3Ar	6Ta	21Ge	25Cn	15Vi	8Sc	17Sg	8Aq	13Pi
7	3Cp	21Aq	12Pi	27Ar	29Ta	15Cn	21Le	13Li	7Sg	15Cp	4Pi	8Ar
9	0Aq	16Pi	6Ar	20Ta	24Ge	11Le	18Vi	11Sc	5Cp	12Aq	29Pi	2Ta
11	25Aq	10Ar	0Ta	14Ge	18Cn	8Vi	16Li	9Sg	2Aq	7Pi	23Ar	26Ta
13	20Pi	3Ta	24Ta	9Cn	14Le	5Li	14Sc	7Cp	28Aq	2Ar	17Ta	20Ge
15	14Ar	27Ta	18Ge	5Le	11Vi	4Sc	14Sg	5Aq	23Pi	26Ar	11Ge	13Cn
17	7Ta	22Ge	12Cn	2Vi	10Li	4Sg	13Cp	2Pi	17Ar	20Ta	4Cn	7Le
19	2Ge	18Cn	10Le	1Li	10Sc	3Cp	10Aq	27Pi	11Ta	13Ge	29Cn	4Vi
21	27Ge	16Le	8Vi	2Sc	10Sg	2Aq	6Pi	21Ar	5Ge	7Cn	25Le	2Li
23	24Cn	15Vi	8Li	2Sg	10Cp	28Aq	1Ar	15Ta	29Ge	2Le	21Vi	28Li
25	21Le	15Li	9Sc	1Cp	7Aq	23Pi	26Ar	9Ge	24Cn	26Le	19Li	28Sc
27	20Vi	14Sc	8Sg	28Cp	3Pi	17Ar	19Ta	3Cn	20Le	26Vi	19Sc	28Sg
29	19Li	12Sg	6Cp	24Aq	27Pi	11Ta	13Ge	29Cn	18Vi	26Li	20Sg	27Cp
31	17Sc		2Aq		21Ar		7Cn	26Le		25Aq		

1933

	Jan	Feb	Mar	Apr	May	Jun	Jul	Aug	Sep	Oct	Nov	Dec
1	9Pi	24Ar	2Ta	16Ge	18Cn	4Vi	9Li	2Sg	25Cp	3Pi	22Ar	26Ta
3	4Ar	18Ta	26Ta	10Cn	12Le	0Li	7Sc	1Cp	24Aq	27Pi	16Ta	20Ge
5	28Ar	12Ge	20Ge	4Le	8Vi	28Li	7Sg	1Aq	22Pi	22Ar	10Ge	14Cn
7	22Ta	6Cn	14Cn	0Vi	5Li	28Sc	7Cp	1Pi	21Ar	17Ta	4Cn	7Le
9	16Ge	1Le	9Le	27Vi	4Sc	29Sg	7Aq	27Pi	13Ar	15Ge	29Cn	2Vi
11	10Cn	27Le	5Vi	26Li	5Sg	29Cp	5Pi	23Ar	15Ta	9Cn	23Le	26Vi
13	5Le	24Vi	3Li	26Sc	5Cp	28Aq	1Ar	18Ta	9Ge	4Le	18Vi	23Li
15	1Vi	21Li	2Sc	25Sg	4Aq	23Pi	27Ar	11Ge	3Cn	28Le	15Li	22Sc
17	27Vi	20Sc	2Sg	24Cp	1Pi	18Ar	21Ta	5Cn	27Cn	24Vi	14Sc	22Sg
19	25Li	18Sg	29Sg	21Aq	27Pi	12Ta	15Ge	29Cn	21Le	21Li	14Sg	23Cp
21	23Sc	16Cp	27Cp	17Pi	21Ar	5Ge	8Cn	23Le	16Vi	18Sc	14Cp	20Pi
23	22Sg	14Aq	24Aq	12Ar	15Ta	0Cn	3Le	20Vi	11Sc	20Sg	13Aq	20Pi
25	21Cp	11Pi	20Pi	6Ta	9Ge	24Cn	1Vi	18Li	9Sg	18Cp	10Pi	16Ar
27	19Aq	7Ar	15Ar	0Ge	3Cn	18Le	29Vi	14Sc	8Cp	16Aq	4Ar	11Ta
29	16Pi		10Ta	24Ge	28Cn	13Vi	28Li	14Sg	9Aq	15Pi	28Ar	5Ge
31	12Ar		4Ge		21Le		11Cp	9Ar		29Ge		

1934

	Jan	Feb	Mar	Apr	May	Jun	Jul	Aug	Sep	Oct	Nov	Dec
1	11Cn	25Le	4Vi	22Li	29Sc	22Cp	1Pi	22Ar	9Ge	12Cn	25Le	27Vi
3	4Le	20Vi	19Vi	29Sc	28Sg	21Aq	29Pi	18Ta	4Cn	6Le	19Vi	22Li
5	28Le	16Li	26Li	17Sg	26Cp	19Pi	26Ar	13Ge	27Cn	29Le	14Li	19Sc
7	23Vi	12Sc	23Sc	16Cp	25Aq	16Ar	21Ta	7Cn	21Le	24Vi	11Sc	17Sg
9	19Li	10Sg	20Sg	14Aq	22Pi	12Ta	16Ge	0Le	15Vi	19Li	8Sg	16Cp
11	16Sc	9Cp	19Cp	12Pi	19Ar	7Ge	10Cn	24Le	10Li	15Sc	7Cp	15Aq
13	15Sg	9Aq	18Aq	9Ar	15Ta	1Cn	3Le	18Vi	5Sc	12Sg	5Aq	14Pi
15	16Cp	8Pi	17Pi	6Ta	10Ge	25Cn	27Le	13Li	1Sg	10Cp	3Pi	12Ar
17	16Aq	7Ar	14Ar	2Ge	4Cn	18Le	21Vi	8Sc	29Sg	8Aq	1Ar	8Ta
19	15Pi	3Ta	11Ta	26Ge	28Cn	12Vi	16Li	5Sg	28Cp	7Pi	29Ar	4Ge
21	12Ar	28Ta	6Ge	20Cn	21Le	7Li	12Sc	3Cp	27Aq	5Ar	25Ta	29Ge
23	8Ta	22Cn	0Cn	14Le	16Vi	3Sc	10Sg	3Aq	26Pi	1Ta	21Ge	24Cn
25	2Ge	16Cn	24Cn	8Vi	12Li	1Sg	9Cp	3Pi	25Ar	0Ge	16Cn	17Le
27	26Ge	10Le	18Le	4Li	9Sc	1Cp	10Aq	3Ar	22Ta	26Ge	9Le	11Vi
29	20Cn		13Vi	1Sc	8Sg	1Aq	10Pi	1Ta	18Ge	20Cn	3Vi	5Li
31	13Le		8Li		7Cp		8Ar	27Ta		13Le		0Sc

1935

	Jan	Feb	Mar	Apr	May	Jun	Jul	Aug	Sep	Oct	Nov	Dec
1	13Sc	3Cp	12Cp	5Pi	14Ar	5Ge	10Cn	23Le	9Li	25Le	0Cp	7Aq
3	11Sg	3Aq	11Aq	5Ar	12Ta	1Cn	4Le	19Vi	3Sc	8Sg	27Cp	5Pi
5	10Cp	3Pi	11Pi	4Ta	10Ge	26Cn	28Le	12Li	28Sc	2Cp	25Aq	4Ar
7	10Aq	3Ar	12Ar	2Ge	6Cn	20Le	22Vi	7Sc	24Sg	0Aq	23Pi	2Ta
9	10Pi	2Ta	10Ta	28Ge	1Le	14Vi	16Li	2Sg	21Cp	29Aq	23Ar	1Ge
11	8Ar	28Ta	7Ge	24Cn	24Le	8Li	11Sc	28Sg	21Aq	29Pi	22Ta	29Ge
13	5Ta	23Ge	2Cn	16Le	18Vi	3Sc	7Sg	27Cp	21Pi	0Ta	21Ge	25Cn
15	1Ge	17Cn	26Cn	10Vi	12Li	29Sc	5Cp	27Aq	21Ar	0Ge	19Cn	20Le
17	26Ge	11Le	20Le	4Li	8Sc	26Sg	4Aq	28Pi	20Ta	28Ge	14Le	14Vi
19	20Cn	5Vi	13Vi	29Li	5Sg	27Cp	4Pi	27Ar	17Ge	25Cn	7Vi	7Li
21	14Le	28Vi	8Li	25Sc	4Cp	24Aq	3Ar	25Ta	13Cn	16Le	0Li	2Sc
23	8Vi	23Li	2Sc	22Sg	4Aq	23Pi	1Ta	21Ge	7Le	21Vi	3Li	26Sc
25	2Li	18Sc	28Sc	18Cp	27Aq	20Ar	28Ta	16Cn	1Vi	3Li	18Sc	23Sg
27	26Li	14Sg	24Sg	16Aq	25Pi	18Ta	26Ge	10Le	25Vi	29Li	14Sg	20Cp
29	22Sc		21Cp	15Pi	24Ar	16Ge	24Cn	4Vi	18Li	25Sc	10Cp	18Aq
31	19Sg		20Aq		21Ta		13Le	27Vi		17Sg		16Pi

1936

	Jan	Feb	Mar	Apr	May	Jun	Jul	Aug	Sep	Oct	Nov	Dec
1	1Ar	23Ta	17Ge	5Le	8Vi	22Li	25Sc	11Cp	1Pi	9Ar	3Ge	10Cn
3	29Ar	20Ge	13Cn	29Le	2Li	16Sc	20Sg	8Aq	0Ar	9Ta	28Ge	6Le
5	27Ta	16Cn	8Le	23Vi	26Li	12Sg	16Cp	6Pi	0Ta	9Ge	25Cn	29Le
7	24Ge	11Le	2Vi	17Li	20Sc	6Cp	13Aq	5Ar	0Ge	7Cn	20Le	28Vi
9	20Cn	6Vi	26Vi	11Sc	14Sg	3Aq	11Pi	4Ta	27Ge	3Le	15Vi	22Li
11	15Le	0Li	20Li	5Sg	10Cp	0Pi	9Ar	2Ge	23Cn	28Le	13Li	16Sc
13	10Vi	23Li	14Sc	0Cp	6Aq	28Pi	7Ta	0Cn	18Le	22Vi	7Sc	9Sg
15	3Li	17Sc	8Sg	25Cp	3Pi	27Ar	6Ge	26Cn	13Vi	16Li	1Sg	4Cp
17	27Li	12Sg	3Cp	23Aq	2Ar	26Ta	5Cn	21Le	7Li	10Sc	25Sg	29Cp
19	22Sc	8Cp	0Aq	22Pi	2Ta	24Ge	2Le	15Vi	1Sc	4Sg	21Cp	25Aq
21	17Sg	6Aq	29Aq	23Ar	1Ge	22Cn	26Le	9Li	25Sc	28Sg	15Aq	22Pi
23	14Cp	6Pi	29Pi	23Ta	0Cn	18Le	21Vi	3Sc	19Sg	22Cp	12Pi	20Ar
25	13Aq	6Ar	0Ta	22Ge	27Cn	13Vi	15Li	28Sc	14Cp	19Aq	11Ar	19Ta
27	12Pi	6Ta	29Ta	19Cn	22Le	7Li	9Sc	23Sg	10Aq	18Pi	11Ta	18Ge
29	11Ar	4Ge	27Ge	14Le	17Vi	1Sc	3Sg	19Cp	9Pi	17Ar	11Ge	18Cn
31	10Ta		23Cn		11Li		28Sg	16Aq		17Ta		15Le

1937

	Jan	Feb	Mar	Apr	May	Jun	Jul	Aug	Sep	Oct	Nov	Dec
1	29Le	14Li	2Li	6Cp	25Aq	1Ar	24Ta	17Cn	25Le	13Li	13Li	17Sc
3	24Vi	8Sc	16Sc	29Sg	3Aq	21Pi	23Ge	15Le	21Vi	11Sc	8Sg	10Sg
5	18Li	1Sg	9Sg	24Cp	28Aq	19Ar	21Cn	12Li	21Vi	11Sc	4Cp	4Cp
7	12Sc	26Sg	3Cp	20Aq	26Pi	19Ta	20Le	8Li	11Sc	25Sg	28Cp	28Cp
9	6Sg	21Cp	29Cp	18Pi	25Ar	19Ge	17Vi	3Sc	5Sg	19Cp	23Aq	22Aq
11	0Cp	17Aq	26Aq	17Ar	26Ta	19Cn	15Li	27Sc	13Li	15Cp	29Sg	17Pi
13	25Cp	15Pi	24Pi	17Ta	26Ge	17Le	11Sc	7Sg	21Sg	23Cp	9Ar	14Ar
15	22Aq	14Ar	23Ar	17Ge	25Cn	14Vi	17Li	1Sg	6Cp	18Aq	6Ar	13Ta
17	19Pi	12Ta	21Ta	15Cn	22Le	7Li	10Sg	25Cp	10Aq	14Pi	5Ta	13Ge
19	17Ar	10Ge	20Ge	11Le	17Vi	1Sc	5Cp	19Pi	6Pi	12Ar	5Ge	13Cn
21	15Ta	8Cn	18Cn	6Vi	11Li	26Sc	28Cp	13Ar	3Ar	11Ta	5Cn	11Le
23	14Ge	5Le	15Le	0Li	5Sc	20Sg	23Aq	11Ta	3Ta	11Ge	4Le	11Vi
25	12Cn	2Vi	11Vi	29Sc	29Sc	14Cp	18Aq	9Ar	1Ge	10Cn	2Vi	7Li
27	10Le	27Vi	7Li	23Sc	23Sg	8Aq	15Pi	8Ta	0Cn	8Le	28Vi	1Sc
29	6Vi		0Sc	17Cp	17Cp	7Pi	12Ar	7Ge	28Cn	5Vi	23Li	25Sc
31	2Li		24Sc		12Aq		10Ta	3Cn		1Li		19Sg

1938

	Jan	Feb	Mar	Apr	May	Jun	Jul	Aug	Sep	Oct	Nov	Dec
1	1Cp	16Aq	25Aq	15Ar	20Ta	13Cn	22Le	13Li	29Sc	1Cp	15Aq	17Pi
3	25Cp	11Pi	21Pi	11Ta	19Ge	13Le	20Vi	9Sc	25Sg	25Cp	9Pi	12Ar
5	19Aq	7Ar	17Ar	9Ge	18Cn	11Vi	17Li	5Sg	21Cp	19Aq	4Ar	9Ta
7	14Pi	4Ta	15Ta	7Cn	17Le	7Li	12Sc	1Cp	16Aq	14Pi	1Ta	8Ge
9	10Ar	2Ge	13Ge	6Le	14Vi	3Sc	6Sg	26Cp	10Pi	9Ar	29Ta	8Cn
11	8Ta	0Cn	11Cn	4Vi	10Li	27Sc	0Cp	20Aq	4Ar	6Ta	28Ge	7Le
13	6Ge	28Cn	9Le	1Li	5Sc	21Sg	24Cp	14Pi	28Ar	4Ge	26Cn	6Vi
15	6Cn	25Le	6Vi	27Li	0Sg	15Cp	18Aq	8Ar	24Ta	2Cn	24Le	4Li
17	6Le	22Vi	5Li	23Sc	24Sg	9Aq	12Pi	2Ta	21Ge	0Le	23Vi	0Sc
19	5Vi	18Li	2Sc	18Sg	18Cp	3Pi	7Ar	27Ta	20Cn	29Le	20Li	25Sc
21	3Li	13Sc	28Sc	12Cp	12Aq	27Pi	2Ta	24Ge	18Le	27Vi	17Sc	19Sg
23	28Li	8Sg	23Sg	6Aq	6Pi	22Ar	28Ta	22Cn	16Vi	24Li	11Sg	14Cp
25	22Sc	6Cp	18Cp	0Pi	0Ar	18Ta	24Ge	19Le	12Li	20Sc	5Cp	7Aq
27	16Sg	0Aq	11Aq	24Pi	24Ar	14Ge	21Cn	15Vi	7Sc	15Sg	29Cp	1Pi
29	9Cp		5Pi	18Ar	18Ta	11Cn	18Le	12Li	3Sg	9Cp	23Aq	25Pi
31	4Aq		29Pi		13Ge		16Vi	9Sc		3Aq		20Ar

1939

	Jan	Feb	Mar	Apr	May	Jun	Jul	Aug	Sep	Oct	Nov	Dec
1	3Ta	24Ge	3Cn	27Le	5Li	26Sc	0Cp	15Aq	0Ar	3Ta	22Ge	0Le
3	1Ge	24Cn	2Le	26Vi	2Sc	22Sg	24Cp	9Pi	24Ar	2Ge	20Cn	29Le
5	1Cn	24Le	2Vi	25Li	0Sg	16Cp	18Aq	3Ar	19Ta	1Cn	18Le	26Vi
7	1Le	24Vi	2Li	22Sc	26Sg	10Aq	12Pi	27Ar	15Ge	0Le	16Vi	24Li
9	1Vi	23Li	1Sc	18Sg	20Cp	4Pi	6Ar	21Ta	12Cn	21Le	14Li	22Sc
11	0Li	19Sc	27Sc	12Cp	14Aq	28Pi	1Ta	19Ge	12Le	21Vi	11Sc	18Sg
13	27Li	14Sg	22Sg	6Aq	8Pi	23Ar	28Ta	18Cn	12Vi	20Li	7Sg	13Cp
15	22Sc	8Cp	16Cp	0Pi	2Ar	19Ta	25Ge	18Le	11Li	19Sc	2Cp	7Aq
17	17Sg	1Aq	9Aq	24Pi	28Ar	17Ge	25Cn	18Vi	9Sc	15Sg	26Cp	1Pi
19	11Cp	25Aq	4Pi	19Ar	24Ta	16Cn	25Le	18Li	6Sg	11Cp	20Aq	26Pi
21	4Aq	19Pi	28Pi	15Ta	22Ge	16Le	25Vi	16Sc	3Cp	6Aq	14Pi	16Ta
23	28Aq	14Ar	23Ar	12Cn	21Cn	15Vi	23Li	12Sg	29Aq	29Pi	13Ar	16Ta
25	22Pi	11Ta	19Ta	10Le	20Le	15Li	6Cp	21Aq	23Pi	8Ta	13Ar	11Cn
27	17Ar	5Ge	16Ge	8Vi	18Vi	9Sc	0Aq	15Pi	18Ar	4Ge	8Le	11Cn
29	12Ta		13Cn	7Li	16Li	5Sg	24Aq	9Ar	13Ta	2Cn	5Vi	10Le
31	9Ge		12Le		15Sc		18Pi	4Ge		0Le		9Vi

1940

	Jan	Feb	Mar	Apr	May	Jun	Jul	Aug	Sep	Oct	Nov	Dec
1	23Vi	15Sc	8Sg	26Cp	12Aq	1Ar	14Ta	1Cn	22Le	0Li	23Sc	0Cp
3	21Li	12Sg	4Cp	20Aq	6Pi	27Ar	10Ge	28Cn	21Vi	29Li	20Sg	24Aq
5	18Sc	7Cp	29Cp	14Pi	1Ar	22Ta	6Cn	24Le	21Li	28Sc	20Cp	24Aq
7	15Sg	2Aq	23Aq	8Ar	25Ar	17Ge	1Le	27Vi	21Sc	28Sg	18Cp	18Pi
9	10Cp	26Aq	17Pi	1Ta	5Ge	24Cn	3Vi	1Sc	24Cp	10Pi	27Ar	5Ta
11	5Aq	20Pi	10Ar	1Ge	1Cn	21Le	14Ge	29Sc	19Aq	13Ar	27Ta	5Ta
13	29Aq	13Ar	4Ta	21Ge	20Cn	21Vi	29Li	21Sg	13Pi	10Ta	25Ge	29Ta
15	23Pi	7Ta	29Ta	17Cn	19Le	21Li	18Sc	16Cp	7Ar	4Ge	21Cn	25Ge
17	17Ar	2Ge	24Ge	15Le	17Vi	17Sc	24Sg	11Aq	1Ta	29Ge	16Le	21Cn
19	11Ta	28Ge	21Cn	13Vi	15Li	15Sg	21Cp	5Pi	26Ta	24Cn	10Vi	15Li
21	7Ge	27Cn	20Le	14Li	14Sc	12Cp	16Aq	29Pi	20Ge	18Le	7Li	15Li
23	4Cn	27Le	20Vi	13Sc	13Sg	8Aq	11Pi	24Ar	14Cn	12Vi	4Vi	14Vi
25	4Le	27Vi	20Li	12Cp	9Cp	2Pi	4Ar	18Ta	8Le	2Li	2Li	11Sc
27	4Vi	27Li	20Sc	9Aq	5Aq	26Pi	28Ar	13Ge	2Vi	6Sc	28Li	22Ar
29	3Li	25Sc	17Sg	4Pi	0Pi	20Ar	22Ta	9Cn	0Vi	0Sc	8Sc	15Ta
31	2Sc		13Cp		24Pi		18Ge	7Le		0Sc		6Aq

1941

	Jan	Feb	Mar	Apr	May	Jun	Jul	Aug	Sep	Oct	Nov	Dec
1	19Aq	3Ar	12Ar	25Ta	29Ge	16Le	23Vi	16Sc	9Cp	16Aq	4Ar	7Ta
3	14Pi	27Ar	5Ta	19Ge	23Cn	13Vi	21Li	11Sg	3Aq	12Pi	29Ar	2Ge
5	8Ar	21Ta	29Ta	14Cn	19Le	11Li	20Sc	7Cp	29Aq	8Ar	24Ta	28Ge
7	1Ta	15Ge	23Ge	10Le	17Vi	11Sc	19Sg	3Aq	24Pi	4Ta	19Ge	23Cn
9	25Ta	11Cn	19Cn	8Vi	16Li	10Sg	18Cp	7Pi	23Ar	25Ta	9Cn	17Le
11	20Ge	8Le	16Le	8Li	16Sc	10Cp	16Aq	0Ar	17Ta	17Ge	13Cn	11Vi
13	16Cn	6Vi	15Vi	8Sc	16Sg	9Aq	12Pi	24Ar	11Ge	5Cn	8Le	5Li
15	13Le	4Sc	14Li	8Sg	16Cp	6Pi	7Ar	18Ta	5Cn	0Le	1Vi	28Li
17	11Vi	4Sc	14Sc	7Cp	13Aq	2Ar	1Ta	14Ge	0Le	4Vi	25Li	4Sg
19	9Li	3Sg	13Sg	5Aq	9Pi	27Ar	25Ta	9Cn	24Le	29Vi	19Sc	27Sc
21	8Sc	0Cp	11Cp	29Aq	2Ar	24Ge	19Ge	5Le	20Vi	25Li	26Sg	4Cp
23	6Sg	23Aq	8Aq	22Pi	26Ar	19Cn	15Cn	1Vi	16Li	20Sc	23Sg	16Pi
25	4Cp	23Aq	2Pi	17Ar	19Ta	15Le	11Le	0Li	13Sc	2Cp	23Sg	15Aq
27	17Pi	17Pi	26Pi	13Ta	16Ge	11Vi	9Vi	27Li	13Sg	20Cp	22Cp	14Pi
29	17Aq		20Ar	9Ge	13Cn	8Li	7Li	25Sc	13Cp	20Aq	22Aq	14Ar
31	21Pi		14Ta		3Le		7Sc	23Sc		9Ge		9Ge

1942

	Jan	Feb	Mar	Apr	May	Jun	Jul	Aug	Sep	Oct	Nov	Dec
1	21Ge	7Le	15Le	3Li	11Sc	29Sg	1Aq	19Ta	21Ge	5Le	7Vi	7Vi
3	15Cn	2Vi	11Vi	2Sc	15Sg	4Aq	11Pi	29Ar	13Ge	15Cn	29Le	2Li
5	10Le	29Vi	9Li	2Sg	10Cp	2Pi	7Ta	21Ge	7Cn	9Le	24Vi	29Li
7	6Vi	26Li	5Sc	0Cp	9Aq	28Pi	2Ta	17Ge	0Le	4Vi	21Li	29Sc
9	2Li	24Sc	5Sg	26Cp	6Pi	24Ar	11Cn	20Cn	25Le	29Vi	20Sc	29Sg
11	29Li	23Sg	4Cp	25Aq	4Ar	21Ta	20Ge	5Le	21Vi	27Li	20Sg	29Cp
13	28Sc	21Cp	2Aq	22Pi	1Ta	16Ge	29Cn	29Le	18Li	26Sc	18Cp	25Aq
15	28Sg	20Aq	29Aq	17Ar	26Ta	10Cn	5Le	23Vi	16Sc	25Sg	18Aq	25Pi
17	27Cp	17Pi	25Pi	12Ta	14Ge	4Le	3Vi	21Li	14Sg	23Cp	15Pi	19Ar
19	26Aq	13Ar	21Ar	6Ge	8Cn	28Le	28Vi	12Sc	21Aq	21Cn	11Ar	16Ta
21	22Pi	8Ta	15Ta	0Cn	2Le	22Vi	12Li	9Sg	9Aq	18Pi	18Pi	1Ge
23	18Ar	2Ge	9Ge	24Cn	26Le	16Li	1Sc	6Cp	8Pi	15Ar	1Ge	4Cn
25	12Ta	25Ge	3Cn	18Le	21Vi	13Sc	0Sg	6Aq	6Ar	10Ta	28Ge	28Cn
27	6Ge	20Cn	27Cn	14Vi	20Li	11Sg	0Cp	6Pi	3Ta	5Ge	22Cn	16Vi
29	29Ge		23Le	11Li	20Sc	12Cp	1Aq	4Ar	27Ta	27Ge	16Le	9Li
31	24Cn		19Vi		20Sg		19Pi	7Ta		23Cn		11Li

1943

	Jan	Feb	Mar	Apr	May	Jun	Jul	Aug	Sep	Oct	Nov	Dec
1	24Li	15Sg	24Cp	17Pi	27Ar	17Ta	12Cn	6Le	20Vi	24Li	13Sc	22Cp
3	22Sc	15Cp	24Cp	17Pi	24Ar	12Ge	15Cn	1Vi	23Li	20Sc	11Cp	20Aq
5	22Sg	15Aq	23Pi	14Ta	20Ta	6Cn	23Li	10Sc	13Sg	10Cp	9Aq	18Pi
7	22Cp	15Pi	23Pi	12Ta	12Ge	0Le	2Vi	18Li	6Sg	14Cp	8Pi	16Ar
9	22Aq	13Ar	21Ar	8Ge	10Cn	24Le	4Sc	3Sg	3Aq	12Pi	4Ta	10Ge
11	21Pi	9Ta	17Ta	2Cn	4Le	18Vi	21Li	10Sc	3Aq	12Pi	4Ta	10Ge
13	19Ar	3Ge	11Ge	26Cn	29Le	16Li	16Sc	9Sg	3Pi	9Ar	2Ge	6Cn
15	13Ta	28Ge	6Cn	19Le	22Vi	9Sc	16Sg	9Cp	3Ar	9Ta	27Ge	29Cn
17	7Ge	20Cn	0Le	14Vi	18Li	8Sg	16Cp	9Aq	1Ta	6Ge	20Cn	17Vi
19	1Cn	15Le	24Le	10Li	15Sc	7Cp	16Aq	9Ar	27Ta	1Cn	13Le	11Li
21	25Cn	10Vi	18Vi	8Sc	14Sg	7Aq	15Pi	7Ta	21Ge	24Cn	7Vi	6Sc
23	18Le	5Li	14Li	4Sg	6Pi	18Ta	6Ar	3Ge	17Cn	25Cn	3Li	6Sc
25	13Vi	0Sc	11Sc	4Cp	10Pi	1Ta	6Ge	11Le	28Li	14Sg	28Li	3Sg
27	7Li	27Sc	6Sg	1Aq	10Pi	1Ta	6Ge	21Cn	23Vi	29Vi	35g	35g
29	3Sc		6Cp	29Aq	7Ar	26Ta	0Cn	8Vi		0Sg	23Sg	1Pi
31	1Sg		4Aq		4Ta		24Cn	8Vi		0Sg		1Pi

1944

	Jan	Feb	Mar	Apr	May	Jun	Jul	Aug	Sep	Oct	Nov	Dec
1	15Pi	7Ta	29Ta	16Cn	18Le	2Li	4Sc	21Sg	12Aq	20Pi	14Ta	21Cn
3	13Ar	3Ge	25Ge	10Le	12Vi	26Li	0Sg	19Cp	1Ar	13Ge	18Cn	18Le
5	10Ta	28Ge	19Cn	4Vi	6Li	22Sc	25Sg	19Aq	21Ta	10Cn	13Le	
7	6Ge	22Cn	13Le	27Vi	0Sc	18Sg	25Cp	19Pi	12Ta	18Ge	5Le	7Vi
9	1Cn	16Le	7Vi	22Li	26Sc	16Cp	24Aq	18Ar	10Ge	15Cn	11Ta	19Ge
11	26Cn	10Vi	1Li	17Sc	2Sg	16Aq	16Ta	5Cn	9Le	23Vi	25Li	
13	19Le	4Li	25Li	12Sg	20Cp	13Pi	22Ar	13Ge	0Le	3Vi	17Li	20Sc
15	13Vi	28Li	20Sc	9Cp	17Aq	11Ar	19Ta	8Cn	24Le	27Vi	11Sc	15Sg
17	7Li	23Sc	15Sg	7Aq	16Pi	9Ta	16Ge	3Le	18Vi	20Li	6Sg	12Cp
19	1Sc	19Sg	13Cp	5Pi	14Ar	6Ge	11Cn	27Aq	13Li	11Li	1Cp	9Aq
21	27Sc	18Cp	11Aq	4Ar	13Ta	2Cn	6Le	21Vi	9Sc	9Sg	29Cp	7Pi
23	23Sg	17Aq	10Pi	4Ta	11Ge	28Cn	0Vi	14Li	0Sg	5Sc	26Aq	5Ar
25	24Cp	18Pi	11Ar	2Ge	7Cn	22Le	24Vi	8Sc	25Sg	2Aq	24Pi	3Ta
27	25Aq	18Ar	10Ta	29Ge	2Le	16Vi	18Li	3Sg	22Cp	0Pi	23Ar	2Ge
29	24Pi	16Ta	8Ge	24Cn	28Cn	10Li	12Sc	29Sg	20Aq	29Pi	22Ta	1Ge
31	23Ar		4Cn		20Vi		8Sg	27Cp		29Ar		26Ge

1945

	Jan	Feb	Mar	Apr	May	Jun	Jul	Aug	Sep	Oct	Nov	Dec
1	8Le	27Vi	6Li	19Sg	7Aq	15Pi	9Ta	1Cn	8Le	27Vi	21Li	27Li
3	3Vi	17Li	25Li	10Sg	14Cp	4Pi	3Ar	7Cn	28Cn	3Vi	18Li	21Li
5	27Vi	11Sc	19Sc	5Cp	10Aq	1Ta	2Ta	4Cn	23Le	27Vi	13Li	
7	21Li	5Sg	13Sg	1Aq	8Pi	2Ta	11Ge	1Le	18Vi	21Li	6Sg	9Cp
9	15Sc	0Cp	9Cp	29Aq	7Ar	1Ge	27Ge	13Li	13Li	15Sc	29Sg	7Aq
11	10Sg	28Cp	6Aq	28Pi	7Ta	28Ge	22Cn	7Vi	9Sg	24Cp	29Pi	
13	7Cp	27Aq	5Pi	28Ar	6Ge	24Cn	16Le	0Sg	5Cp	26Vi	27Ar	27Pi
15	4Aq	27Pi	4Ar	29Ta	6Cn	24Cn	10Vi	0Sc	5Aq	28Cp	17Pi	26Ar
17	3Pi	26Ar	6Ta	28Ge	3Le	18Vi	20Li	4Sg	19Cp	25Aq	16Ar	25Ta
19	2Ar	25Ta	5Ge	24Cn	28Le	11Li	14Sc	29Sg	16Aq	25Pi	15Pi	24Cn
21	0Ta	22Ge	1Cn	19Le	6Sc	8Sg	25Cp	15Pi	23Ar	17Ge	17Ge	24Cn
23	28Ta	18Cn	24Cn	14Vi	16Li	10Sc	3Sg	13Aq	17Ar	15Ar	13Ta	22Le
25	25Ge	13Le	22Le	7Li	10Sc	25Sg	0Aq	21Pi	15Ta	23Ge	13Le	17Vi
27	21Cn	7Vi	17Vi	1Sc	4Sg	21Cp	27Aq	21Ar	14Cn	21Cn	9Vi	12Li
29	11Vi		10Li	25Sc	29Sg	18Aq	26Pi	20Ta	12Ge	17Le	3Li	6Sc
31	11Vi		4Sc		24Cp		24Ar	18Ge		12Vi		29Sc

1946

	Jan	Feb	Mar	Apr	May	Jun	Jul	Aug	Sep	Oct	Nov	Dec
1	11Sg	27Cp	5Aq	24Pi	2Ta	25Ge	1Vi	9Sc	11Sg	24Cp	27Aq	27Aq
3	6Cp	23Aq	2Pi	23Ar	2Ge	25Cn	1Vi	19Li	3Sg	19Aq	15Pi	20Ar
5	1Aq	20Pi	0Ar	23Ta	2Cn	23Le	25Sc	13Sg	26Sg	23Aq	25Cp	20Ar
7	27Aq	18Ar	29Ar	22Ge	0Le	19Vi	23Li	7Cp	20Cp	23Aq	12Ar	19Ta
9	24Pi	17Ta	28Ta	20Cn	17Vi	13Li	5Sg	0Cp	15Aq	20Pi	11Ta	20Cn
11	22Ar	15Ge	26Ge	17Le	10Li	5Sc	25Cp	12Pi	18Ar	11Ge	20Cn
13	20Ta	13Cn	23Cn	13Vi	17Li	2Sg	4Cp	20Aq	9Ar	18Ta	11Cn	0Vi
15	19Ge	10Le	20Le	8Li	11Sc	25Sg	28Cp	16Pi	8Ta	17Ge	10Le	16Vi
17	18Cn	7Vi	16Vi	2Sc	5Sg	19Cp	23Ar	6Ge	0Le	13Le	3Li	12Li
19	16Le	3Li	11Li	26Sc	28Sg	14Aq	20Pi	11Ta	9Cn	13Le	3Li	6Pi
21	12Vi	27Li	5Sc	19Sg	22Cp	9Pi	16Ar	9Ge	2Le	10Vi	27Li	1Sg
23	8Li	21Sc	29Sc	13Cp	17Aq	7Ar	14Ta	8Cn	0Vi	6Li	21Sc	24Sg
25	2Sc	15Sg	23Sg	8Aq	13Pi	6Ta	13Ge	6Le	26Vi	1Sc	15Sg	18Cp
27	27Sc	9Cp	17Cp	4Pi	11Ar	4Ge	13Cn	4Vi	21Li	25Sc	9Cp	12Aq
29	19Sg		12Aq	2Ar	10Ta	3Cn	11Le	1Li	15Sc	19Sg	3Aq	6Pi
31	14Cp		10Pi		10Ge		10Vi	27Li		12Cp		2Ar

1947

	Jan	Feb	Mar	Apr	May	Jun	Jul	Aug	Sep	Oct	Nov	Dec
1	15Ar	7Ge	17Ge	10Le	19Vi	8Sc	15Sg	11Pi	15Ar	5Ge	5Ge	13Cn
3	13Ta	6Cn	16Cn	9Vi	15Li	3Sg	5Cp	20Aq	6Ar	12Ta	3Cn	13Le
5	12Ge	6Le	15Le	6Li	11Sc	26Sg	29Cp	14Pi	2Ta	9Ge	2Le	11Vi
7	13Cn	5Vi	13Vi	2Sc	6Sg	20Cp	22Aq	9Ar	28Ta	7Cn	0Vi	8Li
9	13Le	3Li	11Li	27Sc	0Cp	14Aq	17Pi	5Ta	26Ge	5Le	28Vi	5Sc
11	11Vi	29Li	7Sc	22Sg	23Cp	8Pi	5Ta	25Cn	5Vi	4Vi	25Li	0Sg
13	8Li	24Sc	2Sg	15Cp	17Aq	8Ta	0Cn	0Cn	4Le	2Li	21Sc	25Sg
15	3Sc	18Sg	26Sg	9Aq	12Pi	0Ta	7Ge	0Ta	23Vi	26Li	16Sg	19Cp
17	28Sc	11Cp	20Cp	4Pi	8Ar	28Ta	0Vi	22Li	11Cp	13Aq	
19	21Sg	5Aq	13Aq	0Ar	5Ta	7Le	29Vi	18Sc	21Sg	15Pi	4Pi	13Aq
21	15Cp	0Pi	9Pi	27Ar	5Ge	4Vi	28Le	5Li	13Sg	13Cp	9Aq	1Ar
23	9Aq	26Pi	5Ar	26Ta	4Cn	28Le	5Li	27Sc	7Cp	9Aq	23Pi	26Ar
25	3Pi	22Ar	2Ta	4Le	26Vi	5Li	1Aq	3Pi	18Ar	23Ta
27	29Pi	19Ar	0Ge	23Cn	2Vi	22Li	26Sc	11Cp	25Aq	28Pi	15Ta	24Cn
29	25Ar		28Ge	21Le	17Sc	14Cp	4Aq	19Pi	24Ar	14Ge	22Le
31	23Ta		26Cn		25Li		14Cp	28Aq		21Ta		22Le

1948

	Jan	Feb	Mar	Apr	May	Jun	Jul	Aug	Sep	Oct	Nov	Dec
1	7Vi	28Li	20Sc	6Cp	8Aq	21Pi	24Ar	11Ge	3Le	12Vi	5Sc	11Sg
3	5Li	24Sc	15Sg	0Aq	2Pi	14Ar	20Ta	10Cn	3Vi	9Li	29Sc	8Cp
5	2Sc	19Sg	10Cp	24Aq	26Pi	11Ta	17Ge	9Le	4Li	5Sc	25Sg	5Aq
7	27Sc	13Cp	3Aq	18Pi	21Ar	9Ge	16Cn	9Vi	1Sc	29Sc	20Cp	2Pi
9	22Sg	6Aq	27Aq	12Ar	16Ta	7Cn	16Le	0Sg	5Cp	29Cp	21Pi
11	16Cp	0Pi	21Pi	8Ta	14Ge	6Le	15Vi	5Li	20Sg	17Aq	5Ar	15Ar
13	9Aq	24Pi	16Ar	4Ge	13Cn	5Vi	13Li	2Sc	12Cp	0Aq	14Ar	9Ta
15	3Pi	19Ar	11Ta	1Cn	10Le	4Li	9Sc	28Sc	7Aq	17Pi	17Li
17	27Pi	14Ta	7Ge	0Le	7Vi	5Li	7Sg	23Cp	8Pi	11Ar	27Ta	2Cn
19	22Ar	10Ge	4Cn	27Le	6Li	2Sc	0Sg	17Aq	1Ar	5Ta	21Cn	0Le
21	18Ta	8Cn	3Le	1Le	3Sc	1Li	27Sg	11Pi	25Ar	29Ge	24Le
23	15Ge	8Le	2Vi	25Li	1Sg	18Cp	20Aq	5Ar	21Ta	27Cn	18Le	28Vi
25	15Cn	9Vi	2Li	23Sc	27Sg	14Aq	14Pi	29Ar	16Ge	24Cn	14Vi	23Sc
27	16Le	9Li	1Sc	19Sg	22Cp	6Pi	8Ar	24Ta	13Cn	22Le	15Li	23Sc
29	16Vi	7Sc	28Sc	14Cp	16Aq	0Ar	2Ta	20Ge	12Le	21Vi	23Sc	20Sg
31	15Li		24Sg		10Pi		28Ta	18Cn		20Li		28Vi

1949

	Jan	Feb	Mar	Apr	May	Jun	Jul	Aug	Sep	Oct	Nov	Dec
1	28Cp	13Pi	22Pi	6Ta	10Ge	29Cn	7Vi	1Sc	23Sg	29Cp	15Pi	17Ar
3	23Aq	7Ar	15Ar	1Ge	6Cn	27Le	3Li	29Sc	19Cp	24Aq	9Ar	11Ta
5	17Pi	1Ta	9Ta	26Ge	2Le	25Vi	29Li	26Sg	14Aq	18Pi	2Ta	5Ge
7	11Ar	25Ta	3Ge	21Cn	0Vi	4Sc	26Sc	22Cp	9Pi	12Ar	26Ta	29Ge
9	5Ta	21Ge	29Ge	20Le	29Vi	21Sc	22Sg	18Aq	3Ar	5Ta	20Ge	25Cn
11	0Ge	19Cn	26Cn	20Vi	20Li	21Cn	18Cp	12Pi	26Ar	29Ta	15Cn	19Vi
13	27Ge	18Le	26Le	20Li	18Sc	18Cp	12Aq	6Ar	20Ta	25Ge	12Le	19Vi
15	25Cn	19Vi	27Vi	20Sc	15Sg	13Aq	6Pi	0Ta	14Ge	19Cn	9Vi	17Li
17	25Le	18Li	27Li	18Sg	23Cp	8Pi	0Ar	24Ta	10Cn	16Le	8Li	16Sc
19	22Vi	15Sc	23Sc	13Cp	21Cn	2Ar	24Ar	20Ge	7Le	15Vi	6Sc	13Sg
21	23Li	9Sg	18Sg	7Aq	18Ta	28Ta	19Ta	19Cn	6Vi	14Li	2Sg	9Cp
23	20Sc	9Cp	19Cp	4Pi	6Ar	20Ta	8Cn	16Le	6Li	14Sc	27Sg	3Aq
25	16Sg	4Aq	28Pi	13Cn	19Le	13Vi	20Li	13Vi	2Sg	9Cp	7Pi
27	12Cp	28Aq	7Pi	21Ar	24Ta	12Cn	11Le	8Li	10Sc	28Cp	24Aq	23Pi
29	7Aq	1Ar	15Ta	19Ge	9Le	18Vi	11Sc	4Sg	23Aq	18Pi	19Ta
31	1Pi		24Ar		16Cn		16Cp	3Li		3Pi		19Ta

1950

	Jan	Feb	Mar	Apr	May	Jun	Jul	Aug	Sep	Oct	Nov	Dec
1	1Ge	17Cn	25Cn	14Vi	22Li	10Sc	2Sc	13Pi	28Ar	0Ge	20Cn	18Le
3	26Ge	14Le	22Le	14Li	23Sc	22Aq	8Ar	22Ta	27Cn	9Le	14Vi
5	22Cn	13Vi	21Vi	14Sc	23Sg	16Aq	18Pi	21Ta	25Ge	18Cn	9Vi	11Li
7	19Le	11Li	20Li	12Sg	21Cp	12Pi	4Ar	14Le	0Li	2Li	2Li
9	16Vi	9Sc	20Sc	12Cp	18Aq	4Ar	6Ar	20Ge	6Le	10Vi	5Sc	10Sg
11	14Li	7Sg	18Sg	9Aq	13Pi	7Ge	0Ta	15Cn	2Vi	5Li	1Sg	4Cp
13	12Sc	5Cp	15Cp	7Pi	22Ta	24Ge	11Le	0Li	9Li	9Sc	10Aq
15	11Sg	2Aq	11Aq	28Pi	1Sc	3Sg	29Li	5Li	7Pi
17	9Cp	28Aq	7Pi	22Ar	25Ta	10Cn	15Le	5Li	1Sc	7Cp	28Aq	7Pi
19	6Aq	23Pi	1Ar	16Ta	19Ge	11Vi	3Sc	27Sg	24Pi	1Pi	18Ar
21	2Pi	17Ar	25Ar	9Ge	13Cn	1Vi	8Li	21Pi	18Ar	21Ta
23	27Pi	11Ta	19Ta	2Cn	8Le	14Vi	22Li	25Pi	17Ta	16Vi
25	21Ar	4Ge	13Ge	28Cn	4Vi	26Li	28Cp	12Ar	21Ar	6Ge	8Li	14Sc
27	15Ta	29Ge	7Cn	22Le	2Li	25Sc	12Aq	15Ta	5Sc	13Cp
29	9Ge	3Le	23Vi	2Sc	22Sg	21Pi	6Ta	9Ge	28Sc	13Cp
31	4Cn		0Vi		1Sg		0Pi	16Ar		2Cn		23Vi

1951

	Jan	Feb	Mar	Apr	May	Jun	Jul	Aug	Sep	Oct	Nov	Dec
1	7Li	29Sc	10Sg	3Aq	10Pi	28Ar	16Cb	1Vi	6Li	26Sc	5Sg	5Aq
3	4Sc	28Sg	8Cp	0Pi	6Ar	22Ta	2Ge	25Cn	10Vi	2Sc	0Sg	5Aq
5	1Sg	26Cp	6Aq	28Pi	1Ta	17Ge	26Ge	5Vi	23Li	1Sg	13Cp	3Pi
7	4Cp	26Aq	4Pi	26Ar	26Ta	11Cn	3Sc	0Li	20Sc	29Sg	28Aq	28Pi
9	3Aq	23Pi	1Ar	17Ta	20Ge	4Le	7Vi	13Cn	23Sc	28Cp	20Pi	26Ar
11	2Pi	19Ar	27Ar	11Ge	13Cn	13Sc	17Cp	16Aq	21Ta
13	28Pi	13Ta	21Ta	7Le	23Vi	29Li	23Sc	16Aq	23Pi	12Ta	20Cn
15	23Ar	7Ge	15Ge	26Cn	2Vi	20Vi	2Cp	14Pi	20Ar	7Cn	3Le
17	17Ta	1Cn	9Cn	24Le	28Vi	19Sc	27Sg	21Aq	12Ar	16Ta	3Le	
19	11Ge	25Cn	3Le	0Vi	26Li	28Cp	20Pi	8Ta	11Cn	24Cn	21Vi	
21	5Cn	21Le	29Le	18Li	25Sc	19Cp	7Ge	18Li	5Cn	5Sc	18Le
23	29Cn	17Vi	25Vi	15Sc	25Sg	12Pi	13Cp	4Vi	6Sc	16Li
25	24Le	14Li	23Li	16Sg	25Cp	17Pi	22Ar	16Ta	1Le	24Cn	22Le	8Li	14Sc
27	20Vi	11Sc	22Sc	15Cp	24Aq	13Ar	1Cn	15Le	9Vi	17Vi	6Sc	13Cp
29	17Li		21Sg	14Aq	20Pi	8Ta	10Ge	24Vi	9Vi	12Sc	13Cp
31	15Sc		19Cp		16Ar		4Cn	19Le		12Sc		14Aq

1952

	Jan	Feb	Mar	Apr	May	Jun	Jul	Aug	Sep	Oct	Nov	Dec
1	28Aq	19Ar	10Ta	26Ge	27Cn	11Vi	14Li	2Sg	24Cp	3Pi	27Ar	3Ge
3	26Pi	15Ta	5Ge	20Cn	21Le	6Li	10Sc	0Cp	23Aq	2Ar	23Ta	28Ge
5	23Ar	9Ge	29Ge	13Le	15Vi	1Sc	6Sg	0Aq	24Pi	1Ta	18Ge	23Cn
7	18Ta	3Cn	23Cn	7Vi	10Li	29Sc	7Cp	1Pi	23Ar	29Ta	15Cn	
9	12Ge	27Cn	17Le	2Li	7Sc	0Ar	21Ta	25Ge	23Vi	23Li
11	6Cn	21Le	11Vi	28Li	5Sg	29Aq	12Pi	19Ar	19Cn	3Vi	21Li	
13	0Le	15Vi	6Li	26Sc	4Cp	2Aq	25Pi	2Ta	7Sc	7Vi	19Li	
15	24Le	9Li	1Sc	23Sg	4Aq	2Pi	2Ta	20Ge	5Le	7Vi	21Li	
17	18Vi	5Sc	27Sc	20Cp	3Pi	1Ar	28Ta	14Cn	1Li	4Li	18Vi
19	12Li	1Sg	24Sg	18Aq	2Ar	28Ar	23Ge	8Le	22Vi	1Sc	26Li
21	9Sc	29Sg	22Cp	18Pi	1Ta	24Ta	17Cn	1Vi	17Li	11Ta	22Cp
23	6Sg	0Aq	24Aq	16Ar	27Ta	8Cn	11Le	25Vi	12Sc	18Cp	20Pi
25	6Cp	29Aq	23Pi	13Ta	4Vi	8Sg	8Sg	15Aq	9Pi	15Ta
27	6Aq	29Pi	21Ar	9Ge	28Vi	16Li	13Cp	5Aq	14Aq	12Pi	5Ta	10Ge
29	6Pi	27Ar	18Ta	4Cn	12Li	9Sc	8Aq	3Ar	12Pi	5Ta	6Cn
31	5Ar		13Ge		18Sc		5Pi	1Ar		11Ar		6Cn

1953

	Jan	Feb	Mar	Apr	May	Jun	Jul	Aug	Sep	Oct	Nov	Dec
1	19Cn	3Vi	12Vi	27Li	1Sg	21Aq	28Aq	23Ar	15Ge	20Cn	9Vi	7Li
3	13Le	27Vi	6Li	22Sc	27Sg	19Aq	28Pi	21Ta	10Cn	14Le	29Vi	1Sc
5	7Vi	21Li	1Sc	18Sg	24Cp	17Pi	4Ar	18Ge	5Le	8Vi	22Li	25Sc
7	0Li	15Sc	25Sc	14Cp	22Aq	15Ar	24Ta	13Cn	29Le	2Li	16Sc	21Sg
9	24Li	11Sg	20Sg	11Aq	21Pi	14Ta	21Ge	8Le	23Vi	26Li	10Sg	17Cp
11	20Sc	9Cp	18Cp	11Pi	20Ar	11Ge	16Cn	2Vi	16Li	20Sc	5Cp	14Aq
13	17Sg	9Aq	17Aq	10Ar	18Ta	7Cn	10Le	26Vi	10Sc	14Sg	1Aq	14Pi
15	16Cp	9Pi	17Pi	10Ta	17Ge	2Le	4Vi	20Li	5Sg	10Cp	0Pi	10Ar
17	16Aq	9Ar	16Ar	8Ge	13Cn	28Le	0Li	7Cp	29Aq	8Ta
19	15Pi	8Ta	15Ta	5Cn	8Le	21Vi	9Vi	8Li	0Li	5Pi	29Ar	8Ta
21	14Ar	5Ge	12Ge	0Le	2Vi	15Li	16Sc	5Sg	25Aq	2Aq	26Ta	1Le
23	12Ta	0Cn	9Cn	24Le	24Vi	9Sc	28Vi	2Sg	22Pi	27Pi	5Ta	1Le
25	8Ge	24Cn	3Le	19Vi	19Li	4Sg	3Pi	27Ar	3Ge	28Cn
27	3Cn	18Le	27Le	11Li	14Sc	3Cp	3E	17Ta	5Cn	19Le
29	27Cn		21Vi	6Sc	10Sg	0Aq	9Pi	3Ta	24Cn	13Vi
31	21Le		15Li		7Cp		1Ge		23Le		9Sc

248

1964

	Jan	Feb	Mar	Apr	May	Jun	Jul	Aug	Sep	Oct	Nov	Dec
1	0Le	19Vi	10Li	25Sc	27Sg	11Aq	16Pi	6Ta	29Ge	4Le	29Vi	4Sc
3	28Le	15Li	5Sc	18Sg	20Cp	6Pi	12Ar	5Ge	28Cn	6Vi	25Li	29Sc
5	24Vi	9Sc	29Sc	12Cp	15Aq	3Ar	10Ta	4Cn	26Le	3Li	20Sc	23Sg
7	19Li	3Sg	22Sg	7Aq	11Pi	1Ta	10Ge	3Le	24Vi	29Li	14Sg	16Cp
9	13Sc	26Sg	16Cp	2Pi	8Ar	1Ge	10Cn	2Vi	21Li	24Sc	8Cp	10Aq
11	7Sg	21Cp	11Aq	0Ar	7Ta	1Cn	9Le	0Li	16Sc	18Sg	1Aq	4Pi
13	0Cp	16Aq	8Pi	29Ar	6Ge	1Le	8Vi	26Li	10Sg	12Cp	26Aq	29Pi
15	25Cp	13Pi	6Ar	29Ta	8Cn	29Le	5Li	21Sc	4Cp	5Aq	21Pi	26Ar
17	20Aq	10Ar	5Ta	28Ge	6Le	26Vi	0Sc	14Sg	28Cp	0Pi	18Ar	25Ta
19	17Pi	8Ta	3Ge	26Cn	3Vi	21Li	24Sc	8Cp	22Aq	27Pi	17Ta	25Ge
21	14Ar	7Ge	2Cn	23Le	29Vi	15Sc	17Sg	2Aq	18Pi	25Ar	17Ge	25Cn
23	12Ta	5Cn	29Cn	19Vi	24Li	9Sg	11Cp	27Aq	16Ar	23Ta	17Cn	25Le
25	10Ge	3Le	26Le	15Li	18Sc	2Cp	5Aq	23Pi	14Ta	23Ge	16Le	23Vi
27	9Cn	0Vi	23Vi	9Sc	12Sg	26Cp	0Pi	20Ar	12Ge	21Cn	13Vi	19Li
29	8Le	27Vi	18Li	3Sg	5Cp	21Aq	26Pi	17Ta	9Cn	19Le	9Li	14Sc
31	6Vi		13Sc		29Cp		23Ar	15Ge		16Vi		8Sg

1965

	Jan	Feb	Mar	Apr	May	Jun	Jul	Aug	Sep	Oct	Nov	Dec
1	20Sg	4Aq	12Aq	28Pi	3Ta	25Ge	4Le	27Vi	17Sc	20Sg	4Aq	6Pi
3	13Cp	28Aq	7Pi	25Ar	2Ge	25Cn	4Vi	25Li	12Sg	14Cp	0Ar	0Ar
5	7Aq	23Pi	2Ar	22Ta	2Cn	24Le	2Li	21Sc	6Cp	8Aq	22Pi	23Ta
7	1Pi	18Ar	29Ar	20Ge	29Cn	22Vi	29Li	15Sg	0Aq	2Pi	17Ar	22Ta
9	26Pi	15Ta	25Ta	18Cn	25Le	18Li	24Sc	9Cp	24Aq	26Pi	14Ta	20Ge
11	22Ar	13Ge	23Ge	16Le	21Vi	14Sc	18Sg	3Aq	18Pi	22Ar	13Ge	19Cn
13	19Ta	12Cn	21Cn	15Vi	22Li	11Sg	12Cp	27Aq	14Ar	18Ta	13Cn	17Le
15	18Ge	11Le	20Le	12Li	18Sc	5Cp	6Aq	21Pi	8Ta	11Le	8Ta	17Vi
17	18Cn	11Vi	19Vi	9Sc	13Sg	27Cp	0Pi	16Ar	6Ge	13Cn	6Vi	15Li
19	18Le	10Li	17Li	4Sg	7Cp	21Aq	24Pi	11Ta	2Cn	11Le	4Li	11Sc
21	18Vi	6Sc	14Sc	29Sg	1Aq	15Pi	19Ar	8Ge	0Le	10Vi	1Sc	7Sg
23	15Li	1Sg	9Sg	23Cp	24Aq	9Ar	14Ta	6Cn	29Le	8Li	28Sc	2Cp
25	10Sc	25Sg	3Cp	16Aq	19Pi	6Ta	13Ge	6Le	29Vi	6Sc	23Sg	26Cp
27	5Sg	19Cp	27Cp	11Pi	14Ar	4Ge	12Cn	6Vi	28Li	3Sg	18Cp	20Aq
29	28Sg		21Aq	6Ar	12Ta	4Cn	12Le	6Li	25Sc	28Sg	12Aq	14Pi
31	22Cp		15Pi		10Ge		13Vi	4Sc		22Cp		8Ar

1966

	Jan	Feb	Mar	Apr	May	Jun	Jul	Aug	Sep	Oct	Nov	Dec
1	20Ar	8Ge	17Ge	8Le	18Vi	10Sc	17Sg	4Aq	21Ar	7Ge	10Cn	13Cn
3	16Ta	6Cn	14Cn	8Vi	17Li	7Sg	12Cp	28Aq	12Ta	6Cn	9Le	10Le
5	13Ge	6Le	14Le	8Li	17Sc	4Cp	7Aq	21Pi	6Ge	4Le	6Vi	8Vi
7	13Cn	6Vi	14Vi	7Sc	13Sg	29Cp	1Pi	15Ar	1Ge	2Vi	2Li	4Li
9	13Le	6Li	15Li	5Sg	8Cp	24Aq	25Pi	10Ta	27Ge	29Vi	28Li	29Li
11	13Vi	5Sc	13Sc	1Cp	3Aq	17Pi	19Ar	5Ge	24Cn	26Li	23Sc	23Sc
13	13Li	3Sg	11Sg	26Cp	26Aq	11Ar	13Ta	1Cn	22Le	23Sc	18Sg	3Sg
15	8Sc	26Sg	5Cp	19Aq	21Pi	6Ta	10Ge	0Le	24Vi	23Sg	12Cp	27Cp
17	4Sg	20Cp	29Cp	13Pi	15Ar	1Ge	6Cn	29Le	23Li	19Cp	6Aq	22Aq
19	29Sg	14Aq	22Aq	7Ar	10Ta	29Ge	4Le	28Vi	22Sc	14Aq	0Pi	16Pi
21	23Cp	7Pi	16Pi	2Ta	6Ge	27Cn	2Vi	26Li	19Sg	8Pi	24Pi	10Ar
23	17Aq	1Ar	10Ar	27Ta	4Cn	26Le	0Li	23Sc	15Cp	2Ar	18Ar	4Ta
25	10Pi	25Ar	5Ta	23Ge	4Le	25Vi	28Li	19Sg	9Aq	25Ar	13Ta	29Ta
27	4Ar	20Ta	0Ge	21Cn	4Vi	23Li	25Sc	13Cp	3Pi	20Ta	9Ge	25Ge
29	29Ar		26Ge	19Le	5Li	19Sc	20Sg	7Aq	27Pi	16Ge	7Cn	21Cn
31	24Ta		24Cn		6Sc		13Cp	1Ar		14Cn		21Le

1967

	Jan	Feb	Mar	Apr	May	Jun	Jul	Aug	Sep	Oct	Nov	Dec
1	5Vi	28Li	8Sc	29Sg	4Aq	20Pi	5Ge	22Cn	27Le	20Li	28Sc	28Sc
3	4Li	26Sc	6Sg	25Cp	29Aq	13Ar	0Cn	17Le	27Vi	20Sc	28Sg	28Sg
5	2Sc	23Sg	3Cp	20Aq	23Pi	7Ta	25Cn	13Vi	27Li	21Sg	28Cp	27Cp
7	29Sc	19Cp	28Cp	14Pi	17Ar	2Ge	21Le	12Li	28Sc	21Cp	27Aq	23Aq
9	26Sg	15Aq	23Aq	8Ar	10Ta	28Ge	18Vi	12Sc	28Sg	19Aq	23Pi	19Pi
11	23Cp	8Pi	17Pi	2Ta	5Ge	24Cn	17Li	12Sg	26Cp	16Pi	19Ar	6Ta
13	18Aq	2Ar	11Ar	26Ta	29Ge	22Le	16Sc	11Cp	24Aq	13Pi	28Ar	6Ta
15	12Pi	26Ar	4Ta	20Ge	25Cn	17Vi	19Sc	9Aq	13Pi	28Ar	0Ge
17	6Ar	20Ta	28Ta	15Cn	22Le	16Li	24Sc	16Cp	8Ar	7Ar	25Ge	24Ge
19	0Ta	14Ge	22Ge	12Le	20Vi	16Sc	22Sg	7Pi	4Cn	29Ge	21Le	22Cn
21	24Ta	9Cn	17Cn	11Vi	19Sc	14Sg	7Ta	1Ta	16Ta	18Ge	10Cn	20Vi
23	20Ge	9Le	17Le	10Li	19Sc	11Cp	16Aq	24Ta	16Ta	18Ge	21Le	12Vi
25	17Cn	9Vi	17Vi	11Sc	18Sg	9Aq	12Pi	18Ge	9Cn	4Le	20Vi	9Li
27	16Le	9Li	17Li	10Sg	15Cp	5Pi	5Ar	14Cn	8Le	4Vi	29Vi	8Sc
29	15Vi		17Sc	8Cp	13Aq	28Pi	23Ta	13Ge	8Vi	6Li	29Vi	8Sc
31	14Li		16Sg		8Pi		23Ta	8Cn		5Li		6Cp

1968

	Jan	Feb	Mar	Apr	May	Jun	Jul	Aug	Sep	Oct	Nov	Dec
1	20Cp	9Pi	0Ar	14Ta	17Ge	2Le	7Vi	28Li	1Aq	21Pi	25Ar	25Ar
3	18Aq	4Ar	24Ar	8Ge	11Cn	27Le	4Li	26Sc	20Cp	28Aq	19Ta	19Ta
5	14Pi	28Ar	18Ta	2Cn	5Le	24Vi	2Sc	25Sg	18Aq	24Pi	10Ta	13Ge
7	9Ar	22Ta	12Ge	27Cn	1Vi	22Li	1Sg	24Cp	15Pi	19Ar	4Ge	7Cn
9	2Ta	16Ge	6Cn	21Le	27Vi	21Sc	1Cp	22Aq	11Ar	13Ta	28Ge	0Le
11	26Ta	11Cn	1Le	20Vi	28Li	21Sg	0Aq	20Pi	5Ta	7Ge	22Cn	25Le
13	20Ge	6Le	26Le	18Li	27Sc	20Cp	29Aq	17Ar	0Ge	2Cn	16Le	20Vi
15	15Cn	4Vi	27Vi	20Sc	29Sg	20Aq	25Pi	13Ta	23Ge	26Cn	11Vi	17Li
17	12Le	2Li	26Li	18Sg	27Cp	20Pi	4Ge	9Ge	17Cn	7Sc	15Sg
19	8Vi	1Sc	25Sc	18Cp	27Aq	17Ar	18Ta	4Cn	15Le	7Sc	15Sg
21	6Li	29Sc	24Sg	15Aq	24Pi	13Ta	14Ge	0Le	9Vi	1Li	18Sc	22Sg
23	4Sc	27Sg	22Cp	11Pi	19Ar	9Ge	8Cn	24Le	5Li	27Li	17Sg	22Cp
25	2Sg	25Cp	18Aq	6Ar	14Ta	2Cn	2Le	20Vi	4Sc	27Sc	17Cp	21Aq
27	1Cp	21Aq	14Pi	1Ta	8Ge	26Cn	27Le	17Li	4Sg	26Sg	16Aq	19Pi
29	29Cp	17Pi	8Ar	26Ta	2Cn	20Le	24Vi	15Sc	29Sg	13Pi	15Pi
31	26Aq		3Ta		20Cn		17Li	7Sg		28Cp		8Ar

1969

	Jan	Feb	Mar	Apr	May	Jun	Jul	Aug	Sep	Oct	Nov	Dec
1	10Ge	24Cn	2Le	18Vi	24Li	16Sg	25Cp	18Pi	7Ta	10Ge	24Cn	25Le
3	4Cn	19Le	27Le	15Li	23Sc	15Cp	25Aq	15Ar	2Ge	4Cn	18Le	20Vi
5	28Cn	14Vi	23Vi	13Sc	22Sg	16Aq	23Pi	11Ta	26Ge	28Cn	12Vi	15Li
7	22Le	10Li	20Li	12Sg	22Cp	21Cp	14Pi	8Ge	20Cn	22Le	7Li	11Sc
9	17Vi	7Sc	17Sc	11Cp	20Aq	15Pi	15Ta	0Cn	14Le	16Vi	1Sc	11Sg
11	11Li	5Sg	15Sg	9Aq	17Pi	5Ta	9Ge	23Cn	8Vi	11Li	2Sg	11Cp
13	5Sc	3Cp	14Cp	6Pi	13Ar	0Ge	3Cn	17Le	3Li	9Sc	0Cp	10Aq
15	9Sg	3Aq	14Aq	3Ar	9Ta	24Ge	27Cn	11Vi	29Li	7Sg	29Cp	9Pi
17	9Cp	2Pi	10Pi	29Ar	3Ge	17Cn	20Le	6Li	25Sc	5Cp	28Aq	6Ar
19	9Aq	0Ar	8Ar	24Ta	27Ge	11Le	14Vi	1Sc	23Sg	3Aq	25Pi	2Ta
21	8Pi	26Ar	4Ta	18Ge	21Cn	5Vi	9Li	29Sc	23Cp	2Pi	21Ar	28Ta
23	5Ar	21Ta	28Ta	12Cn	14Le	0Li	5Sc	28Sg	21Aq	29Pi	18Ta	22Ge
25	1Ta	15Ge	23Ge	6Le	8Vi	27Li	2Sg	28Cp	20Pi	18Ar	14Ge	16Cn
27	25Ta	9Cn	16Cn	1Vi	4Li	25Sc	1Cp	27Aq	18Ar	23Ta	9Cn	10Le
29	19Ge		10Le	26Vi	1Sc	24Sg	26Pi	15Ta	11Cn	2Le	4Vi
31	12Cn		5Vi		1Sg		3Pi	24Ar	27Ta	13Cn		28Vi

1970

	Jan	Feb	Mar	Apr	May	Jun	Jul	Aug	Sep	Oct	Nov	Dec
1	10Li	28Sc	8Sg	1Aq	10Pi	27Ta	24Ge	9Vi	11Li	15Sg	24Aq	5Cp
3	6Sc	27Sg	6Cp	29Aq	8Ar	28Ta	18Cn	3Li	8Sc	15Cp	23Pi	3Aq
5	4Sg	27Cp	5Aq	29Pi	6Ta	27Ge	13Le	28Li	8Sg	15Aq	22Ar	1Pi
7	4Cp	27Aq	5Pi	27Ar	3Ge	24Cn	7Vi	23Sc	6Cp	13Pi	19Ta	29Pi
9	4Aq	27Pi	5Ar	24Ta	28Ge	18Le	0Li	18Sg	5Aq	12Ar	15Ge	25Ar
11	4Pi	25Ar	3Ta	20Ge	23Cn	12Vi	24Li	14Cp	4Pi	11Ta	11Cn	21Ta
13	3Ar	21Ta	0Ge	15Cn	17Le	5Li	19Sc	12Aq	3Ar	9Ge	6Le	15Ge
15	29Ar	16Ge	25Ge	9Le	10Vi	29Li	16Sg	12Pi	2Ta	5Cn	0Vi	9Cn
17	25Ta	10Cn	19Cn	2Vi	5Li	22Sc	28Sg	21Aq	15Pi	22Ta	9Cn	12Le
19	19Ge	4Le	12Le	27Vi	29Li	18Sg	9Cp	0Pi	13Ar	18Ge	13Ge	6Le
21	13Cn	28Le	6Vi	22Li	25Sc	15Cp	7Aq	29Pi	12Ta	14Cn	8Le	29Vi
23	7Le	22Vi	0Li	18Sc	22Sg	13Aq	6Pi	29Ar	10Ge	8Le	2Vi	24Li
25	1Vi	16Li	26Li	15Sg	22Cp	12Pi	5Ar	28Ta	6Cn	2Vi	26Vi	18Sc
27	25Vi	12Sc	22Sc	13Cp	22Aq	12Ar	4Ta	25Ge	0Le	26Vi	20Li	13Sg
29	19Li		19Sg	11Aq	21Pi	12Ta	1Ge	20Cn	24Le	20Li	15Sc	9Cp
31	15Sc		16Cp		18Ar		27Ge	14Le		15Sc		13Aq

1971

	Jan	Feb	Mar	Apr	May	Jun	Jul	Aug	Sep	Oct	Nov	Dec
1	27Aq	20Ar	0Ta	20Ge	25Cn	11Vi	15Li	20Sg	12Cp	18Aq	11Ta	19Ta
3	26Pi	18Ta	28Ta	16Cn	19Le	3Li	7Sc	16Cp	10Aq	17Pi	11Ta	19Ge
5	24Ar	15Ge	24Ge	11Le	13Vi	27Li	2Sg	13Aq	10Pi	16Ar	9Ge	17Cn
7	21Ta	11Cn	19Cn	4Vi	6Li	21Sc	26Sg	11Pi	9Ar	16Ta	9Cn	13Le
9	18Ge	5Le	14Le	28Vi	0Sc	17Sg	23Cp	11Ar	9Ta	16Ge	9Ta	8Vi
11	13Cn	0Vi	7Vi	22Li	24Sc	14Cp	21Aq	11Ta	8Ge	14Cn	4Vi	2Li
13	8Le	23Vi	1Li	15Sc	18Sg	9Aq	20Pi	9Ge	4Cn	9Le	28Vi	26Li
15	2Vi	17Li	25Li	9Sg	13Cp	7Pi	18Ar	6Cn	0Le	3Vi	22Li	19Sc
17	26Vi	10Sc	19Sc	7Cp	14Aq	7Pi	16Ta	7Cn	24Le	28Vi	11Sc	10Sg
19	19Li	10Sc	18Vi	4Aq	11Ta	6Ta	18Li	20Vi	18Li	15Sc	9Cn	10Cp
21	14Sc	1Cp	10Cp	2Pi	11Ar	14Cn	11Li	15Sc	15Cn	1Cp	6Aq	3Pi
23	10Sg	0Aq	6Aq	1Ar	10Ta	4Cn	21Vi	6Li	21Vi	6Sg	2Aq	26Pi
25	7Cp	29Aq	8Pi	1Ta	9Ge	28Cn	1Vi	0Sg	4Cp	23Aq	7Sg	1Ar
27	7Aq	0Ar	8Ar	2Ge	8Cn	25Le	9Sc	20Cp	20Cp	21Pi	0Aq	9Ta
29	6Pi		8Ta	2Cn	7Le	21Vi	3Sg	28Sg	20Cp	27Aq	9Ta	0Ta
31	6Ar		7Ge		3Vi		28Sg	26Pi		0Cp		27Ge

1972

	Jan	Feb	Mar	Apr	May	Jun	Jul	Aug	Sep	Oct	Nov	Dec
1	11Cn	29Le	20Vi	5Sc	7Sg	20Aq	24Ar	14Ge	2Le	5Vi	21Li	16Li
3	8Le	24Vi	14Li	28Sc	1Cp	19Aq	19Ta	12Cn	0Vi	1Li	6Li	10Sc
5	4Vi	18Li	8Sc	22Sg	26Cp	15Pi	14Ge	9Le	27Vi	24Li	29Sc	3Sg
7	28Vi	12Sc	2Sg	16Cp	22Aq	14Ar	23Ta	16Cn	9Le	10Li	24Sc	27Sg
9	22Li	6Sg	26Sg	13Aq	19Pi	13Ge	21Cn	10Vi	1Li	14Sc	21Sg	21Cp
11	16Sc	1Cp	21Cp	11Pi	19Ar	13Cn	21Cn	10Vi	1Li	14Sc	21Sg	16Aq
13	10Sg	28Cp	18Aq	10Ar	19Ta	13Le	20Le	8Li	29Li	9Sg	15Cp	11Pi
15	6Cp	25Aq	17Pi	11Ta	20Ge	12Vi	19Vi	3Sc	24Sc	4Cp	2Pi	8Ar
17	2Aq	24Pi	17Ar	11Ge	18Cn	23Sc	7Cp	10Aq	20Cp	7Ge	10Aq	7Ta
19	0Pi	23Ar	17Ta	9Cn	15Le	1Li	3Sc	12Cp	24Aq	5Pi	28Ar	24Li
21	28Pi	23Ta	17Ge	6Le	11Vi	3Sc	12Cp	29Aq	9Ar	24Pi	5Ta	6Cp
23	26Ar	19Ge	13Cn	1Vi	5Li	29Sc	22Pi	27Ar	7Ta	21Ar	1Ge	6Le
25	23Ta	16Cn	9Le	26Vi	29Li	22Sg	16Pi	27Ar	6Ge	20Ta	29Ge	4Vi
27	18Ge	12Le	4Vi	20Li	22Sc	16Cp	10Ar	26Ta	3Cn	17Ge	24Cn	29Vi
29	20Cn	7Vi	13Sc	16Sg	9Aq	3Ar	22Ge	29Cn	13Cn	19Li	24Li
31	16Le		23Li		11Cp		11Cp	0Le		29Le		18Sc

1973

	Jan	Feb	Mar	Apr	May	Jun	Jul	Aug	Sep	Oct	Nov	Dec
1	18Aq	14Cp	22Cp	8Pi	14Ar	7Ge	16Cn	8Vi	27Li	0Sg	13Cp	15Aq
3	24Sg	9Aq	17Aq	4Ar	12Ta	7Cn	15Le	2Li	22Sc	25Sg	13Cp	15Aq
5	18Cp	5Pi	9Pi	2Ta	12Ge	6Le	13Vi	1Sc	16Sg	13Cp	8Aq	10Pi
7	13Aq	11Ar	11Ar	4Ge	13Cn	5Vi	10Li	26Sc	9Cp	11Aq	27Pi	2Ta
9	8Pi	29Ar	10Ta	3Cn	13Le	3Li	5Sc	20Sg	6Pi	6Pi	24Ar	1Ge
11	5Ar	27Ta	8Ge	1Le	9Vi	26Li	28Sc	13Cp	24Aq	28Aq	23Ta	1Cn
13	1Ta	24Ge	6Cn	29Le	6Li	22Sc	22Sg	7Aq	24Pi	7Ta	23Cn	2Le
15	1Ge	24Cn	4Le	24Vi	1Sc	16Sg	16Cp	2Pi	21Ar	24Cn	22Cn	0Vi
17	0Cn	13Vi	10Li	20Li	23Sc	15Ar	0Pi	28Pi	19Ta	7Cn	26Cn	24Li
19	20Vi	28Vi	14Li	8Sc	12Sg	5Pi	4Ar	17Ge	26Cn	18Vi	24Li
21	28Le	17Li	8Sg	12Cp	2Aq	16Le	14Cn	11Sc	24Ar	22Ta	12Vi	13Sc
23	25Vi	10Sc	18Sc	5Cp	4Aq	21Pi	4Ar	22Ta	21Ge	13Cn	11Vi	9Li
25	20Li	28Sc	26Cp	20Aq	25Pi	16Ta	24Ge	18Le	11Vi	11Li	3Sc	7Cp
27	15Sc	28Sg	6Cp	20Aq	25Pi	16Ta	24Ge	18Le	9Li	9Sc	28Sg	0Aq
29	9Sg		24Pi	16Pi	23Ar	16Ge	24Le	16Vi	5Sc	8Sg	22Cp	24Aq
31	2Cp		25Aq		22Ta		24Le	14Li		2Cp		18Pi

1974

	Jan	Feb	Mar	Apr	May	Jun	Jul	Aug	Sep	Oct	Nov	Dec
1	1Ar	20Ta	0Ge	23Cn	2Vi	23Li	29Sc	14Cp	29Aq	2Ar	19Ta	26Ge
3	27Ar	18Ge	28Ge	21Le	0Li	19Sc	23Sg	8Aq	23Pi	27Ar	16Ge	24Cn
5	25Ta	17Cn	27Cn	20Vi	27Li	14Sg	17Cp	2Pi	18Ar	23Ta	14Cn	23Le
7	24Ge	18Le	26Le	18Li	23Sc	9Cp	9Aq	26Pi	13Ta	20Ge	12Le	22Vi
9	25Cn	17Vi	25Vi	15Sc	18Sg	2Aq	5Pi	20Ar	9Ge	17Cn	11Vi	19Li
11	25Le	16Li	23Li	13Sg	12Cp	26Aq	29Pi	16Ta	7Cn	16Le	9Li	16Sc
13	24Vi	12Sc	20Sc	5Cp	6Aq	20Pi	24Ar	13Ge	6Le	15Vi	7Sc	12Sg
15	20Li	7Sg	15Sg	28Cp	0Pi	15Ar	20Ta	12Cn	6Vi	14Li	4Sg	7Cp
17	16Sc	0Cp	9Cp	22Aq	25Pi	12Ta	19Ge	12Le	5Li	12Sc	29Sg	2Aq
19	10Sg	24Cp	2Aq	17Pi	21Ar	10Ge	18Cn	12Vi	4Sc	9Sg	24Cp	25Aq
21	4Cp	18Aq	26Aq	12Ar	18Ta	10Cn	19Le	12Li	1Sg	4Cp	18Aq	19Pi
23	27Cp	12Pi	21Pi	9Ta	16Ge	10Le	19Vi	9Sc	26Sg	28Cp	11Pi	13Ar
25	21Aq	7Ar	17Ar	7Ge	15Cn	9Vi	17Li	5Sg	20Cp	22Aq	6Ar	9Ta
27	15Pi	3Ta	13Ta	7Cn	14Le	7Li	13Sc	29Sg	13Aq	16Pi	1Ta	6Ge
29	10Ar		11Ge	4Le	13Vi	3Sc	8Sg	23Cp	7Pi	10Ar	28Ta	4Cn
31	6Ta		8Cn		10Li		2Cp	7Aq		6Ta		4Le

1975

	Jan	Feb	Mar	Apr	May	Jun	Jul	Aug	Sep	Oct	Nov	Dec
1	19Le	12Li	21Li	11Sg	14Cp	29Aq	0Ar	15Ta	2Cn	9Le	2Li	11Sc
3	18Vi	10Sc	19Sc	6Cp	9Aq	23Pi	24Ar	10Ge	0Le	8Vi	2Sc	9Sg
5	16Li	6Sg	15Sg	1Cp	3Pi	18Ar	19Ta	7Cn	28Le	8Li	1Sg	5Cp
7	13Sc	1Cp	10Cp	24Aq	26Pi	11Ta	16Ge	6Le	28Vi	8Sc	29Sg	1Aq
9	9Sg	25Cp	5Aq	18Pi	21Ar	7Ge	13Cn	6Vi	29Li	7Sg	25Cp	25Aq
11	4Cp	19Aq	28Aq	12Ar	16Ta	4Cn	12Le	6Li	29Sc	5Cp	20Aq	19Pi
13	28Cp	12Pi	22Pi	7Ta	13Ge	3Le	11Vi	6Sc	29Sg	1Aq	15Pi	13Ar
15	22Aq	6Ar	15Ar	2Ge	11Cn	1Vi	11Li	6Sg	27Cp	24Aq	9Ar	7Ta
17	16Pi	0Ta	9Ta	28Ge	8Le	28Vi	9Sc	5Cp	24Aq	17Pi	2Ta	1Ge
19	9Ar	25Ta	3Ge	25Cn	5Vi	25Li	5Sg	29Cp	18Pi	11Ar	26Ta	26Ge
21	4Ta	20Ge	29Ge	23Le	3Li	22Sc	0Cp	23Aq	11Ar	5Ta	22Ge	23Cn
23	1Ge	19Cn	27Cn	22Vi	1Sc	18Sg	24Cp	16Pi	5Ta	2Ge	20Cn	24Le
25	28Ge	20Le	27Le	22Li	0Sg	14Cp	18Aq	9Ar	1Ge	0Cn	21Le	24Vi
27	27Cn	21Vi	29Vi	21Sc	29Sg	9Aq	12Pi	3Ta	29Ge	29Cn	21Vi	23Li
29	27Le		29Li	19Sg	27Cp	3Pi	5Ar	28Ta	28Cn	0Le	18Li	20Sc
31	28Vi		27Sc		17Aq		27Ar	24Ge		1Vi		18Sg

1976

	Jan	Feb	Mar	Apr	May	Jun	Jul	Aug	Sep	Oct	Nov	Dec
1	2Cp	19Aq	19Pi	23Ar	27Ta	21Li	21Le	6Sg	3Pi	3Ar	0Ta	23Ta
3	28Cp	14Pi	4Ar	18Ta	22Ge	16Sc	19Vi	3Cp	2Ar	1Ta	8Ta	23Ta
5	24Aq	8Ar	28Ar	12Ge	16Cn	7Vi	16Li	26Cp	7Vi	26Ta	14Cn	23Le
7	18Pi	1Ta	22Ta	7Cn	13Le	8Li	15Sc	22Aq	0Ar	15Ta	17Ge	17Cn
9	12Ar	25Ta	16Ge	16Le	11Vi	4Sc	13Sg	5Aq	21Pi	24Ar	8Ge	12Cn
11	5Ta	20Ge	11Cn	2Vi	10Li	4Sg	10Cp	0Pi	15Ar	18Ta	2Cn	7Le
13	0Ge	17Cn	9Le	1Li	10Sc	3Cp	5Aq	24Pi	9Ta	11Ge	27Cn	3Vi
15	26Ge	16Le	8Vi	1Sc	10Sg	0Aq	0Pi	19Ar	3Ge	5Cn	22Le	0Li
17	23Cn	15Vi	9Li	1Sg	9Cp	26Aq	24Pi	13Ta	28Ge	1Le	20Vi	28Li
19	21Le	15Li	9Sc	0Cp	6Aq	21Pi	19Ar	7Ge	22Cn	28Le	18Li	28Sc
21	20Vi	14Sc	7Sg	27Cp	1Pi	15Ar	13Ta	1Cn	19Le	26Vi	19Sc	27Sg
23	19Li	11Sg	5Cp	22Aq	25Pi	9Ta	7Ge	28Cn	18Vi	26Li	20Sg	27Cp
25	17Sc	8Cp	0Aq	16Pi	19Ar	3Ge	2Cn	25Le	18Li	26Sc	20Cp	24Aq
27	14Sg	3Aq	25Aq	10Ar	12Ta	28Ge	28Cn	23Vi	18Sc	26Sg	16Aq	20Pi
29	11Cp	28Aq	19Pi	4Ta	8Ge	24Cn	26Le	22Li	18Sg	25Cp	12Pi	14Ar
31	7Aq		13Ar		4Cn		25Le	22Sc		22Aq		8Ta

1977

	Jan	Feb	Mar	Apr	May	Jun	Jul	Aug	Sep	Oct	Nov	Dec
1	20Ta	4Cn	12Cn	29Le	5Li	28Sc	7Cp	29Aq	17Ar	19Ta	3Cn	6Le
3	14Ge	29Cn	7Le	27Vi	4Sc	26Sg	1Aq	23Pi	13Ta	15Ge	1Le	4Vi
5	8Cn	26Le	4Vi	26Li	3Sg	24Cp	26Aq	17Ar	9Ge	12Cn	29Le	1Li
7	4Le	23Vi	3Li	25Sc	2Cp	22Aq	20Pi	11Ta	5Cn	9Le	27Vi	28Li
9	0Vi	21Li	2Sc	25Sg	0Aq	18Pi	15Ar	6Ge	23Cn	7Vi	25Li	26Sc
11	27Vi	19Sc	0Sg	23Cp	27Aq	13Ar	9Ta	1Cn	23Le	6Li	24Sc	25Sg
13	24Li	18Sg	29Sg	18Aq	22Pi	7Ta	3Ge	26Cn	21Vi	6Sc	23Sg	24Cp
15	23Sc	16Cp	26Cp	16Pi	20Ar	1Ge	27Ge	23Le	12Li	6Sg	23Cp	22Aq
17	22Sg	15Aq	23Aq	10Ar	13Ta	26Ge	23Cn	21Vi	21Sc	6Cp	21Aq	19Pi
19	21Cp	10Pi	19Pi	4Ta	7Ge	22Cn	21Le	21Li	21Sg	6Aq	18Pi	15Ar
21	19Aq	6Ar	14Ar	28Ta	1Cn	19Le	22Vi	22Sc	21Cp	4Pi	13Ar	10Ta
23	15Pi	0Ta	8Ta	22Ge	25Cn	17Vi	21Li	23Sg	19Aq	0Ar	8Ta	3Ge
25	10Ar	24Ta	2Ge	16Cn	21Le	17Li	22Sc	22Cp	15Pi	25Ar	1Ge	27Ge
27	4Ta	17Ge	25Ge	11Le	18Vi	16Sc	22Sg	21Aq	11Ar	19Ta	25Ge	21Cn
29	28Ta		20Cn	7Vi	16Li	16Sg	22Cp	18Pi	5Ta	13Ge	18Cn	15Le
31	22Ge		15Le		13Sc		20Aq	14Ar		7Cn		9Vi

1978

	Jan	Feb	Mar	Apr	May	Jun	Jul	Aug	Sep	Oct	Nov	Dec
1	22Vi	11Sc	22Sc	15Cp	24Aq	15Ar	20Ta	5Cn	19Le	22Vi	10Sc	17Sg
3	18Li	10Sg	20Sg	14Aq	22Pi	10Ta	14Ge	28Cn	13Vi	18Li	8Sg	16Cp
5	16Sc	9Cp	19Cp	11Pi	18Ar	4Ge	8Cn	22Le	8Li	14Sc	6Cp	15Aq
7	15Sg	8Aq	18Aq	8Ar	13Ta	28Ge	2Le	16Vi	4Sc	12Sg	5Aq	14Pi
9	15Cp	8Pi	16Pi	5Ta	8Ge	23Cn	25Le	11Li	1Sg	10Cp	3Pi	11Ar
11	16Aq	6Ar	14Ar	0Ge	2Cn	16Le	19Vi	7Sc	29Sg	8Aq	1Ar	7Ta
13	14Pi	2Ta	9Ta	25Ge	25Cn	10Vi	14Li	6Sg	28Cp	7Pi	27Ar	2Ge
15	11Ar	26Ta	4Ge	18Cn	20Le	5Li	11Sc	3Cp	27Aq	5Ar	24Ta	28Ge
17	6Ta	20Ge	28Ge	12Le	2Vi	1Sc	9Sg	1Aq	24Pi	2Ta	19Ge	23Cn
19	0Ge	14Cn	22Cn	6Vi	10Li	28Sc	7Cp	29Aq	21Ar	28Ta	13Cn	15Le
21	24Ge	8Le	16Le	0Li	6Sc	26Sg	6Aq	27Pi	17Ta	22Ge	7Le	9Vi
23	17Cn	3Vi	11Vi	0Sc	5Sg	25Cp	5Pi	24Ar	12Ge	16Cn	0Vi	3Li
25	12Le	28Vi	7Li	27Sc	5Cp	25Aq	4Ar	19Ta	6Cn	9Le	25Vi	29Li
27	6Vi	25Li	5Sc	27Sg	6Aq	24Pi	1Ta	14Ge	0Le	3Vi	21Li	26Sc
29	2Li		3Sg	27Cp	5Pi	23Ar	28Ta	9Cn	24Le	28Vi	18Sc	25Sg
31	28Li		1Cp		4Ar		23Ge	2Le		23Li		25Cp

1979

	Jan	Feb	Mar	Apr	May	Jun	Jul	Aug	Sep	Oct	Nov	Dec
1	10Aq	3Ar	11Ar	1Ge	4Cn	18Le	20Vi	5Sc	23Sg	0Aq	23Pi	2Ta
3	10Pi	1Ta	9Ta	26Ge	29Cn	12Vi	14Li	1Sg	21Cp	29Aq	23Ar	0Ge
5	8Ar	27Ta	5Ge	21Cn	22Le	6Li	9Sc	28Sg	20Aq	29Pi	22Ta	27Ge
7	4Ta	21Ge	0Cn	15Le	16Vi	0Sc	6Sg	27Cp	21Pi	29Ar	19Ge	23Cn
9	0Ge	15Cn	24Cn	8Vi	10Li	28Sc	4Cp	26Aq	21Ar	28Ta	15Cn	18Le
11	24Ge	9Le	18Le	3Li	5Sc	24Sg	4Aq	26Pi	19Ta	24Ge	10Le	11Vi
13	18Cn	3Vi	12Vi	27Li	3Sg	25Cp	4Pi	24Ar	16Ge	20Cn	4Vi	5Li
15	12Le	27Vi	6Li	24Sc	2Cp	24Aq	4Ar	21Ta	11Cn	14Le	27Vi	29Li
17	6Vi	21Li	1Sc	20Sg	29Cp	0Ta	4Ta	17Ge	5Le	7Vi	21Li	25Sc
19	0Li	16Sc	26Sc	17Cp	27Aq	22Pi	27Ta	13Cn	0Vi	1Li	15Sc	21Sg
21	24Li	13Sg	23Sg	15Aq	27Pi	22Ar	22Ge	8Le	24Vi	25Li	13Sg	19Cp
23	20Sc	12Cp	21Cp	15Pi	28Ar	17Ta	17Cn	2Vi	17Li	20Sc	10Cp	18Aq
25	18Sg	11Aq	20Aq	13Ar	20Ta	8Cn	11Le	16Sg	7Aq	16Pi	14Pi	—
27	18Cp	12Pi	19Pi	11Ta	17Ge	11Le	5Vi	19Li	11Sc	16Sg	7Aq	16Pi
29	18Aq		19Ar	8Ge	12Cn	5Vi	29Vi	13Sc	5Sg	10Cp	5Pi	14Ar
31	18Pi		17Ta		6Le		22Li	9Sg		9Pi		9Ge

1980

	Jan	Feb	Mar	Apr	May	Jun	Jul	Aug	Sep	Oct	Nov	Dec
1	23Ge	10Le	1Vi	15Li	18Sc	5Cp	25Pi	18Ta	9Cn	16Le	0Le	26Vi
3	19Cn	4Vi	24Vi	9Sc	13Sg	3Aq	24Ar	16Ge	4Le	11Vi	24Le	21Li
5	14Le	28Vi	18Li	4Sg	9Cp	2Pi	24Ta	14Cn	0Vi	6Li	18Li	13Sc
7	8Vi	21Li	12Sc	29Sg	5Aq	27Pi	22Ge	11Le	24Vi	0Sc	11Sc	7Sg
9	1Li	15Sc	6Sg	25Cp	3Pi	26Ar	20Cn	7Vi	18Li	24Sc	5Sg	0Cp
11	25Li	9Sg	2Cp	22Aq	2Ar	25Ta	18Le	2Li	11Sc	17Sg	29Sg	24Cp
13	20Sc	5Cp	28Cp	22Pi	3Ta	24Ge	15Vi	29Li	5Sg	11Cp	23Cp	18Aq
15	16Sg	6Aq	26Aq	24Ar	3Ge	22Cn	11Li	24Sc	28Sg	5Aq	18Aq	14Pi
17	14Cp	6Pi	29Pi	22Ge	16Le	19Vi	2Li	11Pi	1Li	24Vi	4Le	10Vi
19	13Aq	6Ar	29Ar	21Ge	0Sc	10Aq	18Pi	18Aq	14Pi	14Ge	4Le	10Vi
21	12Pi	5Ta	28Ta	17Cn	21Le	6Sc	10Cp	17Pi	1Ge	0Cn	29Cn	8Li
23	11Ar	3Ge	26Ge	13Le	16Vi	0Sg	4Aq	11Ar	26Ge	26Cn	24Le	3Sc
25	9Ta	29Ge	21Cn	6Vi	8Li	23Sg	28Aq	5Ta	22Ge	24Le	20Vi	29Sc
27	6Ge	24Cn	16Le	0Li	2Sc	18Cp	24Pi	2Ge	19Cn	22Vi	16Li	26Sg
29	2Cn	19Le	9Vi	24Li	25Sc	14Aq	22Ar	0Cn	18Le	20Li	11Sc	22Cp
31	27Cn		3Li		22Sg		21Ta	29Cn		19Sc		16Aq

1981

	Jan	Feb	Mar	Apr	May	Jun	Jul	Aug	Sep	Oct	Nov	Dec
1	10Sc	24Sg	2Cp	20Aq	25Pi	19Ta	28Ge	6Li	9Sc	23Sg	26Cp	—
3	4Sg	20Cp	27Cp	17Pi	25Ar	17Ge	27Cn	15Vi	3Cp	17Cp	20Aq	26Pi
5	29Sg	17Aq	24Aq	17Ar	26Ta	16Cn	11Li	25Sc	19Sg	11Aq	14Ar	—
7	24Cp	15Pi	23Pi	17Ta	26Ge	16Le	20Vi	21Sc	7Pi	21Cp	7Pi	14Ar
9	21Aq	13Ar	21Ar	17Ge	25Cn	12Vi	7Li	11Sg	15Sc	16Ag	13Ar	13Ta
11	19Pi	11Ta	20Ta	16Cn	22Le	7Li	19Sc	5Cp	23Sg	8Aq	18Ar	—
13	17Ar	10Ge	19Ge	12Le	16Vi	1Sc	1Sg	29Cp	17Aq	2Pi	5Ta	13Ta
15	15Ta	8Cn	18Cn	6Vi	8Li	24Sc	27Sg	23Aq	11Pi	26Pi	28Ta	5Le
17	14Ge	14Le	1Li	4Sc	18Sg	13Cp	2Ta	11Ge	4Le	10Vi	4Le	10Vi
19	12Cn	0Vi	9Vi	25Vi	13Cp	8Aq	14Pi	5Ta	8Ge	10Cn	0Vi	7Li
21	9Le	25Vi	4Li	19Li	7Aq	2Pi	7Ar	28Ta	3Cn	5Le	25Vi	3Sc
23	5Vi	20Li	28Li	15Sc	3Pi	27Pi	2Ta	25Ge	0Le	2Vi	21Li	29Sc
25	0Li	15Sc	22Sc	6Cp	11Aq	0Ar	9Ta	3Cn	24Le	29Vi	15Sc	17Sg
27	24Li	7Sg	13Sg	1Aq	0Ar	29Ar	28Ta	7Cn	20Li	25Li	8Sg	11Cp
29	17Sc		10Cp	4Ar	4Ar	29Ta	7Cn	0Le	28Li	5Le	5Aq	—
31	12Sg		5Aq		4Ta		5Le	24Vi		11Sg		0Pi

1982

	Jan	Feb	Mar	Apr	May	Jun	Jul	Aug	Sep	Oct	Nov	Dec
1	13Pi	4Ta	14Ta	8Cn	16Le	6Li	10Sc	25Sg	9Aq	12Pi	1Ta	8Ge
3	9Ar	2Ge	12Ge	5Le	12Vi	1Sc	5Sg	18Cp	2Pi	5Ar	26Ta	6Cn
5	7Ta	1Cn	11Cn	3Vi	9Li	25Sc	28Sg	12Aq	26Pi	0Ta	24Ge	6Le
7	6Ge	0Le	9Le	29Vi	5Sc	19Sg	22Cp	7Pi	21Ar	26Ta	24Cn	6Vi
9	6Cn	28Le	7Vi	28Li	13Cp	13Cp	16Aq	1Ar	21Ge	2Cn	25Le	29Li
11	6Le	26Vi	4Li	20Sc	22Sg	6Aq	10Pi	29Ar	21Ge	22Vi	23Vi	29Li
13	4Vi	22Li	29Li	14Sg	14Cp	0Pi	3Ta	25Ge	18Le	26Vi	19Li	25Sc
15	1Li	16Sc	24Sc	7Cp	10Aq	26Pi	1Ta	25Cn	18Le	26Vi	15Sc	18Sg
17	26Li	10Sg	18Sg	5Aq	4Pi	8Ar	28Ta	24Cn	14Li	14Li	9Sg	12Cp
19	20Sc	4Cp	11Cp	26Aq	1Ar	27Ta	0Cn	24Le	14Li	19Sc	3Cp	5Aq
21	12Pi	5Ta	28Ta	17Cn	6Sc	21Sg	10Cp	17Vi	7Sc	2Sg	27Cp	24Aq
23	8Cp	23Aq	1Pi	20Ar	28Ta	22Cn	0Vi	5Sg	7Cp	27Sg	24Aq	23Pi
25	25Cp	19Pi	28Pi	20Ta	15Sc	29Sg	12Cp	17Vi	9Ar	17Ta	15Pi	19Aq
27	27Aq	16Ar	26Ar	18Ge	19Vi	24Li	9Sg	23Cp	25Aq	11Ar	18Ar	16Ta
29	23Pi		25Ta	18Cn	16Li	19Sc	3Cp	17Aq	18Ar	7Ta	16Ge	16Ge
31	20Ar		24Ge		13Sc		27Cp	14Ar		5Cn		16Cn

1983

	Jan	Feb	Mar	Apr	May	Jun	Jul	Aug	Sep	Oct	Nov	Dec
1	1Le	24Vi	2Li	21Sc	24Sg	8Aq	10Pi	26Ar	14Ge	22Cn	15Vi	24Li
3	1Vi	21Li	0Sc	16Sg	18Cp	2Pi	4Ar	21Ta	11Cn	21Le	12Li	21Sc
5	29Vi	17Sc	27Sc	10Cp	12Aq	26Pi	29Ar	18Ge	10Le	21Vi	10Sc	16Sg
7	26Li	12Sg	23Sg	4Aq	6Pi	21Ar	26Ta	18Cn	12Vi	21Li	7Sg	13Cp
9	21Sc	6Cp	17Cp	28Aq	0Ar	18Ta	25Ge	18Le	10Vi	18Sg	18Sc	24Li
11	15Sg	29Cp	11Aq	22Pi	26Ar	15Ge	25Cn	19Vi	10Sc	15Sc	15Vi	24Li
13	4Vi	29Li	10Li	16Sc	15Sg	8Aq	10Pi	26Ar	14Ge	22Cn	15Vi	24Li
15	2Aq	17Pi	26Pi	15Ta	22Ge	24Cn	0Vi	18Li	6Sg	9Cp	13Aq	19Ar
17	26Aq	12Ar	21Ar	14Ge	22Cn	24Le	28Vi	15Sc	1Cp	4Aq	7Pi	12Ta
19	20Pi	8Ta	18Ta	10Cn	19Le	22Vi	25Li	9Sg	25Cp	27Aq	1Ar	6Ge
21	15Ar	5Cn	13Cn	5Vi	15Li	18Sc	20Sg	3Cp	19Aq	21Pi	25Ar	1Cn
23	11Ta	3Cn	13Cn	6Vi	15Li	4Sg	7Cp	22Aq	7Ar	11Ta	1Cn	9Le
25	26Aq	12Ar	14Vi	14Vi	24Vi	22Sc	8Ge	8Vi	29Cp	24Le	28Sc	9Vi
27	9Ge	2Vi	11Vi	7Sg	1Aq	16Pi	0Ar	28Ta	3Vi	7Cp	28Le	7Li
29	9Cn		10Li	7Sg	11Cp	16Pi	0Ar	28Ta	3Vi	26Vi	26Li	7Li
31	9Vi		7Sc		26Cp		13Ar	15Le		1Li		1Sg

1984

```
      Jan    Feb    Mar    Apr    May    Jun    Jul    Aug    Sep    Oct    Nov    Dec
 1   14Sg    0Aq   21Aq    5Ar    9Ta   26Ge   27Vi   20Sc   27Sg   13Aq   16Pi
 3    9Cp   24Aq   15Pi    0Ta    4Ge   24Cn    2Vi    3Li   17Sg   22Cp    8Pi   10Ar
 5    3Aq   18Pi    8Ar   24Ta    0Cn   22Le    1Li   24Sc   13Cp    2Aq    1Ar    8Ta
 7   27Aq   11Ar    2Ta   20Ge   27Vi    0Sc   20Sg    8Aq   11Pi   25Ar   28Ta

 9   21Pi    6Ta   27Ta   16Cn   18Le   18Li   27Sc   16Cp    2Pi    5Ar   19Ta   16Pi
11   15Ar    1Ge   23Ge   14Le   17Sc   11Aq    9Sc   26Vi   29Sc    6Cp   19Ge   16Le
13   10Ta   28Ge   20Cn   14Vi   23Li   14Sg   19Cp   19Ar   14Ge   15Vi   16Le
15   15Ge   26Cn   20Le   14Li   14Sg   18Aq    0Ar   14Ta   11Cn   14Li

17    4Cn   27Le   20Vi   13Sc   19Sg    6Aq    8Pi   22Ar    8Ge   12Cn    4Vi   13Li
19    3Le   27Vi   20Li   11Sg   13Cp   12Ge   16Ta    9Ge   14Cn   22Li   10Sg
21    4Vi   27Li   19Sc    7Cp   10Aq   24Pi   26Ar   11Ge    0Le    8Vi   2Sc   10Sg
23    3Li   24Sc   16Sg    4Aq   8Pi    0Ar   20Ta    8Cn    0Li    8Sc   11Sg   7Cp

25    1Sc   20Sg   12Cp   2Aq   28Pi   13Ta   16Ge    6Le   0Li   29Sg   4Aq
27   28Sc   15Cp    6Aq   20Pi   22Ar   11Ge   0Cn   6Vi   7Sc   5Cp   29Aq   29Aq
29   23Sg    9Aq    0Pi   14Ar   17Ta   5Cn   13Le   6Li   2Sg   22Aq   24Pi
31   18Cp          23Pi          13Ge          12Vi   6Sc          1Ar          17Ar
```

1985

```
      Jan    Feb    Mar    Apr    May    Jun    Jul    Aug    Sep    Oct    Nov    Dec
 1   29Ar    2Ge    9Le   16Vi   19Sg    9Aq   27Pi    3Cn    6Le   17Cn
 3   23Ta    9Cn   17Cn    8Vi   16Li   10Sg   17Cp    6Pi   21Ar   23Ta    7Cn   12Le
 5   18Ge    7Le   15Le    8Li    5Sc   16Sg    6Aq   25Ar    8Ge   11Cn   28Le    5Li
 7   15Cn    6Vi   15Vi    8Sc   16Sg    6Aq   10Pi   25Ar    8Ge   11Cn   28Le    5Li

 9   13Le    6Li   15Li   8Sc   15Cp    2Ar    8Ta    3Cn   6Vi    1Sc   4Sc
11   11Vi    4Sc   14Sc    6Cp   11Aq   27Pi   29Ar   12Ge   2Vi   3Vi   25Li   4Sc
13    9Li    2Sg   13Sg    4Aq    8Pi    0Ar   12Ta   22Cn   3Le   24Vi   3Sc   3Aq
15    8Sc   29Sg    9Cp   27Aq   1Ar   14Ta   17Ge   3Le   24Vi   3Sc   26Sg   3Aq

17    5Sg   25Cp   5Aq   21Pi   24Ar   8Ge   0Li   11Li   3Sg   5Sg   0Pi
19    3Cp   21Aq   0Pi   14Ar   18Ta   3Cn   1Pi   9Sc   22Sc   5Cp   26Aq   26Pi
21   29Cp   16Pi   24Pi   9Ta   27Ge   6Vi   11Pi   1Sg   22Cp   17Pi   26Aq
23   25Aq   10Ar   18Ar   6Ge   23Cn   7Li   27Sc   19Cp   7Pi   10Ar   13Ta

25   19Pi    3Ta   12Ta   2Ge   23Vi   2Sc   15Aq   20Pi   5Ta   7Ge
27   13Ar   27Ta   6Ge   28Cn   28Le   22Sc   22Cp   11Pi   18Ar   28Ta   1Cn
29    7Ta          0Cn   24Le   20Sc   28Sg   14Pi   5Ar   18Ar   18Ge
31    1Ge          26Cn          25Li          26Cp          1Ge          22Le
```

1986

```
      Jan    Feb    Mar    Apr    May    Jun    Jul    Aug    Sep    Oct    Nov    Dec
 1    5Vi   26Li    7Sc    0Cp    9Aq   27Pi    1Ta   15Ge   29Cn    2Vi   21Li   28Sc
 3    5Li   24Sc    5Sg   28Cp    5Pi   22Ar   24Ta   18Cn   26Le   29Vi   20Sc   29Sg
 5   29Li   22Sg    3Cp   25Aq    0Ar   17Ta   15Ge   18Le   28Le   27Li   21Sc   29Cp
 7   28Sc   21Cp    1Aq   20Pi   24Ar    9Ge   12Cn   3Le   17Li   25Sc   19Cp   27Aq

 9   27Sg   19Aq   28Aq   15Ar    6Ta   24Ge   0Le   13Vi   24Le   24Sg   19Cp   24Pi
11   26Cp   16Pi   24Pi   10Ta   1Ge   1Vi   11Li   13Sg   23Cp   14Pi   20Ar
13   25Aq   11Ar   19Ar   4Ge   27Vi   12Ge   0Vi   13Vi   23Cp   14Pi   20Ar
15   21Pi    6Ta   14Ta   27Ge    0Le   17Vi   17Sg   10Aq   17Pi    5Ta   8Ge

17   16Ar   29Ta    7Ge   21Cn   22Sc   16Cp    5Ar   9Ta   29Sc   2Cn
19   10Ta   23Ge   1Cn   16Le   21Sg   0Ta   9Ta   27Sg   9Le   21Cn
21    3Ge   18Cn   25Cn   13Vi   19Cp   1Pi   13Pi   0Ta   25Ta   29Ge   11Le   26Cn
23   27Ge   13Le   21Le   11Li   19Sc   25Aq   24Ge   29Sg   1Aq   25Ta   27Ge   14Vi

25   22Cn   10Vi   19Vi   11Sc   18Pi   6Vi   0Sc   10Li
27   18Le    8Li   17Li   11Sg   19Cp   28Sc   22Sc   20Aq   3Pi   28Cp
29   15Vi          17Sc   10Cp   18Aq   4Ar   10Vi   6Li   1Li
31   12Li          16Sg          14Pi          7Li                        7Cp
```

1987

```
      Jan    Feb    Mar    Apr    May    Jun    Jul    Aug    Sep    Oct    Nov    Dec
 1   22Cp   14Pi   22Pi   10Ta   14Ge   28Cn   0Vi   16Li   6Sg   14Cp   8Pi   16Ar
 3   22Aq   12Ar   20Ar   6Ge   8Cn   24Li   14Li   6Sg   21Ar   23Ta   3Cn
 5   20Pi    7Ta   16Ta   0Cn   24Li   10Sg   10Sg   5Aq   12Pi   3Pi   3Ta   3Cn
 7   16Ar    0Ge   10Ge   24Cn   25Le   11Li   16Sc   9Cp   3Pi   1Ar   29Ta   3Cn

 9   11Ta   26Ge   4Cn   18Le   20Vi   9Sc   15Sg   9Aq   0Ta   8Ta   29Le   21Le
11    5Ge   19Cn   27Cn   12Vi   17Li   7Sg   9Pi   9Ar   26Ta   5Ge   24Cn   21Le
13   29Ge   13Le   21Le   8Li   15Sc   7Cp   26Ar   9Ge   23Ge   3Cn   7Vi   9Li
15   23Cn    8Vi   17Vi    5Sc   13Sg    7Aq   15Pi   16Li   21Cn   23Ge   7Vi    9Li

17   17Le    3Li   13Li   4Sg   6Pi   12Le   15Cn   9Le   11Vi   27Li   1Sc
19   11Vi   29Li   11Sc   2Cp   12Aq   9Ta   9Ta   25Ge   9Le   11Vi   27Li   1Cp
21    6Li   25Sc    7Sg   0Aq   10Pi   24Pi   13Pi   3Vi   6Li   18Vi   3Vi   6Li
23    3Sc   25Sg   5Cp   28Aq   6Ar   24Ta   28Ge   0Li   27Vi   27Li   23Sg   1Aq

25    1Sg   23Aq   4Aq   26Pi   6Vi   0Sc   1Pi
27    0Cp   23Aq   3Pi   23Ar   27Ta   13Ge   1Li   19Sc   5Sg   27Sg   18Pi   26Ar
29    0Aq          1Ar   19Ta   22Ge   6Le   16Sc   16Sg   5Cp   27Pi   26Ar
31    0Pi          27Ar          16Cn          4Li   22Sc          23Aq
```

1988

```
      Jan    Feb    Mar    Apr    May    Jun    Jul    Aug    Sep    Oct    Nov    Dec
 1    5Ge   21Cn   11Le   25Vi   29Li   17Sg   25Cp   19Pi   11Ta   17Ge    4Le    5Vi
 3   29Ge   14Le    5Vi   20Li   25Sc   15Cp    2Ar    8Ge    4Cn   28Le   29Vi
 5   24Cn    8Vi   29Vi   15Sc   22Sg    3Aq    9Ge   23Cn   1Vi   7Le   21Vi   23Li
 7   17Le    2Li   23Li   11Sg   21Cp   15Aq   21Ge   1Vi   1Vi   7Li   21Vi   23Li

 9   11Vi   26Li   18Sc    8Cp   17Aq    1Ar    8Ge   22Le   25Vi    9Sc   14Sg
11    5Li   21Sc   14Sg    6Aq   6Aq   9Ta   1Le   18Li   6Sc   25Vi   1Cp   14Sg
13    0Sc   18Sg   12Cp   5Pi   5Ar   19Ge   5Cn   18Sc   6Sc   25Vi   1Cp   7Pi
15   26Sc   17Cp   11Aq   4Ar   12Ta   27Ge   4Le   19Vi   3Sc   9Li   1Cp   7Pi

17   24Sg   18Aq   11Pi   3Ta   7Ge   26Cn   29Cn   1Vi   4Cp   26Aq   5Ar
19   24Cp   18Pi   11Ar   1Ge   1Ge   5Cn   23Le   6Li   0Pi   23Aq   3Ta
21   25Aq   17Ar   9Ta   27Ge   27Ge   12Le   3Vi   6Li   3Cp   9Sc   29Pi   1Ge
23   24Pi   15Ta   6Ge   22Cn   24Cn   22Vi   27Li   6Sc   20Aq   21Sc   22Ar

25   22Ar   11Ge   1Cn   16Le   18Le   7Li   22Sc   6Cp   20Pi
27   19Ta    6Cn   26Cn   10Vi   10Vi   1Sc   27Sg   21Aq   28Ta   16Cn   19Le
29   14Ge    0Le   20Le    3Li   4Li   25Sc   21Sg   6Li   6Li   11Ge   13Vi
31    8Cn          13Vi          3Sg          6Li                       7Li
```

1989

```
      Jan    Feb    Mar    Apr    May    Jun    Jul    Aug    Sep    Oct    Nov    Dec
 1   19Li    3Sg   12Sg    0Aq   8Pi   1Ta   10Ge   0Le   17Vi   19Li    4Sg    8Cp
 3   13Sc    0Cp   8Cp   26Aq   2Ar   11Ge   26Ge   8Li   13Sc   28Sg    3Aq
 5    9Sg   28Cp    6Aq   26Pi   1Ta   9Cn   26Ge   26Ge   11Sc   13Sc   23Cp   29Aq
 7    6Cp   27Aq    5Pi   29Ar   7Ta   23Cn   24Vi   14Li   25Sc   19Pi   26Pi

 9    4Aq   27Pi    5Ar   29Ta   5Cn   22Le   8Sc   23Sg   27Cp   19Ar
11   3Pi   26Ar   5Ta   27Ge   1Le   18Li   2Sg   28Aq   24Ge   25Ar
13    2Ar   24Ta    4Ge   24Cn   28Le   13Sc   27Sg   16Ar   23Pi   17Ta   3Ge
15    0Ta   20Ge   1Cn   18Le   22Vi   13Sg   23Ar   23Cp   23Ar   17Ta   3Ge

17   27Ta   17Cn   26Cn   12Vi   14Li   28Sc   2Cp   14Ta   15Cn   20Le
19   24Ge   12Le   20Le   5Li   8Sc   22Aq   10Aq   0Pi   21Ta   6Ge   6Ge   10Li
21   20Cn    6Vi   15Vi   1Sc   8Sc   20Cp   27Aq   20Ar   0Vi   10Li
23   15Le   29Vi    8Li   24Sc   1Sg   8Li   28Vi   19Ta   11Ge   7Li   10Li   3Sc

25    9Vi   23Li   18Sg    5Pi   24Ar   17Ge   7Le   10Vi   25Li   27Sc
27    3Li   17Sc   13Cp   10Aq   12Ta   20Ge   14Cn   8Vi   25Li   25Li   19Sg   17Cp
29   27Li          21Sg   10Aq   18Pi   12Ta   20Ge   9Le   25Vi   28Li   9Sc   13Aq
31   21Sc          17Cp          17Ar          17Cn   4Vi                      13Aq
```

1990

```
      Jan    Feb    Mar    Apr    May    Jun    Jul    Aug    Sep    Oct    Nov    Dec
 1   26Aq   18Ar   28Ar   22Ge   29Cn   17Vi   21Li   9Sg   22Aq   19Ta
 3   23Pi   16Ta   27Ta   20Cn   26Le   12Li   14Sc   28Sg   14Aq   9Pi   11Ta
 5   21Ar   15Ge   25Ge   16Le    8Sc   8Sg   11Pi   11Pi   7Ge   18Le
 7   20Ta   13Cn   23Cn   11Vi   15Li    0Sg   2Aq   19Ar   17Ta   13Cn   28Le   18Le

 9   19Ge   10Le   19Le    6Li   9Sc   26Sg   25Pi   7Ta   15Vi   9Le   15Vi
11   17Cn    6Vi   14Vi   0Sc   2Sg   18Cp   9Le   6Ge   15Cn   1Li   5Sc
13   15Le   1Li   9Li   24Sc   26Sg   26Ge   26Ge   12Ge   9Cn   4Le   21Vi   5Sc
15   11Vi   25Li   3Sc   18Sg   17Sg   13Cp   10Aq   19Vi   3Sc   5Sg   3Aq

17    5Li   19Sc   27Sc   11Cp   15Aq   4Ar   14Ta    8Cn   29Le    4Li   22Sg
19   29Li    8Sg   21Sg    6Aq   12Pi   4Ta   25Sc   6Le   18Vi   1Sc   14Sg   16Cp
21   23Sc    8Cp   15Cp    3Pi   10Ar   4Ge   12Cn   3Vi   9Li   23Sc   0Aq
23   17Sg    3Aq   11Aq   0Ar   9Ta   5Cn   11Le   0Li   15Sc   18Sg   5Pi

25   12Cp   1Pi   9Pi   1Ta   10Ge   3Le   8Vi   24Li   10Cp   26Aq   1Ar
27    9Aq   29Pi   8Ar   1Ge   9Cn   0Vi   4Li   22Pi   5Ar   27Ta
29    6Pi          8Ta   0Cn   6Le   25Vi   29Li   12Sg   0Pi   19Ar   27Ta
31    4Ar          8Ge          5Vi          23Sc          6Cp                28Ge
```

1991

```
      Jan    Feb    Mar    Apr    May    Jun    Jul    Aug    Sep    Oct    Nov    Dec
 1   13Cn   4Vi   12Vi   1Sc   8Cp   20Aq   7Ar   28Ta   7Cn   0Vi    7Li
 3   12Le    2Li   9Li   25Sc   28Sg   15Pi   0Ta   28Ge   4Le   23Vi   3Sc
 5   10Vi    7Sc   5Sc   19Sg   28Sg   1Ar   8Ta   9Cn   2Vi   24Li   23Vi   3Sc
 7    7Li   22Sc   0Sg   13Cp   15Aq   1Ar   8Ta   0Cn   24Le   1Li   20Sc   23Sg

 9    2Sc   16Sg   23Sg   7Aq   10Pi   6Ge   0Le   23Vi   28Li   28Li
11   26Sc   9Cp   25Sg   7Aq   28Ta   7Le   18Li   9Cp   11Aq
13   19Sg    3Aq   21Cp   2Pi   6Ar   28Ta   7Le   18Li   9Cp   11Aq
15   13Cp   29Aq   7Pi   26Ar   6Ge   28Cn   7Li   25Li   11Sg   13Cp   26Aq   29Pi

17    7Aq   24Pi   4Ar   25Ta   4Cn   21Sc   1Sc   15Sg   8Aq   21Pi   25Ar
19    1Pi   19Ar   4Ar   25Ta   3Le   15Sc   5Sg   15Aq   16Pi   21Pi   25Ar
21   28Pi   19Ta   0Ge   23Cn   3Vi   25Vi   23Aq   30Ga   18Pi   14Ge   14Cn   22Cn
23   24Ar   7Ta   25Te   4Cn   3Li   1Sg   2Aq   18Pi   18Ga   26Pi   14Ga   22Cn

25   22Ta   16Cn   26Cn   18Vi   23Li   9Sc   14Ar   21Ta   1Tc   14Ar   21Vi
27   21Ge   14Le   24Le   14Li   18Sc   6Sg   11Ta   19Ge   9Le   19Ge   21Vi   21Li
29   21Cn          21Vi   9Sc   12Sg    0Pi   0Pi   14Ta   6Li   10Vi   10Vi   18Sc
31   20Le          18Li          6Cp                25Pi   14Ta   16Le                13Sc
```

1992

```
      Jan    Feb    Mar    Apr    May    Jun    Jul    Aug    Sep    Oct    Nov    Dec
 1   26Sc   11Cp    1Aq   16Pi   19Ar    8Ge   16Cn   10Vi    2Sc    7Sg   23Cp   25Aq
 3   20Sg    4Aq   26Aq   14Ar   18Ta    6Cn   13Le    2Li   26Sc   20Cp   11Pi
 5   14Cp   28Aq   19Pi    9Ta   15Ge    2Le   9Vi   27Li   7Sc   15Vi   1Sc   13Ar
 7    7Aq   22Pi   14Ar   3Ge   11Cn   5Vi   13Li   7Sc   15Vi   1Sc   13Ar

 9    1Pi   17Ar   10Ta   0Cn   10Sc   27Sg   12Aq   15Pi   0Ta   4Ge
11   25Pi   13Ta   6Ge   28Cn   0Sc   6Sg   6Pi   0Aq   4Ge   2Cn
13   20Ar   10Cn   4Cn   27Le   19Cp   15Aq   0Ar   4Ta   23Ge   0Le
15   17Ta          0Sc   26Vi   21Sg   25Cp   9Pi   24Ar   29Ta   9Li   1Li

17   15Ge   8Le   2Vi   24Li   14Le   18Ga   3Ar   20Ta   3Ar   20Ta   16Vi   27Vi
19   15Cn   8Vi   1Li   21Sc   25Ge   10Aq   12Pi   1Li   16Vi   23Cn   16Vi   27Vi
21   15Le   8Li   0Sc   17Sg   20Cp   3Pi   3Li   0Sc   24Li   29Li   13Sc   19Sc
23   15Vi          6Sc   13Cp   17Aq   27Pi   1Ta   19Ge   11Le   21Vi   15Sc   19Sg

25   14Li   1Sg   6Aq   7Pi   2Ar   27Ta   11Vi   11Vi   11Vi   12Vi   6Cp
27   12Sc   0Pi   0Aq   27Ta   19Ge   25Ge   18Le   1Aq   5Sg   18Ga
29   9Sg   29Pi   24Pi   24Ar   27Ta   18Le   18Li   11Sc   0Sg   15Sg   3Pi
31   5Sg                3Pi          24Ta          24Le   18Li                11Cp
```

1993

```
      Jan    Feb    Mar    Apr    May    Jun    Jul    Aug    Sep    Oct    Nov    Dec
 1    8Ar   23Ta    2Ge   21Cn   29Le   23Li    2Sg   12Cp    7Pi   10Ar   24Ta   28Ge
 3    3Ta   20Ge   28Ge   18Le   26Vi   19Sc   28Sg   6Aq   1Ar   5Ta   19Ge   24Cn
 5   29Ta   18Cn   26Cn   19Vi   23Li   16Sg   25Cp   0Pi   24Ar   27Ta   14Cn   21Le
 7   26Ge   16Le   24Le   16Li   20Sc   13Cp   20Aq    4Ar   18Ta   21Ge   11Le

 9   25Cn   15Vi   19Sc   19Sc   12Aq   14Pi   3Ar   13Ge   17Cn   8Vi   17Li
11   24Le   14Li   27Li   18Sc   12Aq   14Pi   8Ta   9Ca   13Le   16Sg   8Ge   8Vi
13   24Vi   13Sc   26Sc   17Sg   9Pi   5Ar   26Ta   6Le   11Vi   14Li   7Li
15   22Li   12Sg   22Sg   8Aq   18Pi   24Ar   26Ta   6Le   11Vi   14Li   7Sg

17   19Sc    8Cp   21Cp   2Sc   12Le   22Cp   21Ca   12Le   6Sc   14Sg   6Cp   10Aq
19   15Sg    5Aq   17Aq   25Pi   28Ar   16Ge   0Vi   6Sc   14Sg   6Cp   5Pi
21   11Cp    1Pi   11Aq   19Ar   18Ta   10Cn   11Sc   2Cp   6Aq   21Pi   29Pi
23    5Aq   20Pi   29Pi    1Ta   18Ge   9Le   18Vi   9Li   29Sg   25Pi

25   29Aq   24Ar   9Ge   12Cn   7Vi   9Sc   5Cp   22Aq   25Pi   5Ta   17Ta
27   23Pi    7Ta   17Ar   12Ge   15Sc   5Cp   22Aq   25Pi   9Ta   17Ta
29   17Ar   7Ta   17Ar   10Vi   1Li   4Sc   0Aq   16Pi   18Ar   3Ge   4Cn
31   11Ta          8Cn          9Li          8Cp   25Aq          12Ta                 4Le
```

1994

	Jan	Feb	Mar	Apr	May	Jun	Jul	Aug	Sep	Oct	Nov	Dec
1	18Le	11Li	20Li	13Sg	20Cp	8Pi	11Ar	24Ta	8Cn	12Le	2Li	10Sc
3	16Vi	9Sc	20Sc	11Cp	17Aq	2Ar	4Ta	18Ge	3Le	10Vi	2Sc	10Sg
5	14Li	7Sg	17Sg	7Aq	11Pi	26Ar	28Ta	13Cn	2Vi	9Li	2Sg	10Cp
7	12Sc	4Cp	14Cp	2Pi	5Ar	20Ta	23Ge	9Le	0Li	9Sc	2Cp	9Aq
9	10Sg	0Aq	10Aq	26Pi	29Ar	14Ge	17Cn	7Vi	29Li	8Sg	0Aq	6Pi
11	8Cp	26Aq	5Pi	20Ar	23Ta	8Cn	11Le	5Li	27Sc	7Cp	27Aq	1Ar
13	5Aq	21Pi	0Ar	14Ta	17Ge	4Le	5Vi	3Sc	26Sg	4Aq	22Pi	25Ar
15	1Pi	15Ar	23Ar	8Ge	11Cn	0Vi	1Li	1Sg	25Cp	0Pi	16Ar	19Ta
17	25Pi	9Ta	17Ta	2Cn	7Le	27Vi	6Sc	29Sg	20Aq	25Pi	10Ta	12Ge
19	19Ar	2Ge	11Ge	26Cn	3Vi	26Li	5Sg	28Cp	15Pi	19Ar	4Ge	6Cn
21	13Ta	27Ge	5Cn	24Le	1Li	25Sc	3Cp	24Aq	11Ar	13Ta	27Ge	1Le
23	7Ge	23Cn	1Le	22Vi	1Sc	24Sg	1Aq	20Pi	5Ta	7Ge	22Cn	26Le
25	2Cn	21Le	29Le	22Li	1Sg	23Cp	28Aq	14Ar	28Ta	0Cn	16Le	23Vi
27	29Cn	21Vi	29Vi	23Sc	2Cp	20Aq	24Pi	8Ta	22Ge	25Cn	13Vi	20Li
29	27Le		29Li	22Sg	29Cp	16Pi	18Ar	2Ge	16Cn	20Le	11Li	19Sc
31	26Vi		29Sc		25Aq		12Ta	28Ge		18Vi		18Sg

1995

	Jan	Feb	Mar	Apr	May	Jun	Jul	Aug	Sep	Oct	Nov	Dec
1	3Cp	25Aq	3Pi	21Ar	24Ta	8Cn	11Le	29Vi	20Sc	29Sg	22Aq	29Pi
3	3Aq	22Pi	0Ar	15Ta	17Ge	2Le	6Vi	25Li	18Sg	27Cp	19Pi	24Ar
5	1Pi	17Ar	24Ar	9Ge	11Cn	26Le	1Li	22Sc	16Cp	25Aq	15Ar	19Ta
7	27Pi	11Ta	19Ta	3Cn	5Le	22Vi	29Li	22Sg	15Aq	22Pi	10Ta	13Ge
9	22Ar	5Ge	13Ge	27Cn	0Vi	19Li	27Sc	21Cp	13Pi	19Ar	5Ge	7Cn
11	15Ta	29Ge	7Cn	22Le	25Vi	18Sc	27Sg	19Aq	10Ar	14Ta	29Ge	1Le
13	9Ge	23Cn	1Le	19Vi	21Li	19Sg	27Cp	19Pi	6Ta	8Ge	23Cn	25Le
15	3Cn	19Le	27Le	17Li	19Sc	21Cp	27Aq	16Ar	1Ge	2Cn	16Le	19Vi
17	28Cn	16Vi	25Vi	17Sc	19Sg	24Aq	24Pi	11Ta	24Ge	26Cn	11Vi	15Li
19	23Le	13Li	23Li	16Sg	21Cp	24Pi	20Ar	5Ge	18Cn	21Le	7Li	13Sc
21	20Vi	11Sc	22Sc	15Cp	19Aq	22Ar	14Ta	28Ge	13Le	18Vi	5Sc	13Sg
23	17Li	9Sg	20Sg	13Aq	19Pi	16Ta	7Ge	22Cn	8Vi	14Li	5Sg	13Cp
25	14Sc	8Cp	18Cp	9Pi	14Ar	29Ta	2Cn	17Le	15Sc	12Sc	5Cp	13Aq
27	12Sg	6Aq	16Aq	5Ar	9Ta	23Ge	26Cn	12Vi	12Sc	1Sg	5Sg	2Aq
29	12Cp		13Pi	0Ta	2Ge	17Cn	21Le	8Li	0Sg	10Cp	2Pi	9Ar
31	11Aq		8Ar		26Ge		16Vi	6Sc		8Aq		4Ta

1996

	Jan	Feb	Mar	Apr	May	Jun	Jul	Aug	Sep	Oct	Nov	Dec
1	16Ta	1Cn	20Cn	6vi	9Li	28Sc	7Cp	1Pi	22Ar	27Ta	13Cn	15Le
3	10Ge	25Cn	15Le	1Li	6Sc	25Sg	7Aq	0Ar	19Ta	21Ge	7Le	8Vi
5	4Cn	19Le	10Vi	27Li	5Sg	28Cp	7Pi	28Ar	17Ge	15Cn	1Vi	2Li
7	28Cn	13Vi	5Li	25Sc	3Cp	27Aq	5Ar	23Ta	11Cn	9Le	25Vi	28Li
9	22Le	8Li	3Sc	23Sg	2Aq	25Pi	1Ta	18Ge	5Le	3Vi	20Li	25Sc
11	16Vi	4Sc	28Sc	21Cp	0Pi	21Ar	26Ta	12Cn	0Vi	28Vi	16Sc	23Sg
13	11Li	1Sg	26Sg	20Aq	28Pi	17Ta	21Ge	6Le	24Vi	24Li	14Sg	22Cp
15	8Sc	0Cp	25Cp	18Pi	24Ar	12Ge	15Cn	29Le	19Li	20Sc	12Cp	21Aq
17	6Sg	0Aq	24Aq	15Ar	20Ta	6Cn	9Le	23Vi	15Sc	18Sg	11Aq	19Pi
19	6Cp	29Aq	22Pi	11Ta	15Ge	0Le	2Vi	18Li	13Sg	17Cp	9Pi	17Ar
21	6Aq	28Pi	20Ar	7Ge	9Cn	24Le	26Vi	14Sc	11Cp	16Aq	7Ar	14Ta
23	6Pi	26Ar	16Ta	1Cn	3Le	17Vi	21Li	11Sg	10Aq	15Pi	4Ta	9Ge
25	4Ar	21Ta	11Ge	26Cn	27Le	12Li	17Sc	9Cp	9Pi	13Ar	1Ge	3Cn
27	0Ta	16Ge	5Cn	19Le	21Vi	8Sc	14Sg	8Aq	7Ar	9Ta	26Ge	27Cn
29	25Ta	9Cn	29Cn	13Vi	15Li	5Sg	13Cp	7Pi	4Ta	5Ge	21Cn	21Le
31	19Ge		23Le		9Sc		14Aq	4Ar		0Cn		16Vi

1997

	Jan	Feb	Mar	Apr	May	Jun	Jul	Aug	Sep	Oct	Nov	Dec
1	28Vi	14Sc	23Sc	13Cp	22Aq	15Ar	23Ta	12Cn	27Le	0Li	15Sc	19Sg
3	23Li	10Sg	19Sg	9Aq	18Pi	10Ta	17Ge	6Le	21Vi	25Li	11Sg	15Cp
5	18Sc	9Cp	17Cp	7Pi	15Ar	4Ge	10Cn	0Vi	15Li	18Sc	8Cp	13Aq
7	16Sg	9Aq	17Aq	6Ar	13Ta	28Ge	4Le	24Vi	8Sc	13Sg	5Aq	11Pi
9	16Cp	9Pi	17Pi	5Ta	9Ge	22Cn	28Le	18Li	2Sg	9Cp	3Pi	9Ar
11	16Aq	9Ar	17Ar	3Ge	4Cn	16Le	21Vi	12Sc	26Sg	6Aq	29Pi	8Ta
13	16Pi	7Ta	16Ta	1Cn	28Cn	10Vi	15Li	7Sg	21Cp	5Pi	28Ar	6Ge
15	14Ar	3Ge	12Ge	28Cn	21Le	4Li	9Sc	4Cp	26Aq	5Ar	28Ta	4Cn
17	11Ta	28Ge	8Cn	23Le	15Vi	28Li	5Sg	1Aq	24Pi	6Ta	27Ge	1Le
19	7Ge	23Cn	2Le	17Vi	9Li	23Sc	3Cp	0Pi	24Ar	6Ge	24Cn	27Le
21	2Cn	16Le	26Le	11Li	4Sc	20Sg	2Aq	1Ar	24Ta	5Cn	20Le	22Vi
23	26Cn	10Vi	19Vi	4Sc	29Sc	18Cp	2Pi	1Ta	23Ge	2Le	14Vi	16Li
25	19Le	4Li	13Li	29Sc	24Sg	18Aq	1Ar	29Ta	21Cn	28Le	8Li	10Sc
27	13Vi	28Li	7Sc	24Sg	22Cp	18Pi	1Ta	26Ge	18Le	23Vi	2Sc	4Sg
29	7Li		1Sg	20Cp	21Aq	18Ar	1Ge	22Cn	12Vi	17Li	26Sc	28Sg
31	1Sc		29Sg		21Pi		29Ge	16Le		11Sc		25Cp

1998

	Jan	Feb	Mar	Apr	May	Jun	Jul	Aug	Sep	Oct	Nov	Dec
1	9Aq	2Ar	12Ar	5Ge	11Cn	28Le	0Li	14Sc	28Sg	2Aq	23Pi	1Ta
3	8Pi	1Ta	11Ta	2Cn	8Le	22Vi	24Li	8Sg	24Cp	29Aq	22Ar	1Ge
5	6Ar	29Ta	9Ge	28Cn	3Vi	16Li	18Sc	2Cp	22Aq	29Pi	23Ta	1Cn
7	4Ta	26Ge	6Cn	23Le	28Vi	10Sc	12Sg	28Cp	21Pi	29Ar	23Ge	0Le
9	2Ge	22Cn	2Le	17Vi	22Li	4Sg	7Cp	25Aq	21Ar	29Ta	21Cn	26Le
11	29Ge	17Le	26Le	10Li	15Sc	28Sg	2Aq	24Pi	21Ta	28Ge	18Le	21Vi
13	25Cn	11Vi	19Vi	4Sc	9Sg	24Cp	29Aq	24Ar	21Ge	25Cn	14Vi	15Li
15	21Le	5Li	13Li	28Sc	4Cp	20Aq	27Pi	24Ta	20Cn	21Le	9Li	9Sc
17	15Vi	28Li	7Sc	22Sg	0Aq	18Pi	27Ar	24Ge	16Le	15Vi	3Sc	2Sg
19	8Li	22Sc	1Sg	18Cp	28Aq	18Ar	27Ta	22Cn	11Vi	9Li	27Sc	27Sg
21	2Sc	16Sg	26Sg	15Aq	28Pi	18Ta	27Ge	19Le	5Li	3Sc	21Sg	22Cp
23	27Sc	12Cp	22Cp	13Pi	28Ar	18Ge	25Cn	14Vi	29Li	27Sc	15Cp	18Aq
25	22Sg	9Aq	20Aq	14Ar	28Ta	16Cn	22Le	9Li	23Sc	21Sg	11Aq	15Pi
27	20Cp	7Pi	20Pi	13Ta	26Ge	12Le	18Vi	3Sc	17Sg	16Cp	8Pi	12Ar
29	18Aq		20Ar	13Ge	24Cn	7Vi	12Li	27Sc	11Cp	11Aq	6Ar	10Ta
31	18Pi		20Ta		20Le		5Sc	21Sg		8Pi		10Ge

1999

	Jan	Feb	Mar	Apr	May	Jun	Jul	Aug	Sep	Oct	Nov	Dec
1	24Ge	15Le	24Le	11Li	14Sc	28Sg	2Aq	20Pi	12Ta	21Ge	14Le	20Vi
3	23Cn	12Vi	20Vi	5Sc	8Sg	23Cp	28Aq	17Ar	11Ge	20Cn	10Vi	15Li
5	21Le	7Li	15Li	29Sc	1Cp	17Aq	23Pi	15Ta	9Cn	17Le	6Li	10Sc
7	17Vi	1Sc	9Sc	23Sg	25Cp	13Pi	20Ar	13Ge	7Le	13Vi	1Sc	4Sg
9	11Li	25Sc	3Sg	17Cp	21Aq	10Ar	19Ta	13Cn	4Vi	9Li	25Sc	27Sg
11	5Sc	19Sg	27Sg	12Aq	17Pi	8Ta	19Ge	13Le	1Vi	6Li	19Sc	21Cp
13	29Sc	13Cp	21Cp	9Pi	16Ar	8Ge	18Cn	9Vi	26Li	28Sc	13Sg	15Aq
15	23Sg	9Aq	17Aq	8Ar	16Ta	8Cn	17Le	4Li	20Sc	22Sg	7Cp	10Pi
17	18Cp	7Pi	15Pi	8Ta	17Ge	6Le	14Vi	0Sc	14Sg	16Cp	1Pi	6Ar
19	14Aq	5Ar	14Ar	8Ge	16Cn	6Vi	10Li	24Sc	8Cp	10Aq	27Pi	4Ta
21	11Pi	5Ta	14Ta	8Cn	14Le	1Li	5Sc	18Sg	2Aq	6Pi	26Ar	4Ge
23	9Ar	2Ge	13Ge	4Le	10Vi	26Li	28Sc	12Cp	28Aq	4Ar	26Ta	4Cn
25	7Ta	0Cn	11Cn	1Vi	20Sc	7Aq	25Pi	7Ta	25Pi	7Aq	25Pi	2Ta
27	6Ge	27Cn	8Le	26Vi	0Li	19Sc	6Ta	3Pi	27Ar	23Ta	26Cn	4Le
29	4Cn		3Vi	20Li	23Sc	7Cp	7Pi	3Ar	23Ta	2Cn	24Le	3Vi
31	2Le		29Vi		17Sg		7Pi	28Ar		0Le		25Li

2000

	Jan	Feb	Mar	Apr	May	Jun	Jul	Aug	Sep	Oct	Nov	Dec
1	7Sc	21Sg	11Cp	25Aq	29Pi	19Ta	28Ge	21Le	13Li	17Sc	2Cp	4Aq
3	8Pi	15Cp	5Aq	21Pi	27Ar	19Ge	20Cn	15Vi	5Sc	11Sg	24Cp	28Aq
5	24Sg	9Aq	0Pi	18Ar	26Ta	19Cn	14Le	9Li	29Sc	5Cp	20Aq	22Pi
7	18Cp	4Pi	26Pi	16Ta	25Ge	18Le	14Sc	29Sg	0Aq	14Pi	18Ar
9	12Aq	29Pi	23Ar	15Ge	24Cn	16Vi	22Li	24Aq	10Ar	15Ta
11	7Pi	26Ar	20Ta	14Cn	22Le	13Li	17Sc	2Cp	16Aq	19Pi	7Ta	13Ge
13	2Ar	23Ta	18Ge	12Le	19Vi	8Sc	26Cp	11Pi	15Ar	5Ta	6Ge	13Cn
15	29Ar	22Ge	17Cn	9Vi	16Li	2Sg	20Aq	9Ar	4Cn	13Le
17	27Ta	21Cn	15Le	6Li	11Sc	26Sg	2Ta	7Ge	10Cp	3Le	12Vi
19	27Ge	20Le	13Vi	2Sc	6Sg	20Cp	23Aq	9Ar	29Ta	8Cn	1Vi	9Li
21	27Cn	18Vi	10Li	27Sc	29Sg	14Aq	17Pi	2Ge	25Cn	29Vi	5Sc
23	26Le	15Li	6Sc	21Sg	23Cp	8Pi	12Ar	2Ge	25Cn	4Vi	26Ta
25	24Vi	11Sc	1Sg	15Cp	17Aq	3Ar	9Ta	1Cn	24Le	2Li	21Sc	25Sg
27	21Li	5Sg	25Sg	9Aq	11Pi	9Ar	29Ar	17Sc	19Cp	13Aq
29	15Sc	29Sg	19Cp	3Pi	7Ar	28Ta	6Cn	0Vi	21Li	25Sc	11Cp	13Aq
31	9Sg		13Aq		3Ta		6Le	29Vi		20Sg		6Pi

253

INDEX

Illustration credits

All illustrations Fabbri Publications except the following:
Kevin Jones Associates: 6(m), 8, 9, 10, 11, 12, 13, 14, 15, 16/17, 18, 27 (both), 28 (all), 29, 37(m), 42 (br), 43(b), 61(t), 63, 69, 72, 75, 76(b), 77(both), 83(b), 85, 87(tl), 91, 92(r), 93, 94, 99(b), 100, 101, 102, 109(both), 117, 118, 124, 125, 131(b), 132, 133, 134, 140, 141, 148, 149, 153(b), 156, 157, 162, 163, 164, 176, 178, 182, 184, 188, 190, 194, 196, 199, 201, 206, 209, 211, 212, 218, 220, 224, 226, 230, 235, 236, 238, 241, 243.
Michael Fuller: 32(t), 37(t), 37(b), 38(both), 39(all), 40(all), 41(both), 42(t), 43(t), 44, 45(both), 46(t), 47(both), 49, 51, 55(r), 56(l), 58(r), 59, 61(b), 62, 68, 76(t), 83(t), 92(tl), 99(t), 107, 115, 123, 131(t), 139, 147, 155.
Wilson Design Associates: 36.

Picture Credits

Corbis UK Ltd: 58, 73(l), 105(l), 137(r), 161(l); John Heseltine 22; David Lees 23; Francis G. Mayer 24, 113(r); The State Russian Museum 25; The Corcoran Gallery of Art 26; Gail Mooney 30; Gianni Dagli Orti 31, 42(bl), 56; National Gallery Collection 32, 65(both); Roger Ressmeyer/1989/NASA 33; Macduff Everton 46; Roger Wood 54, 55, 60; Historical Picture Archive 64; Bettmann/UPI 73(r), 145(r), 161(r); Bettmann 81(both), 89(both), 97, 113(l), 121(both), 129(l), 137(l), 145(l), 153, 245; Bettmann/Reuter 97(r); Austrian Archives 105(r); Leonard de Selba 129(r).